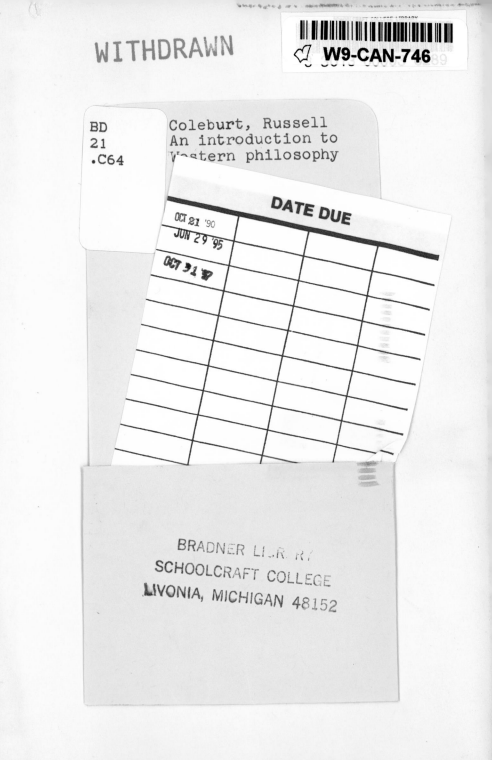

AN INTRODUCTION TO

WESTERN PHILOSOPHY

AN INTRODUCTION TO WESTERN PHILOSOPHY

by *RUSSELL COLEBURT*

SHEED & WARD · NEW YORK

© Copyright 1957, Sheed & Ward Inc.

Library of Congress Catalog Card # 57–10177

Second Printing, 1962

Manufactured in the United States of America

DEDICATION

To my pupils from 1947 to 1957, many of whom unwittingly—but I hope not too unwillingly—have connived at the production of this book.

CONTENTS

CONTENTS

INTRODUCTION

A beginner's introduction to philosophy has no obvious justification, like a similar introduction to arithmetic, for example, or chess. There are certain simple truths about arithmetic and chess which hold good for the expert, however far advanced, and they do not need to be restated at a later stage; the multiplication table does not have to be revised, however much its implications may be developed; the moves of the pieces in chess remain the same, whoever handles them.

It is not so with philosophy. Here the approach is, in a sense, from the opposite direction: from the complex to the simple, not from the simple to the complex. The simplest truths are often the profoundest; but it is only after painstaking analysis of complexities that these simple truths become more than truisms:

> ... the end of all our exploring
> Will be to arrive where we started
> And know the place for the first time.

Philosophy, therefore, as Socrates knew so well, has special traps for the beginner; it is so easy to take a short cut and imagine that you have arrived at your destination. On the other hand, if oversimplification is liable to delude the amateur, overelaboration has often entangled the expert; and the beginner, under the guidance of the expert, can easily become lost in the undergrowth before he is really aware of the ground which he is supposed to be covering. There is something to be said, then, for the view that the beginner should be given a quick look round by the amateur. That is the main justification for my writing this book.

There is also a special consideration which arises from the particular conditions of our time. Philosophy, according to its Greek derivation, means "love of wisdom." The wise man is presumably one who has grasped something of the truths and values of human experience. Philosophy, therefore, began as the search for wisdom in this sense. Inevitably, as it developed, it became caught up in particular problems, some of which are highly technical. In modern English philosophy, it is rather the method by which the problems are examined that is technical, but technical it certainly is. Two consequences follow for the innocent inquirer; firstly, he may be discouraged by what he reads and feel either that he cannot understand it or that he was looking for something different; secondly, even if he masters the technique which is applied to analyzing the problems, he may well fail to get the problems themselves into perspective.

Finally, there is a more general point, which is not confined to the difficulties of beginners. I do not believe that wisdom is attained by too exclusive a concentration on any particular problem; obviously, the deeper our thought, the nearer we shall get to the truth, but we must always retain the widest possible focus. From the very beginning, "philosophy" has been suspected, even ridiculed, by "commonsense," and often rightly so; for the philosophers have too often been fanatics obsessed with a particular line of reasoning which the intensity of their thought has distorted. There is a real sense in which the history of philosophy is the history of half-truths which have subsequently to be readjusted by lesser men. Thus perhaps more wisdom is to be gained by reflecting upon the often contradictory views of great thinkers than upon pinning one's faith too exclusively to any single philosophical system. And thus the specialist must from time to time stand back from the picture and look at it as a whole, while the novice, approaching it for the first time, must try to absorb it in the round, as it were, before he gets too close.

Since this book is intended for beginners and covers a wide field, it cannot be expected to deal exhaustively with any of the questions that are raised, many of which are problems of extreme difficulty to which no facile answer can be given. I am well aware that there are very serious dangers in this treatment, dangers of shallowness and loose thinking, of surrendering intellectual integrity to vague generalizations inadequately thought out. Even worse, truth may seem to be a vague patchwork which provokes an emotional or at best semi-rational response rather than be seen as something definite and inescapable that arrests and determines our minds. The reader must judge for himself, and indeed it is earnestly hoped that he will think very carefully whether these dangers have been avoided. For this book is a historical study and not a history. Every attempt will be made to be objective in giving the views of the philosophers whom we examine—and this the novice will have to accept on trust—but every reader must use his own judgment on the thoughts and problems that are presented. If truth means anything at all, it must be something objective for every man to grasp for himself according to his capacity; it is sheer nonsense to talk of private truths, each essentially different for every individual. On the other hand, truth cannot be served up for all to take on face value; though the same truth exists for all, its existence must be largely external until each man has made it his own by a process of hard and sincere thinking.

Professional philosophers may feel that I have been somewhat arbitrary in what I have chosen to discuss and the relative space that I devoted to each topic; I can only plead that in such matters a writer has to rely on his own judgment, and this is one of those cases where no two men would judge alike. It is important, however, that the beginner should realize at the start the limitations of my method, and that an introduction, by its very nature, is never final. I would also warn him that though my approach may strike him as somewhat eclectic, picking, it might seem, from this philosopher and that, I do not wish to advocate eclecticism as a kind of philosophy of my own. I do believe that philosophical wisdom is to be won by trying to see what is true in all the great thinkers of the past, but I am far from suggesting that this is an easy task, still less that a book such as mine is a substitute for the rigorous study of original texts.

On the contrary, it is my hope that this book may make such a study possible for those who might otherwise be baffled by the difficulty of philosophical writing, and profitable for those who might otherwise be discouraged by the disagreement among philosophers themselves. If this book has a message, it is that the study of philosophical disagreement against the background of human experience does not merely sharpen the mind, but enriches it and lends constructive assistance in the difficult art of living.

Here, of course, I am talking of the natural approach by reason. I would be the last to suggest that the limited human mind is capable of exhausting the whole of reality. Moreover, I believe that Christianity can, on divine authority, give a new depth, a new dimension almost, to what we know by reason and can add much that we can never know by reason. But I do not believe that faith dispenses us from using our reason to the utmost on the natural plane. Of course, since faith, from the Christian point of view, sheds new light on the object for which reason is searching, the thought of a man who has this faith will be of a different quality from that of a man who has not; a man cannot un-think what he believes to be true. Indeed, in this book I hope to show the effect that the birth of Christ had on the way men reasoned; to ignore it would be artificial and absurd. It must be emphasized, how-ever, that this is a study of philosophy, not of religion. It appeals to rea-son and not to faith. I hope, therefore, that those who are unable to accept Christian doctrine will not, simply on that account, feel that it is outside their field or makes unfair demands on their credulity.

It may be helpful if I say a word or two about the plan of this book. When I started teaching philosophy to beginners, I found myself in a dilemma: if I took the great philosophers one by one in their chrono-logical order, the problems became confused or forgotten: it was not easy, for example, to see the development from Platonic to Aristotelian metaphysics, when Platonic psychology and Aristotelian logic had intervened; on the other hand, if I took the great problems independ-ently, it was not easy to sort out the philosophers, still less to see how the views of each hung together and were related to those which I have adopted in this book.

I have attempted to take as much advantage as possible of the obvious fact that the two approaches often coincide: all philosophers and, to some extent, all ages have made their own special contribution to cer-tain particular problems; moreover, these contributions have tended to become more specialized in the course of time. Thus, it was possible to begin with the Greeks and the broadest, as well as the most impor-tant, problem of all philosophy—the problem of the One and the Many. This problem reaches its climax with the teaching of Christian philosophers—especially of St. Thomas Aquinas, who was the greatest systematic philosopher of medieval times and is still the most influential representative of that period.

So far, I had concerned myself almost entirely with metaphysics; in fact, in order to limit the size of this book, I have throughout given metaphysics the priority. On the other hand, no part of philosophy is self-contained; so in Part II, I have tried to reveal the most fundamental points about which a man must decide if he is to apply his metaphysical beliefs to his own conduct and life in society. The early philosophers again served to introduce these points in their simplest form, especially as far as the nature of man is concerned. In the same section, I have given a brief account of the theories of Kant and Mill (who, from their opposite points of view, represent the two most important extremes of ethical thought), and an even briefer account of Hegel and Marx, whose political thought has had such an influence on our modern world. This book, therefore, does not attempt to give an outline of the history of ethical and political thought as such.

Part III was the easiest to plan. The problem of knowledge is still very much with us; in fact, from the time of the rise of physical science in the seventeenth century, it has been our characteristic modern problem, and its development from Descartes to the present day runs on a fairly well defined course.

This development has recently reached a climax in the form of a challenge to the whole of traditional metaphysics. In Part IV, therefore, I have tried to give an account of this challenge. To illustrate it in terms of a particular problem and at the same time in order to examine in some detail that problem which much of the thought considered in this book can least afford to ignore, I have added a short essay on causality, which forms an appendix to the second chapter. Readers who find this difficult to follow can omit it without losing the thread of the book. In fact, in the third and last chapter, I have summarized the main lines of thought in the book by way of suggesting a more general reply to the attack on metaphysics.

There still remained two sets of problems that play a very important part in this controversy but which could not easily be fitted into the historical outline that I was trying to give: problems about free will and evil. I have, therefore, dealt with these separately in a final appendix to the book as a whole.

Throughout, I have not hesitated to jump the centuries when it seemed relevant to do so, especially when some points of modern thought have suggested themselves; it is idle to study the past if we cannot see its relevance to the present. Similarly, I have given a number of cross-references wherever it seemed profitable to do so; thus, the beginner who may have forgotten some point to which I refer, can easily look it up without having to consult the index. I have dropped this practice in the last chapter, where the number of references necessary would only have led to confusion.

Where possible, I have quoted at length from original works in order that the reader may gather something of the actual language used by the philosopher in question and not be entirely dependent on my version of his thought; the selection itself is, of course, bound to be arbitrary, but I have tried to choose those passages which are most famous as well as being most representative. I might further add in passing that I have printed short quotations within quotation marks, and, in such cases, where I have used italics they belong to the original text and are not mine.

I owe a great debt of gratitude to Dom Illtyd Trethowan, who read this book in manuscript and made many helpful suggestions. I should also like to record my thanks to Mr. Ian Davie for some useful criticism of my account of Wittgenstein. Needless to say, in expressing my thanks I do not wish to involve my friends in any criticism that may be leveled against the views that I have offered; in fact, I have no doubt that in many cases they would side with the critics.

AN INTRODUCTION TO

WESTERN PHILOSOPHY

PART ONE

THE ONE AND THE MANY

1. THE BEGINNING OF WESTERN PHILOSOPHY

In the history of literature, poetry comes before prose; in the early days of civilization the buoyancy of life is reflected on its multicoloured surface in sharp contrasts of light and shade that suggest the depths that lie beneath; it is not until the waters become more still that men begin to plumb these depths and charter the regions below. So in Ionia on the coast of Asia Minor, where Greek culture began, the dawn breaks in about the ninth century B.C. with the freshness and brightness of Homer. Yet we recognize the Homeric poems, as we have them, to be the climax of a long bardic tradition; with all their simplicity and directness, their sense of the joy and the pathos of human life, there is a more sophisticated playfulness, when the somewhat scandalous tales of the gods and goddesses are told, which suggests that men are outgrowing them. Many of these myths do indeed have profound things to say about the mysteries of birth and death and the like, but they are too vague and too crude for the maturing Greek mind. So, by the sixth century, Miletus, one of the principal cities of Ionia, had become the center of a more analytical approach to such problems.

Thales (who died in 545 B.C.) was the prototype of all philosophers: he fell into a well while gazing at the stars. (But he was shrewd enough, when with the aid of his meteorological knowledge he foresaw a bad year coming for the olive crops, to make a corner in the olive market so that everybody had to buy from him at high prices.)

Academically, Thales is interesting because he was the first to look for a single cause of everything. The mature intellect seems naturally to be dissatisfied with a disjointed knowledge. Indeed, the human mind

3

seems scarcely able to act at all without either pulling to pieces or building up into a larger whole. Give us a single thing to work upon, say a rose, and we divide it up into its various parts—its stem, leaves, thorns, blossom and so on—or enumerate the characteristics it has in likeness or in contrast with other flowers—as for example its size, scent, or colour. Give us several things, say a collection of animals in a field, and we parcel them up into their respective species and say that we see cows, sheep, chickens and a horse.

So the scientist examines the behavior of things, enumerates their characteristics, and classifies them so that he is able to predict their future behavior or make use of the powers that he finds latent within them, while the philosopher examines the meaning and reason for things, trying to find what lies behind it all, so that when he discovers the true aim of life, he may direct his life according to that aim. Both men examine the relations between the particular things that they see, until they grasp some coherent pattern which makes sense of the behavior of these things as a whole.

The word "science" nowadays suggests an empirical, or experimental, examination of material things; philosophy deals rather with the immaterial reality that can be deduced by reason but cannot be discovered by the senses, or, if it is begging the question to presuppose such a reality, philosophy asks whether such a reality exists; for, by definition, it is not to be apprehended by the senses, and therefore reason alone can give the answer. In early times there was no such clear distinction between the two methods (and, incidentally, we are getting confused about it again today), so that Thales was at once scientist and philosopher. His conclusion was that water was the fundamental cause for which he was looking, presumably because it can become hard or soft by freezing or evaporation, and thus become all things. His question was more interesting than his answer.

The same is true of the other Milesians: Anaximenes, for example, took air, the food of life as it were, as his first principle. More subtle, if more obscure, Anaximander argued that water was merely one of the elements into which and out of which another element changed; there must be other elements no less fundamental than water, otherwise everything would simply be water; there could be nothing else for things to be. Anaximander saw that you could not explain several elements of the same kind in terms of one of them; you must rather look for something of an entirely different nature and on a different level of reality. Thus by a process of pure reasoning he found what he called TO APEIRON, "that which is unlimited" or, perhaps we ought to say, that which has the limitation of no particular nature—that which is no particular thing: "It is," he says, "neither water nor any other of the so-called elements, but a nature different from them and infinite, from which arise all the heavens and worlds within them." The answer is not a clear one and perhaps not immediately helpful, but the process of reasoning is immensely significant.

The sword is sometimes mightier than the pen; at least the conquest of Ionia by the Persians in 546 B.C. put an end to the intellectual activity there, and those Greeks who wished to live and think in peace sailed away to South Italy and Sicily, where they had already established colonies. Here, in the second half of the sixth century, Pythagoras, who had come from the island of Samos, founded a most interesting society, a sort of religious sect given to a mysticism and metaphysics that were both based on mathematics; indeed, they claimed that mathematics purged the soul, possibly because of its value as an abstract intellectual discipline, but perhaps also because of its connection with music, which always played a large part in ancient mysticism and had a special significance in their own philosophy.

As a religious sect, they lived together in "lodges," were subjected from time to time to very serious persecutions, and were forbidden to eat beans. This, apparently, was not merely an asceticism, but scholars are divided as to whether the prohibition was based on the metaphysical grounds that beans had souls or the more pragmatic, empirical reason that when consumed they reacted at least unlike ordinary inanimate matter. The point about beans having souls was important, because the Pythagoreans believed in metempsychosis—that is, that souls after death were born again in a new body, whether human, animal, or even, apparently in some cases, vegetable. Thus there is the story that Pythagoras once stopped a man beating a dog because, as he said, he recognized the voice of a friend.

Aristotle, on whose account most of our knowledge of early philosophy is based, stresses the part that mathematics played in Pythagorean thought: "They thought," he tells us, "that its principles were the principles of all things." It is easy to see the connection between mathematics and music; the pitch, for example, of a plucked string can be described in terms of the frequency at which the string vibrates, and the volume in terms of the distance which the string travels at each vibration. It is less easy to appreciate the bald statement that

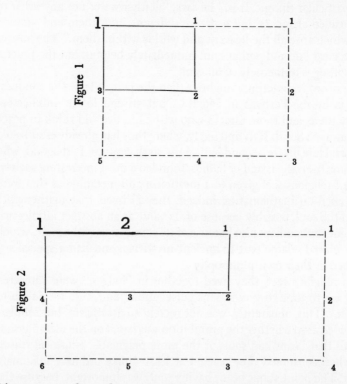

things are numbers; the connection seems to lie in the fact that numbers were visualized spatially. Thus the number 1 is thought of as a point and 2 as a line; similarly, squares can be produced by starting with the number 1 and adding successive odd numbers (1, 4, 9, 16, etc. —*vid.* Fig. 1), rectangles by starting with 2 and adding successive even numbers (6, 12, 20, etc.—*vid.* Fig. 2); thus, ideally at least, any shape, and so any physical thing, can be expressed in numerical terms.

Pythagoras becomes even more obscure when he extends this significance of numbers to abstract ideas; one can see that there is a sort of symmetrical perfection about the number 4 that might suggest Justice; there is an intelligible, if Freudian, symbolism in representing Male by 3 and Female by 2, and consequently marriage by 5; but it is less obvious why 7 should stand for Opportunity, and so with many others.

Figure 3

Behind all this was Pythagoras's development of Anaximander. It was not enough vaguely to suggest that all things proceeded from the Unlimited (TO APEIRON); it had to be pinned down, as it were, in the finite. Thus for Pythagoras Limit (TO PERAS) had always to be linked with the Unlimited for any given thing to exist; reality, therefore, was a mixture of the two. Everything, then, was in a sense part of the whole from which all proceeded, and at the same time that particular thing and not something else. This, again, is reflected in mathematics, where all numbers are either odd (limited) or even (unlimited). The combination of the two could be seen in its most perfect form in a figure representing the numbers 1 to 4, the sum of which comes to 10, in terms of which all larger numbers may be said to be expressed (*vid*, Fig. 3). This figure, known as the TETRAKTUS, became the sacred symbol of the Pythagoreans.

The reader may be forgiven if he is a little bemused by this account of the Pythagorean school, with all its obscurities and curious mixture of the profound and the naïve. But as we study the awakening of the

Western mind, we can perhaps learn far more from the Pythagoreans than from the logical conundrums of some of the more systematic thinkers who followed.

Pythagoras's genius was pre-eminently that of a mathematician, and indeed it was not surprising that he should attempt to explain everything in terms of his own science. His theory that things are numbers may sound absurd, but there are physicists today who seem to claim that their science says all that there is to be said about the universe, and that this information in fact amounts to a series of mathematical formulae. These formulae (to describe the atom, for example) are of immense importance, but, as a scientist has recently shown,* they represent the measurement of forces; at the moment it is not at all clear what these forces are; the physicist can tell us much about how the material world behaves, but he can tell us little about its nature, for the nature of a thing cannot be measured.

On the other hand, Pythagoras is most stimulating as a thinker because he inquired about the whole of reality with the whole of his mind. The result was that his discoveries led to no mere academic approval; his thought was not just admired as an interesting theory, but inspired a way of life in which many followers found their ideal. He showed further that the human mind has many ways of approaching truth—the way of the abstract analytical thinker with his careful calculation and logic, the way of the poet with his intuitive flair for discerning significant resemblances and symbolic connections, and the way of the mystic with his direct experience of reality that is beyond analysis. It is certainly very rare for one man to be pre-eminent in all three fields, but it is arguable that no man can make much headway in any one unless he takes some account of the other two. Otherwise he must stultify the natural exercise of his own mind. It is hoped that this point may become clearer as we proceed.

We have seen the Pythagorean attempt to give some coherent, if groping, account of the unity and diversity of things, but there is one aspect of reality, as we know it through our senses, which is not so convenient for the mathematician; it is always changing. "All things

* E. F. Caldin, *The Power and Limits of Science*, London, Chapman & Hall, 1949.

are flowing" (PANTA REI) was what worried Heraclitus of Ephesus (who flourished a little before 500 B.C.). "You cannot step twice into the same river," he said, and if it comes to that, we might say that you cannot sit down twice on the same chair, since every chair is in process of decay and so ever changing; science, too, tells us that it is not that solid object which we took it to be. How then can we refer to any particular thing at all? Before you can say "chair," something different has appeared, and it will never be the same chair again.

Heraclitus trusted his reason more than his senses, and concluded that his senses must be mistaken, or at least that there was something intrinsically unstable about material things which made it impossible to say anything about them with any certainty, except that they were unstable. Pure reason, however, could discover permanent truths; above all, it demanded some underlying reality that did not change, some immutable unity behind the diversity, or, to put it more accurately, a unity of which the diversity was really the manifestation.

The One, therefore, as Heraclitus called it, must exist in the tension of opposites; for without such a tension there would be nothing to set things moving. It might also be called "fire"; for "fire is want and surfeit"; the world is "an everlasting fire with measures of it kindling and measures going out in more or less equal proportions." Ultimately, all things are manifestations of the same truth: "Good and ill are one," or, more picturesquely: "Swine wash in the mire and barnyard fowls in the dust"; again: "To God all things are fair and good and right, but men hold some things right and some things wrong,"—a convenient solution of what we are to know as the problem of evil.

Heraclitus, then, believed in the ideas that he formed with his mind rather than in the information directly given to him by his senses. Technically, this is known as idealism, the opposite of realism, which, unlike idealism, believes that the world which we have before us is, in the fullest sense, real and true. Philosophers can usually be divided into followers of the one school or the other. One of the great problems of human knowledge which we shall have to examine is bound up with this curious relationship between the direct and vivid impacts on our senses which often mislead us and the indirect, toilsome inferences of our reason in which alone we ultimately seem to trust—

unless in the process of abstraction they have become too empty of content to be worth trusting at all.

Idealist though he was, Heraclitus in a very real sense anticipated modern theories of matter, according to which the atom is no hard little ball, as it used to be imagined, but an organization of forces held together by the attraction by which the electron is drawn towards its opposite power, the proton. At any rate, he brought home one great problem: if change persists everywhere, what permanency is there to change?

Another idealist, Parmenides of Elea (c. 515–445 B.C.), brought home the same problem by very different means. He had not the splendid imagination that gave rise to Heraclitus's vision of the world as a great furnace ever being kindled and quenched, but he had a hard logical mind which faced up to its conclusions, however surprising they might seem.

For Parmenides change and plurality must be an illusion. All that you could say is that the One is; if you hold that anything else exists or comes into being, you are up against a dilemma: if anything is, it comes out of being or not-being; if out of being, it already is; if out of not-being, it is nothing, since nothing comes out of nothing. The reader may feel that he is being tricked by this apparently too facile argument, but there are at least two real difficulties here.

On the question of plurality, the existence, that is, of many different things, we may put the problem: granted this underlying unity for which all the Greek philosophers so far had been looking, granted that the true or ultimate reality is one, in what sense can we say that one particular thing differs from another? For that very difference, if it is anything at all, must itself be contained in the one reality and therefore be identical with the rest. It is this difficulty which has led many people to adopt the view of Pantheism, namely that God is the sum total, as it were, of all existence,

> In which all beings live with God, themselves
> Are God, existing in the mighty whole
> As indistinguishable as the cloudless East
> At noon is from the cloudless West, when all
> The hemisphere is one cerulean blue.

On the question of change, the problem can be put in a different way: if a cow eats grass, we say that the grass has changed into cow, that the grass has, in some wonderful manner, become cow; but this seems to suggest that there has come into being a new thing, cow, in place of the old thing, grass, which seems like substitution rather than change; it is as though some unseen hand had snatched away the grass and put cow into its place, as I might pull up tulips and plant daffodils instead. Where there is change, that which changes, the subject of the verb, must in some way retain its identity; but if it retains its identity, how can it change in any fundamental sense? The scientist, indeed, can identify the chemicals in the grass which have passed into the cow. And the chemicals can be reduced to various combinations of a comparatively small number of atoms. But is there nothing more to be said about material things than that?

Anaxagoras, who was born at Clazomenae in Asia Minor in about 500 B.C., thought this was about as much as you could say. He agreed with his contemporary, Empedocles of Acragas, that things are made up of indestructible material particles. Just as the modern scientist holds that there are a limited number of types of atoms (ninety-two, in point of fact), so Anaxagoras believed that there was a limited variety of material particles which were ultimate and underived. In actual things, these varieties were mixed up, so that one particular type predominated: "In everything," he said, "there is a portion of everything." Thus if grass becomes cow, there must have been a portion of cow already in the grass; by eating grass, the cow, already consisting predominantly of cow particles, becomes more of a cow, though, presumably, as she goes on eating grass, she becomes more and more of a grassy cow.

Anaxagoras, however, was no crude materialist; for it is to him we owe the great thought that if things are as conveniently arranged as they seem to be, it must be the work of a transcendent mind (NOUS), a mind, that is to say, that is aloof and apart from the world it arranges: "Mind has power over all things both greater and smaller." "Mind is infinite and self-ruled, and is mixed with nothing, but is alone, itself by itself." Later, as we shall see, we find Socrates complaining that Anaxagoras did not follow up this theory as he might have done, but it was the signal for great advances in Greek thought. As Hegel puts it: "With Anaxagoras, a light, if still a weak one, begins to dawn, because the understanding is now recognized as the principle."

Before these advances were made, Greek philosophy had to face a challenge to its very existence. Nobody had been able to give a very satisfactory answer to Thales's question as to the fundamental nature of the universe. The Pythagoreans had made an ingenious attempt to combine their mathematical knowledge with the mystique of Orphism, a cult brought to Greece from the East, which perhaps did most at that time to satisfy the need for personal religious experience; but their rational theology was hardly likely to stand the test of time. The Eleatics of Parmenides's school with their insoluble conundrums had brought philosophical speculation to the verge of absurdity. Meanwhile, there had been great political and social developments in what is now known as classical Greece. From the feudal system of Homeric times the Greeks had passed through the oppressive rule of princes enriched by an ever-increasing trade, and through the rule of sovereigns who had headed the revolt of the people against such oppression, until they had gradually evolved something like a party system. By the fifth century most of the cities were ruled either by a democratic or oligarchic party; the Ionian cities, like Athens, were for the most part democratic; the Dorian, like Sparta, were oligarchic. It was, incidentally, unlike our modern versions of the party system in that from time to time a bloody revolution took place, where we have general elections. At Athens, however, thanks to the constitutional insight of her sixth-century sovereigns and the personality and wisdom of her leading citizen, Pericles, democracy had been firmly established —a democracy, moreover, in which every citizen played a responsible part in the government. Socially and economically similar advances had been made: trade was extensive and prosperous; the arts, especially sculpture, architecture and drama, which demand a communal effort and appreciation, flourished as perhaps never before or since. Man was at the height of his power. Small wonder that the great Athenian dramatist, Sophocles, should write the famous ode of the *Antigone* which begins: "Many are the wonders of the world, but none is more wonderful than man."

At the same time, men were traveling far and wide, and horizons were being extended. They saw how other races lived. The pages of Herodotus, the gossip column and recording unit of the ancient world, brought to those who had to stay at home fascinating tales of the fabulous riches of Eastern kings and the amazing customs and beliefs of outlandish peoples.

Philosophy is rarely the fruits of success. A new type of learned man came on the scene, the purveyor of popular education. These sophists, as they were called (men, that is to say, who claimed to be wise), travelled about Greece, those with a name managing to find a niche for themselves at Athens, teaching "practical wisdom." They thought that the detached pursuit of absolute truth had been proved to be a wild-goose chase. The Greeks had always assumed that their code of morality was something imprinted by nature on the human heart, but men like Herodotus had shown that cannibals, for example, made a religious ritual of what the Greeks had considered to be most un-natural conduct. It was all a question of custom (NOMOS); nature (PHYSIS) acted purely in the biological sphere; she controlled the physical laws of operations like eating and drinking; she did not even regulate the diet. Morality was what you made it, or at least what your city found it convenient to make for you.

The sophists, therefore, set out to prepare young men for the practical life they were to lead. Above all they taught them rhetoric, the art of public speaking and argument; in the intensely communal life of the time, the ability to plead a case or to put forward a policy in public committee was what brought the greatest influence and glory.

The greatest figure of this movement was Protagoras of Abdera (who was born in 481 B.C.) with his famous dictum: "Man is the measure of all things." By this he probably did not mean to advocate the anarchy of an excessive individualism, but to put forward the view that man is the greatest being of whom we have any real knowledge and that therefore standards of behaviour are not to be sought in some arbitrary, external code, but rather in the needs and desires that man is known to have. In other words, his view of morals was relative rather than absolute. He believed that morality should adapt itself to the needs and customs of the time and contained no law that was rooted in the nature of things and therefore binding in all circumstances. He would agree that it is proper to say, as men often do nowadays, that such and such a moral principle is "out of date" or "hardly for people like us." Or, to give a more particular example, people who argue that divorce should be allowed because they cannot bear the thought that unhappy couples should be forbidden to remarry are arguing, like Protagoras, relatively, whereas those who would forbid it on the grounds that it is against the law of God are arguing from an absolute standpoint. It is possible, of course, to believe in absolute moral standards and to consider that these are not contravened by divorce; but we are not here concerned with the morality of this particular question; we merely illustrate the two different kinds of reasoning on which men base their views on moral problems.

In such problems, the first and fundamental question must be: do we appeal to an absolute norm or not? This is the question that will be examined in our next chapter. It is, of course, merely one aspect of the larger question which emerges from early Greek thought: can we discover any fixed pattern of reality which (1) enables us to form meaningful propositions that will always be true, irrespective of time or place, and (2) at the same time does justice to the changing face of nature as we know and understand it in our daily lives? In short, whether it is a question of actions or of things, whether we are considering the force of any particular moral obligation or the value and purpose of any particular object of experience, can we give a rational account of the One which will make sense of our experience of the Many?

2. THE FIRST STAGE IN A RATIONAL SYNTHESIS: SOCRATES

The phrase "rational synthesis" is convenient rather than pleasing. "Synthesis" means "a putting-together." Truth was being broken up by the sophists. This chapter will examine the attempts of Socrates (c. 470–399 B.C.) to put it together again, at least as far as ethical problems are concerned, and to replace the conventional values that the sophists were destroying by the lasting values to be discovered in the nature of human life itself.

Socrates was a young man at the peak of Athenian splendour and lived to see that splendour fade in the defeat and collapse of the Athenian Empire at the end of the fifth century. Even in his early days, however, he had never been taken in by the transient prosperity of his city. He had distrusted the spirit of the times, the complacency of his fellow citizens, and above all the confident claims of the sophists to teach all the wisdom that was needed for life.

The story is well known of how a friend asked the oracle at Delphi who was the wisest man in Greece and was given the answer: "Socrates." We are told that Socrates was puzzled when told of this and then concluded that he must be the wisest in that he alone knew how ignorant he was. He used to make much of this "ignorance," asking simple questions which tied people up when they tried to give the answers, and thus showed how ignorant they were too.

On the other hand, he was no aloof intellectual who played no part in the practical life of his own city. Rather, he trained himself in that true state of detachment by which a man is able to carry out his daily tasks superbly well because he is, as the Greeks would say, truly "master of himself." In Plato's *Symposium*, Alcibiades, one of Socrates's favorite companions, tells of the days when he and Socrates went on military service together:

All this, as I should explain, happened before he and I went on the expedition to Potidaea; there we messed together, and I had the opportunity of observing his extraordinary power of sustaining fatigue and going without food when our supplies were intercepted at any place, as will happen with an army. In the faculty of endurance he was superior not only to me but to everybody; there was no one to be compared to him. Yet at a festival he was the only person who had any real powers of enjoyment, and though not willing to drink, he could if compelled beat us all at that, and the most wonderful thing of all was that no human being had ever seen Socrates drunk; and that, if I am not mistaken, will soon be tested. His endurance of cold was also surprising. There was a severe frost, for the winter in that region is really tremendous, and everybody else either remained indoors, or if they went out had on no end of clothing, and were well shod, and had their feet swathed in felt and fleeces: in the midst of this, Socrates, with his bare feet on the ice, and in his ordinary dress, marched better than any of the other soldiers who had their shoes on, and they looked daggers at him because he seemed to despise them.

I have told you one tale, and now I must tell you another, which is worth hearing, of the doings and sufferings of this enduring man while he was on the expedition. One morning he was thinking about something which he could not resolve; and he would not give up, but continued thinking from early dawn until noon—there he stood fixed in thought; and at noon attention was drawn to him, and the rumour ran round the wondering crowd that Socrates had been standing and thinking about something ever since the break of day. At last, in the evening after supper, some Ionians out of curiosity (I should explain that this was not in winter but in summer), brought out their mats and slept in the open air that they might watch him and see whether he would stand all night. There he stood all night as well as all day and the following morning; and with the return of light he offered up a prayer to the sun, and went his way. I will also tell, if you please—and indeed I am bound to tell—of his courage in battle; for who but he saved my life? Now this was the engagement in which I received the prize of valour: for I was wounded and he would not leave me, but he rescued me and my arms; and he ought to have received the prize of valour which the generals wanted to confer on me partly on account of my rank, and I told them so (this Socrates will not impeach or deny), but he was more eager than the generals that I and not he should have the prize. There was another occasion on which he was very noticeable; this was in the flight of the army after the battle of Delium, and I had a better opportunity of seeing him than at Potidaea as I was myself on horseback, and therefore comparatively out of danger. He and Laches were retreating as the troops were in flight, and I met them and told them not to be discouraged, and promised to remain with them; and there you might see him, Aristophanes, as you describe, just as he is in the streets of Athens, stalking like a pelican, and rolling his eyes, calmly contemplating enemies as well as friends, and making very intelligible to anybody, even from a distance, that whoever attacks him will be likely to meet with a stout resistance; and in this way he and his companion escaped—for these are the sort of persons who are never touched in war; they only pursue those who are running away headlong. I particularly observed how superior he was to Laches in presence of mind. Many are the wonders of Socrates which I might narrate in his praise; most of his ways might perhaps be paralleled in others, but the most astonishing thing of all is his absolute unlikeness to any hunman being that is or ever has been.*

We cannot vouch for the details of this story, but it seems beyond dispute that Socrates had remarkable powers of physical endurance, was temperate but not abstemious in his habits, and that he enjoyed mystical experience. He had a great sense of his mission in life to teach the truth and, like St. Joan of Arc, heard voices that encouraged him to carry it out.

In the end, he died for his convictions. As Athenian power suffered reverse after reverse, so the standards of her public life decayed: military leaders were made the scapegoats of the national disgrace and the estates of rich citizens were confiscated to make up for the public money that had been squandered. As a member of the senatorial committee, Socrates had refused to agree to the illegal, if useful, expedient by which the eight generals who had commanded at the battle of Arginusae were to be given a combined trial. Later, he had refused to

* Plato, *Symposium*, 219e–221c (tr. Jowett).

take part in the arrest of one, Leon of Salamis, whose property had been marked down by the politicians. So, in the course of time, charges were trumped up against him: they alleged that he had introduced new religious practices and corrupted the young. When the inevitable verdict was given and he was sentenced to death, he did not take advantage of the opportunity to "escape" from prison into exile which the Athenians were still merciful enough to provide in such circumstances, but spurning to by-pass the law to which he still believed himself to be subject, he calmly awaited his death. Plato, in a dialogue called the *Phaedo*, tells us of his last moments; he puts the story in the mouth of Phaedo who addresses his friend, Echecrates:

Now the hour of sunset was near, for a good deal of time had passed while he was within. When he came out, he sat down with us again after his bath, but not much was said. Soon the jailer, who was the servant of the Eleven,* entered and stood by him, saying: To you, Socrates, whom I know to be the noblest and gentlest and best of all who ever came to this place, I will not impute the angry feelings of other men, who rage and swear at me, when, in obedience to the authorities, I bid them drink the poison—indeed, I am sure that you will not be angry with me; for others, as you are aware, and not I, are to blame. And so fare you well, and try to bear lightly what must needs be—you know my errand. Then bursting into tears he turned away and went out.

Socrates looked at him, and said: I return your good wishes and will do as you bid. Then turning to us, he said, How charming the man is: since I have been in prison he has always been coming to see me, and at times he would talk to me, and was good to me as could be, and now see how generously he sorrows on my account. We must do as he says, Crito; and therefore let the cup be brought, if the poison is prepared: if not, let the attendant prepare some.

Yet, said Crito, the sun is still upon the hill-tops, and I know that many a one has taken the draught late, and after the announcement has been made to him, he has eaten and drunk, and enjoyed the society of his beloved; do not hurry—there is time enough.

Socrates said: Yes, Crito, and they of whom you speak are right in so acting, for they think that they will be gainers by the delay; but I am right in not following their example, for I do not think that I should

* The police authorities at Athens.

gain anything by drinking the poison a little later; I should only be ridiculous in my own eyes for sparing and saving a life which is already forfeit. Please then to do as I say, and not to refuse me.

Crito made a sign to the servant, who was standing by; and he went out, and having been absent for some time, returned with the jailer carrying the cup of poison. Socrates said: You, my good friend, who are experienced in these matters, shall give me directions how I am to proceed. The man answered: You have only to walk about until your legs are heavy, and then to lie down, and the poison will act. At the same time he handed the cup to Socrates, who in the easiest and gentlest manner, without the least fear or change of colour or feature, looking at the man with all his eyes, Echecrates, as his manner was, took the cup and said: What do you say about making a libation out of this cup to any god? May I, or not? The man answered: We only prepare, Socrates, just as much as we deem enough. I understand, he said: but I may and must ask the gods to prosper my journey from this to the other world—even so—and so be it according to my prayer. Then raising the cup to his lips, quite readily and cheerfully he drank off the poison. And hitherto most of us had been able to control our sorrow; but now when we saw him drinking, and saw too that he had finished the draught, we could no longer forbear, and in spite of myself my own tears were flowing fast; so that I covered my face and wept, not for him, but at the thought of my own calamity in having to part from such a friend. Nor was I the first; for Crito, when he found himself unable to restrain his tears, had got up, and I followed: and at that moment, Apollodorus, who had been weeping all the time, broke out in a loud and passionate cry which made cowards of us all. Socrates alone retained his calmness: What is this strange outcry? he said. I sent away the women mainly in order that they might not misbehave in this way, for I have been told that a man should die in peace. Be quiet then, and have patience. When we heard his words we were ashamed, and restrained our tears; and he walked about until, as he said, his legs began to fail, and then he lay on his back, according to the directions, and the man who gave him the poison now and then looked at his feet and legs; and after a while he pressed his foot hard, and asked him if he could feel; and he said, No; and then his leg, and so upwards and upwards, and showed us that he was cold and stiff. And he felt them himself, and said: When the poison reaches the heart, that will be the end. He was beginning to grow cold about the groin, when he uncovered his face, for he had covered himself up, and said—they were his last words—he said: Crito,

cock to Asclepius; will you remember to pay the debt? The debt
be paid, said Crito; is there anything else? There was no answer to
this question; but in a minute or two a movement was heard, and the
attendants uncovered him; his eyes were set, and Crito closed his eyes
and mouth.

Such was the end, Echecrates, of our friend; concerning whom I may
truly say, that of all the men of his time whom I have known, he was
the wisest and justest and best.*

We have gone into some biographical detail here, because Socrates
is the supreme example of a man who hammered out his principles
with his own unaided reason and lived by them without regard to the
consequences. This in itself is a major contribution to philosophy; it
conveys in a most direct manner that philosophical speculation is not
an end in itself but a means of discovering the right way of life.

Now, most of what we know about Socrates's philosophy has its
source in the dialogues of Plato; so that it is difficult to distinguish
between the thought of Socrates and Plato's own development of it.
The matter is of historical rather than philosophical importance, so
we make no apology for assuming a convenient division between the
two which, while obviously a simplification, seems to be as likely a
solution as can be found.

The first lesson which Socrates set out to teach, in opposition to the
sophists, was that the human mind can be satisfied by nothing less
than unchanging, objective truth. Where was such truth to be found?
It could not be discovered in relation to particulars like individual
horses, men, or political constitutions. You might say: "That horse is
lame," or: "The Athenian constitution is good," but these statements
would no longer be true if the horse recovered from its lameness or
the Athenian constitution changed its character. As Heraclitus had
said, all such things are in a state of flux.

On the other hand, if you made statements about the species as a
whole rather than any single member of the species, the result was very
different: you could say: "Horses have ears" or: "Constitutions like the

* Plato, *Phaedo*, 116b. seq. (tr. Jowett).

present Athenian constitution are good" with the knowledge that if your statement were true today, it would be bound to be true tomorrow. You had gotten below the flux on the surface and discovered a level where the pattern remained unchanged. Socrates held that if you could not make general statements that were really founded in the facts of reality, you could not reason at all; for all reasoning was in terms of such general statements and presupposed such a foundation. We might add that even if you say: "General statements cannot be objective" or, as some modern philosophers put it: "General statements are mere tautologies," these statements themselves are general and presumably held to be objectively true.

It is admittedly not so easy to see how to test the truth of such propositions and to see what is the relation between them and the particulars to which they refer. Socrates at any rate worked on the principle that if you examined the particulars in their various instances, you could discover properties and relations which enabled you to make valid statements about them; it was probably left to Plato to work out a metaphysical system that justified this technique.

If then any practical question arose—and Socrates was most interested in practical, especially moral, questions—he would apply the famous Socratic method. For example, if some generals asked him about the education of their sons, as we see in the *Laches*, he would try to discover what virtue they wished their sons to have, and this would lead on to the discussion of courage. To discover the nature of true courage, they would examine examples of it in widely different contexts (courage in the face of the enemy, in the endurance of pain, in resistance to temptation and so on) until, by removing false or confused ideas of it, they had thus come to see what courage really was. Thus Socrates worked on the principle that if you sifted your everyday speech about things, you could discover much about the nature of those things which was implied by your speech about them, and, indeed, without which such speech could have no significance. It would be absurd to talk about "courageous people" unless you believed that some definite meaning could be given to those words. Owing to the imperfection of the human mind, such Socratic inquiries often led to no definite answer in the end, but much light was thrown on the subject on the way. Socrates did not profess to give all the answers, but he did attempt to teach men the value of looking for them, and above all the folly of assuming that you know them already. From the start, he had insisted that the first stage of wisdom consists in appreciating your own ignorance.

At this point, it would perhaps be appropriate to suggest that there are no answers to philosophical problems in the sense in which there are answers to problems in mathematics. This is not to say that philosophy inevitably leads to scepticism, the belief that certainty can never be attained, but rather to prevent such a conclusion by a warning that we must not look for the wrong things and then be disappointed when we cannot find them. It would be a bold man who claimed to explain the whole of reality, but it is no less foolish to say that nothing can be gained by attempting to do so. It is, in fact, the height of absurdity to devote all one's intellectual powers to proving that the intellect has no power at all. Socrates proved that the genuine search for truth may not result in any watertight system constructed with the rational precision of a theorem in geometry, but does lead to convictions for which a man may be prepared to lay down his life.

As we have seen (p. 11) the world first began to make sense for Socrates when he read Anaxagoras's theory that it was the work of a mind, but he was bitterly disappointed with Anaxagoras's failure to work out the consequences of this view. Plato, in the *Phaedo*, makes Socrates tell us the story himself:

Then I heard someone reading, as he said, from a book of Anaxagoras, that mind was the disposer and cause of all, and I was delighted at this notion, which appeared quite admirable, and I said to myself: If mind is the disposer, mind will dispose all for the best, and put each particular in the best place; and I argued that if any one desired to find out the cause of the generation or destruction or existence of anything, he must find out what state of being or doing or suffering was best for that thing, and therefore a man had only to consider the best for himself and others, and then he would also know the worse, since the same science comprehended both. And I rejoiced to think that I had found in Anaxagoras a teacher of the causes of existence such as I desired, and

I imagined that he would tell me first whether the earth is flat or round; and whichever was true, he would proceed to explain the cause and the necessity of this being so, and then he would teach me the nature of the best and show that this was best; and if he said that the earth was in the centre, he would further explain that this position was the best, and I should be satisfied with the explanation given, and not want any other sort of cause. . . .

What expectations I had formed, and how grievously was I disappointed! As I proceeded, I found my philosopher altogether forsaking mind or any other principle of order, but having recourse to air, and ether, and water, and other eccentricities. I might compare him to a person who began by maintaining generally that mind is the cause of the actions of Socrates, but who, when he endeavored to explain the causes of my several actions in detail, went on to show that I sit here because my body is made up of bones and muscles; and the bones, as he would say, are hard and have joints which divide them, and the muscles are elastic, and they cover the bones, which have also a covering or environment of flesh and skin which contains them; and as the bones are lifted at their joints by the contraction or relaxation of the muscles, I am able to bend my limbs, and this is why I am sitting here in a curved posture—that is what he would say; and he would have a similar explanation of my talking to you, which he would attribute to sound, and air, and hearing, and he would assign ten thousand other causes of the same sort, forgetting to mention the true cause, which is, that the Athenians have thought fit to condemn me, and accordingly I have thought it better and more right to remain here and undergo my sentence; for I am inclined to think that these muscles and bones of mine would have gone off long ago to Megara or Boeotia—by the dog they would, if they had been moved by their own ideas of what was best, and if I had not chosen the better and nobler part, instead of playing truant and running away, of enduring any punishment which the state inflicts. There is surely a strange confusion of causes and conditions in all this. It may be said, indeed, that without bones and muscles and the other parts of the body I cannot execute my purposes. But to say that I do as I do because of them, and that this is the way in which mind acts, and not from the choice of the best, is a very careless and idle mode of speaking. I wonder that they cannot distinguish the cause from the condition, which the many, feeling about in the dark, are always mistaking and misnaming.*

* Plato, *Phaedo*, 97b–99b (tr. Jowett).

The gist of the matter is, then, that if the universe is the work of a mind, everything in it must have a purpose; mind, as mind, does not act irrationally. If we wish, therefore, to know the nature of anything, we must ask, What is its purpose or function?

If we apply this question to man, we find (Socrates thought) two distinct levels of being, each with its own function, but with the one subordinated to the other. On one level, man eats, drinks and reproduces his species like the animals; on the other, he distinguishes between truth and error, between right and wrong, is able to conjure up the past in the present, and acts more or less according to reason rather than instinct. The aim of the first is physical health and well-being; the aim of the second is the well-being of the intellectual or spiritual element, and this must mean life away from the change and uncertainty of the material world in a world where reality can be seen and known as it truly is.

These aims will be in conflict unless the soul, the rational principle in man, keeps the life of the body subordinate to its own life. In this world, man must keep his physical appetites in check and become as independent as possible of physical needs. At death, the soul is freed from the shackles of the body. If a man has lived well, if in his life he has purified his soul from physical preoccupations, he will be in a fit state to pass on to the spiritual world and will live, now perfectly happy, in a home that is fitting to its nature; for unless there is such a world and such an end for the proper life of the soul, no sense can be made either of the nature of the soul or of moral experience.

If, however, a soul has led a bad or indifferent life, after passing through the waters of forgetfulness and suffering a period of punishment, it will be born again in a new body, whether animal or human; the best of these souls will be born into a noble form of human life, the worst into the lowest form of animal life, and all the others in various intermediate states according to their condition at death.

The details of this, of course, Socrates does not pretend to know, but he suggests them in an avowedly mythical form. The principle which he wishes to emphasize is that one's own life now and hereafter is quite literally what one makes of it: if the economy of the universe is rational, everything must live in circumstances that are fitting to it; the corrupted soul must go on living in a corrupted state, but the soul that has become purified from corruption can live in an uncorrupted state that is appropriate to its nature and condition.

It follows from all this that man's most pressing need is the care of his soul. We have seen how Socrates himself carried this into practice. Moreover he felt it his duty to assist others in the same task. He liked to refer to himself as a midwife who helped a man to bring to birth the knowledge that lay confused within him.

"Knowledge" may seem an odd word in this context; but Socrates held that virtue and knowledge were the same: a man who knows what is right will do it; no man chooses evil as such. Virtue, therefore, can be taught; that is to say, a man can be given a real insight into truth and goodness. Aristotle disagreed with this equation of virtue and knowledge: "Socrates," he contended, "forgot the irrational part of the soul." It will throw considerable light on Socrates's thought if we examine this point in some detail.

We might put the problem this way: Do we do what we know to be wrong? If we do not, it is difficult to see how we can feel guilt or be justly reproved for what we have done. "I did not know that it was wrong" may not be a valid excuse in law, but it is generally felt to have some force in ordinary life: ignorance, if it is not in itself culpable, is usually considered a legitimate plea. When we wish to condemn a man, we say: "He knew that it was wrong, but he did it." We can imagine a situation that would prompt this remark: the man tells a lie to save his face; he knows that he ought to tell the truth, but he lets this sense of obligation slip into the background and blurts out what it is easier for him to say. If he is morally sensitive, a blush on his cheek reveals that he is still very much conscious of what he ought to be doing. He seems, in fact, to have the knowledge without the virtue.

Suppose, however, that we consider a man who is not morally sensitive but a hardened liar. He will not blush. He may even tell lies without adverting to the fact that it is wrong. Are we then to say that the hardened liar is less guilty than he who tells a lie with a greater sense of the wrong that he is doing? Is it always true that the more clearly a man knows his sin, the more reprehensible he is?

The problem is yet more complex if we also consider the case of a man brought up in a bad environment, so that he hardly developed his moral sense at all. Should we blame him as much as the hardened liar, who has much the same knowledge of what he is doing when he tells his lie, but has lost his moral sensitivity through his own fault?

The answer seems to be that we regard these two latter states of conscience as equally bad in themselves, but we blame the hardened liar, while we call the other man unfortunate. Neither is virtuous. On the other hand, our blushing liar would not be called unfortunate (at least, not in the same sense), but he would be blamed, though perhaps not as much as the hardened liar, for his lie may be but a single offence. Of the three, however, surely it is the blushing liar, the man whose conscience is still sensitive, whom we should think to be the least lacking in virtue.

It seems from this that a sensitive conscience is indispensable to true virtue. Is this a state of the will or of the intellect? A sensitive conscience does not seem to be the same thing as an informed conscience: just as a man may know what is right and not do it, so he may wish to do what is right and not know what that may be. At the risk of being tedious, let us consider what we should say of this latter type of man. Let us put it this way: Is it virtuous to do the wrong thing for the right reason? To offer an extreme case, most of us, whether teetotallers or not, would hardly admire a man who went round pulling down bars and cocktail lounges because he felt it his duty to do so. Or again, we do not feel that Don Quixote is a hero because he charges alone into a flock of sheep that he takes to be evil men. Of course, we do not blame him, for he cannot help his folly; he is like the morally insensitive man brought up in a bad environment: we should not blame him, but we should not think him virtuous.

Admittedly, these are extreme cases. Often we do praise a man who "sticks up for his principles," whether we agree with his principles or not; but these principles must be reasonable to some extent. In other words, if he does the wrong thing, it must at least be the sort of thing that would be done by a rational person trying to do the right thing. The aim and ideal of any moral action must be to do the right thing for the right reason. Objective rightness and motive both play an essential part. A man who acts without taking the trouble to find out what is right is condemned. In fact, when we say that he acts for the right reason, we mean, among other things, that he has done his best to discover what the right action is. He must even, as we have said, make a sensible shot at it: to say "he meant well" is often a dubious compliment. It seems, then, that a conscience must be sensitive and informed for a man to be virtuous. The intellect plays a very definite part.

At the same time, this part played by the intellect can be ambiguous. Sometimes we seem to accept a line of reasoning and act upon it, but then say afterwards: "I knew that it was wrong all the time." Our assent to the argument had not been at the deepest level; the logic had seemed sound, but we never felt that we had grasped the truth of it in the fullest sense. To use Cardinal Newman's phraseology, we gave it a notional assent, not a real assent. Often, we do not give this real assent to a moral argument until we are faced with the practical question ourselves. In peace-time, for example, we may accept the arguments for the view that it is a duty to fight for one's country; when war comes, we can see whether our assent was notional or real, whether we had treated the problem as a kind of intellectual exercise, or whether we had faced up to its true reality and fully grasped the principle in question.

Now according to Aristotle, virtue is a condition of soul which is acquired by a series of good acts. It is not an act in itself, but the virtuous soul is reliable when it has occasion to act, because, in a close combination of act and will, it sees what is right and does it. Its actions flow spontaneously, as it were, from the moral principles which it has fully grasped, and the proof that it has grasped them lies in the fact that, when put to the test, it has carried them out.

Such knowledge of right has reached the depths of the human person, and we should contend that on this level the distinction between will and intellect is misleading. We are reminded of Aristotle's own definition of choice which he calls "desireful reason" or "reasonable desire." An act of choice, then, like any other fully human act, is made by the complete person. In the same way, the condition of true virtue is the condition of a person below the level where any clear distinction between intellect and will applies. It is a condition that is rational in the deepest sense. It has little to do with learning or powers of rational analysis. A simple person can be of the highest virtue.

To sum up, we have admitted that distinctions between the choice of the will and the reasoning of the intellect can be made near the surface, as it were, of a man's mind. We have shown that, nonetheless, virtue, however imperfect, must include knowledge at every stage. We have made use of Newman's distinction between notional and real assent. It seems that the more imperfect knowledge is, the more notional it is. Similarly, the more imperfect virtue is, the more purely it is a question of will, a question of making choices that are dimly felt to be right.

On the other hand, the deeper virtue goes, the more closely it seems to be identified with knowledge, until, in persons of the highest virtue, to know what is right is to do it. Such persons may be an ideal. It may be that in practice "the irrational parts of the soul," as Aristotle puts it, are always with us. But Socrates might answer that just in so far as the soul is irrational it is lacking in virtue. Taking the terms absolutely, it remains true to say that virtue is knowledge.

We said at the beginning of the chapter (p. 15) that Socrates set out to replace the conventional values that the sophists were destroying by the lasting values to be discovered in the nature of human life itself. We also said that he looked for permanent truths in the general statements that could be made about the changing particulars of which we have experience. Since, then, there was something constant which could be described as "human nature," there had to be some constant laws according to which human nature would reach its fullest development, and these laws were the moral values that Socrates sought. Since these values are rooted in human nature, they cannot be reduced to a number of conventions by which various communities have happened to live. They are absolute and unchanging.

What, then, of the sophists' claim that different people in fact live by different rules? If Socrates is right, how can we account for the wide divergency of human standards of behaviour? Consider our own disputes today about divorce, for example, or euthanasia, or the limits of political liberty! Numerous races have had the custom of exposing unwanted children at birth; yet many would think this evil. Today it is not unknown for badly deformed babies to be despatched by the surgeon's knife when they are born; many think this evil, while others claim that not to do so is immoral.

The first answer must be that it is not the same thing to claim, as Socrates did, that there are objective moral values, and to claim, as

Socrates did not, that these values are understood in the same way by all; in fact, Socrates was always emphasizing the corruption of human nature as we find it. Secondly, ethics, as we call the science of moral behaviour, is a practical science, and, perhaps more often than they think, people agree about principles but disagree about their application. For example, no community, as far as I know, has thought it right to kill indiscriminately, though many may interpret the wrongfulness of homicide differently: some have always been ready to kill strangers or even the more useless members of their own tribe; in more civilized races, some people allow killing in self-defence, in a just war, or as a judicial punishment for certain crimes; others have condemned killing in every circumstance. We may feel that the application of the principle has sometimes been very wide of the mark, but would contend that it has always been at least dimly felt to be there, however ill-informed or insensitive the public conscience may have been. For example, every language has a word for "murder," and equally for "stealing," "lying," "disloyalty" and so on, and all these words convey moral disapproval. Where such things have apparently been countenanced, has there not always been some special reason for it, whether we think it a good one or not? Baby girls, for example, have not been just disposed of like kittens, but exposed (to avoid the stain of direct killing), where a surplus population could not be fed; deformed babies have been knifed to prevent their suffering pain as they grow up.

We conclude, then, that all races have acted as if there were objective moral values, and that there has been considerable agreement as to what these values are.

So much, then, for the appeal to history. More fundamentally, let us revert to the question of whether or not any sense can be made of any moral statement if absolute, objective moral values are denied. We have already seen (p. 26) that for an action to be right in the fullest sense, it must be both objectively right and done from the right motive, and that "right motive" includes the notion that there is an objective right which we have done our best to discover. Let us now reflect a little further on our own self-knowledge and use of moral terms.

All moral statements include the idea of obligation; the words "ought" and "duty," in fact, are normally used to express this relation: "You ought not to do this"; "This ought not to be allowed"; "I felt it to be my duty." In fact, these words "duty" and "ought" are unique; they cannot be expressed in terms of anything else. Our moral code may be based on this system of ethics or that; we may say with Jeremy Bentham that it is our duty to promote the greatest happiness of the greatest number, and that all moral principles can be reduced to that fundamental principle; but we are not thereby explaining what we mean by duty; we are merely offering a yardstick or criterion by which, in any particular case, we can tell what our duty is. In Bentham's statement, the word "duty" is a known quantity that has to be imported to give meaning to his sentence. Bentham is not saying that duty means "to promote the greatest happiness" etc.; for that would reduce his principle to a tautology; it would be like saying: "To promote the greatest happiness of the greatest number is to promote the greatest happiness of the greatest number." The truth is that "duty" has a meaning of its own which we all understand but cannot analyze. The idea of "duty" and "ought" cannot be conveyed in other terms. A child without a moral sense could never be taught it. We teach children to be good by appealing to the moral sense that they already have. (We may appeal to other senses at the same time, but this is purely secondary: a right use of punishment may awaken the moral sense and strengthen it; it can never instil it from the start.)

There are philosophers who contend that this sense of duty is really no more than an emotion: when we say that a course of action is right or wrong, we are merely giving it a kind of grunt of approval or disapproval; it is something purely subjective that results from our upbringing or is one of the inherited characteristics of our race (cf. pp. 184 f.). Let us test this opinion by an appeal to self-knowledge.

Let the reader think of some important moral choice in his life, when he has felt a duty to do something and a strong attraction not to do it. Can that sense of duty be explained away as an emotion signifying approval? Was it similar to the emotional attractions that urged him not to do his duty? Can he sincerely deny that he knew that he had an obligation which no attraction or repugnance, no sense of approval or disapproval could remove? Even if we explain away our own duties in this manner, we are quick to show indignation when we suffer for what we consider to be somebody else's lack of moral sense. Such indignation about others would be ridiculous if it meant nothing more than that we grunted differently about the same things. In fact, all our language on moral matters, the very words that we use, like "praise," "blame," "responsibility," "obligation" and so forth, make nonsense if we deny that we are all fundamentally bound by the same law. In any survey of human life, surely nothing can be more significant than that we all know what we mean by "right" and "wrong," that many have laid down their lives on principles affecting their application, and that most attempts to throw light upon them tell us less than we already know.

We have considerably elaborated on Socrates's teaching, but this teaching itself was a painstaking elaboration of three simple and closely connected points:

1) human nature, unlike particular human beings, can be made the subject of general statements which are always true or false independently of time and space;

2) moral values, rooted in this human nature, are derived from an unchanging law which marks the path for human perfection;

3) virtue consists in a real knowledge of these values.

In the moral sphere, then, the answer to the problem of the One and the Many lies in human nature itself and the phenomenon of conscience. The moral experience of individual men implies a law that is binding on all. We can discover more about this law by analyzing the language that we use in moral questions and by examining human nature and trying to discover wherein its perfection lies.

3. THE SYNTHESIS COMPLETED: PLATO'S IDEALISM

Apart from a brief reference to the fundamental principles by which he worked, we confined our treatment of Socrates to the sphere of ethics, because it is generally agreed that ethics was his primary concern. This is not, of course, to deny that a man's principles of conduct must be based on his view of reality as a whole or, to use the technical word, his metaphysics. In fact, Socrates's teaching was the result of his metaphysical belief in the immortality of the soul and its potential happiness. This belief, as we have seen, was itself based on the nature of human knowledge and moral experience, neither of which made any sense to him unless he assumed the existence of an absolute truth wherein alone he could find an aim and purpose for his existence. As far as we can tell, it was left to Plato (c. 428–348 B.C.) to work out in more detail what we may call the metaphysics of Socrates's ethical teaching.

Before we proceed, we must point out another historical difficulty: even supposing that we make a simple distinction between the thought of Plato and that of Socrates, that thought itself is not easy to piece together; for, although we have a number of Plato's dialogues, these dialogues were popular expositions of his philosophy and are not written in any systematic form. Personally, I believe that even if we had Plato's thought, as we have Aristotle's, in the form of lecture notes, we should not be all that much the wiser. Aristotle was essentially a biologist, who was accustomed to classifying things scientifically according to their genera and species; Plato was much more in the tradition of his master, Socrates: he too had a touch of the visionary about him which made him suspicious of systems.

An interesting point in this connection is Plato's device of putting some of his most difficult thought into the form of a myth. Some scholars hold that this was merely a means of making it more digestible for the general reader. It seems, however, more likely that Plato felt that the ordinary method of discursive reasoning—of reasoning, that is, by clear and distinct logical stages—could not adequately convey his meaning: it was neater and more exact, but would lead either to oversimplification or to impossible obscurity; it was better to hint at his meaning rather than try to analyze it. Plato himself seems to suggest this when he introduces the famous simile of the sun in Book VI of the *Republic*; we shall quote this at length in a moment, so that the reader can judge for himself.

Plato was born at Athens or Aegina about 428 B.C. From the age of about twenty he had known Socrates, but he was never one of his regular disciples. In about 388 B.C. he founded at Athens the famous Academy, which might be described as the first European university; students came from various parts of the classical world to study philosophy, mathematics, astronomy, physics and other kindred subjects; it was unlike the "practical" training of the sophists, and rhetoric was not on the syllabus; the disinterested pursuit of knowledge was the only aim. This knowledge could, of course, and ought to, be put to practical use, but that is not what the sophists—or for that matter modern educationists—mean when they talk about "practical training." Members of the Academy, for example, were sometimes asked to frame constitutions for new states that were being founded. Plato himself went to Syracuse to educate the king's nephew, and returned again later to give his advice when that nephew himself became king.

We have seen (p. 20) that according to Socrates permanent truth was to be found only in general statements: particular things change, but species do not change. For convenience, let us use the word "particular" to describe the members of a class or type and the word "universal" to describe that class or type to which particulars belong; thus my dog Caesar is a particular of the universal "dog," or Everest is a particular of the universal "mountain." According to this terminology (which is the usual one in philosophy), it is statements about universals that are permanently true.

This was the point from which Plato began, and he argued somewhat like this: knowledge must be of what is (which we call "reality"); if reality is to be known, we must be able to make statements about it which contain permanent, objective truth; if this truth is to be permanent, it must refer to a reality which is itself permanent; this permanence can be found in the universal, but not in the particular; universals, therefore, constitute the true reality.

For Plato the universal is the real essence or nature of a thing; it is the thing-in-itself, as he often likes to describe it. When, for example, a woman says "Just like a man!" she means that this behaviour reveals the very essence of the male sex; it is masculinity personified. Plato had the same feeling about all particulars: they were merely imperfect revelations of the universal that lay, as it were, in the background; they were mere approximations to the thing-in-itself. Plato, then, like Heraclitus (vid. p. 9), could be considered an idealist.

When we say that a thing is real, we mean that it exists. According to Plato, these universals, these Forms or Ideas as he called them, had an existence of their own in a different world from this. Of course, if we assume a different world, we must also assume that "this-world" language does not apply to it; Plato did not think of the Forms as existing literally "in a place" at all; but we are forced to put it in these words with the necessary mental qualification. Broadly speaking, Plato held that every particular which we experience in this world can be referred to its universal type or Form which has a different kind of existence not-in-this-world.

If universals alone are real in the fullest sense, what of particulars? In what sense, the reader will already be asking, does this world exist at all in Plato's eyes? He thought of this world as but a flimsy copy of the world of Forms; material things are really but an unsubstantial shadow of what is truly real; just as our souls are dulled and made insensitive to truth by contact with our bodies, so the true essence or nature of anything exists but darkly and obscurely in contact with matter; matter, we might say, is an opaque substance which prevents the full light of the Form from shining into it.

This, of course, is scarcely more than metaphor. What precisely did Plato believe the relation between the universal and the particular to be? Here again we have to face the difficulty of language: just as the language of this world is inadequate for describing the world of Forms, so it is unable to convey the relation between that world and this. Plato sometimes talks of "sharing" or "participation" and sometimes more vaguely of "imitation" (MIMESIS). When he says that the particular shares or participates in the universal, he is unwilling, it seems, to drain this world of too much reality; when he says that the particular is an imitation of the universal, he reminds us that, when all is said and done, the title "real" can be applied to the particular only by courtesy. Of the things of this world only the soul can rightfully claim to be fully real.

The Forms themselves do not all have equal status. They are hierarchically arranged under a principle of unity, called the Good in the *Republic* and the Beautiful in the *Symposium*. As far as we know, Plato did not work out this hierarchy in any detail, but apparently the more general the universal, the nearer it stood to the principle of unity which was the most general of all; thus, for example, one might put in ascending order the universals "triangle," "three," "one." In this example (which is mine, not Plato's), we can see that the higher Form makes intelligible the lower: thus, if we know what "one" is, we know what "three" is; if we know the meaning of "three" and "angle" (assuming that "angle" has the same status as "three"), we can understand "triangle."

It seems clear, at any rate, that this principle of intelligibility was essential to the hierarchy. In fact, the whole point of the sun simile in the *Republic* is that the Good gives intelligibility to the intelligible world (or the world of the mind) as the sun gives light to the visible world; in other words, the Forms themselves are intelligible only in the light of the higher principle which co-ordinates them. We might say that nothing can be intelligible except in so far as it can be seen in relation to that which is the ultimate good of all, and this must be Goodness itself.

If this is obscure, we can only leave Plato to speak for himself. In the

Republic, Socrates has been discussing the education of the "Guardians" who are to rule this ideal state. In the final stage of their education, they must have knowledge of the Good, but Socrates, as we have already said (p. 33), falters when it comes to analyzing the Good and suggests instead the simile of the sun; Socrates is the narrator in this dialogue, and here he is reporting his conversation with Glaucon:

Still, I must implore you, Socrates, said Glaucon, not to turn away just as you are reaching the goal; if you will only give such an explanation of the good as you have already given of justice and temperance and the other virtues, we shall be satisfied.

Yes, my friend, and I shall be at least equally satisfied, but I cannot help fearing that I shall fail, and that my indiscreet zeal will bring ridicule upon me. No, sweet sirs, let us not at present ask what is the actual nature of the good, for to reach what is now in my thoughts would be an effort too great for me. But of the child of the good who is likest him, I would fain speak, if I could be sure that you wished to hear—otherwise, not.

By all means, he said, tell us about the child, and you shall remain in our debt for the account of the parent.

I do indeed wish, I replied, that I could pay, and you receive, the account of the parent, and not, as now, of the offspring only; take, however, this latter by way of interest,* and at the same time have a care that I do not render a false account, although I have no intention of deceiving you.

Yes, we will take all the care that we can: proceed.

Yes, I said, but I must first come to an understanding with you, and remind you of what I have mentioned in the course of this discussion, and at many other times.

What?

The old story, that there is a many beautiful and a many good, and so of other things which we describe and define; to all of them the term "many" is applied.

True, he said.

And there is an absolute beauty and an absolute good, and of other things to which the term "many" is applied there is an absolute; for they may be brought under a single idea, which is called the essence of each.

Very true.

* A word-play upon *Tokos*, which means both "offspring" and "interest."

The many, as we say, are seen but known, and the ideas are known but not seen.

Exactly.

And what is the organ with which we see the visible things?

The sight, he said.

And with the hearing, I said, we hear, and with the other senses perceive the other objects of sense?

True.

But have you remarked that sight is by far the most costly and complex piece of workmanship which the artificer of the senses ever contrived?

No, I never have, he said.

Then reflect: has the ear or voice need of any third or additional nature in order that the one may be able to hear and the other to be heard?

Nothing of the sort.

No, indeed, I replied; and the same is true of most, if not all, the other senses—you would not say that any of them requires such an addition?

Certainly not.

But you see that without the addition of some other nature there is no seeing or being seen?

How do you mean?

Sight being, as I conceive, in the eyes, and he who has eyes wanting to see; colour being also present to them, still unless there be a third nature specially adapted to the purpose, the owner of the eyes will see nothing and the colours will be invisible.

Of what nature are you speaking?

Of that which you term light, I replied.

True, he said.

Noble, then, is the bond which links together sight and visibility, and great beyond other bonds by no small difference of nature; for light is their bond, and light is no ignoble thing?

Nay, he said, the reverse of ignoble.

And which, I said, of the gods in heaven would you say is the lord of this element? Whose is that light which makes the eye to see perfectly and the visible to appear?

You mean the sun, as you and all mankind say.

May not the relation of sight to this deity be described as follows?

How?

Neither sight nor the eye in which sight resides is the sun?

No.

Yet of all the organs of sense the eye is most like the sun?

By far the most like.

And the power which the eye possesses is a sort of effluence which is dispensed from the sun?

Exactly.

Then the sun is not sight, but the author of sight who is recognized by sight?

True, he said.

And this is he whom I call the child of the good, whom the good begat in his own likeness, to be in the visible world, in relation to sight and the things of sight, what the good is in the intellectual world in relation to mind and the things of mind:

Will you be a little more explicit? he said.

Why, you know, I said, that the eyes, when a person directs them towards objects on which the light of day is no longer shining, but the moon and stars only, see dimly, and are nearly blind; they seem to have no clearness of vision in them?

Very true.

But when they are directed towards objects on which the sun shines, they see clearly and there is sight in them?

Certainly.

And the soul is like the eye: when resting upon that on which truth and being shine, the soul perceives and understands, and is radiant with intelligence; but when turned towards the twilight of becoming and perishing, then she has opinion only, and goes blinking about, and is first of one opinion and then of another, and seems to have no intelligence?

Just so.

Now, that which imparts truth to the known and the power of knowing to the knower is what I would have you term the idea of good, and this you will deem to be the cause of science, and of truth in so far as the latter becomes the subject of knowledge; beautiful, too, as are both truth and knowledge, you will be right in esteeming this other nature as more beautiful than either; and, as in the previous instance, light and sight may be truly said to be like the sun, and yet not to be the sun, so in this other sphere, science and truth may be deemed to be like the good, but not the good; the good has a place of honour yet higher.

What a wonder of beauty that must be, he said, which is the author of science and truth, and yet surpasses them in beauty; for you surely cannot mean to say that pleasure is the good?

God forbid, I replied; but may I ask you to consider the image in another point of view?

In what point of view?

You would say, would you not, that the sun is not only the author of visibility in all visible things, but of generation and nourishment and growth, though he himself is not generation?

Certainly.

In like manner the good may be said to be not only the author of knowledge to all things known, but of their being and essence, and yet the good is not essence, but far exceeds essence in dignity and power.

Glaucon said, with a ludicrous earnestness: By the light of heaven, how amazing!

Yes, I said, and the exaggeration may be set down to you; for you made me utter my fancies.*

Socrates now continues with another simile, the simile of the line. The interpretation of this is difficult and would take us into new depths where the issue would only be further confused. However we apply the simile of the line in detail, it is clear that it suggests a very sharp division between the world of the senses and the world of the mind: the former can at best produce in us a vague kind of belief (PISTIS); it is only in the latter that we come to grips with truth in the full sense of the word, whether it be by understanding (DIANOIA)—the fruits of discursive reasoning—or intuitive knowledge (NOESIS), which is the highest form of knowledge and the ultimate aim of the human mind; intuitive knowledge is the direct knowledge of the Forms, including the Knowledge of the Good, without which, as we have seen, these Forms are not intelligible. ("Intuition," of course, has nothing to do with "instinct," although nowadays the two are sometimes confused: the Latin verb *intueor* means "I look at," and an intuition is a direct view of truth, as it really is.)

This brings us to the end of Book VI of the *Republic*. Book VII opens with a more homely parable, the famous simile of the cave. This takes a much broader sweep over the whole condition of human life and describes the ignorance of those who are completely immersed in the world of sense, the difficulty of breaking out of this state of igno-

---

* Plato, Republic, VI, 506d–509c (tr. Jowett).

rance (the state of belief or PISTIS described in the simile of the line),
and the difficulty, once one has broken out, of enlightening those who
have not yet done so. Here is the passage:

And now, I said, let me show in a figure how far our nature is enlightened or unenlightened: Behold! human beings living in an under-
ground den, which has a mouth open towards the light and reaching
all along the den; here they have been from their childhood, and have
their legs and necks chained so that they cannot move, and can only
see before them, being prevented by the chains from turning round
their heads. Above and behind them a fire is blazing at a distance, and
between the fire and the prisoners there is a raised way; and you will
see, if you look, a low wall built along the way, like the screen which
marionette players have in front of them, over which they show the
puppets.

I see.

And do you see, I said, men passing along the wall carrying all sorts
of vessels, and statues and figures of animals made of wood and stone
and various materials, which appear over the wall? Some of them are
talking, others silent.

You have shown me a strange image, and they are strange prisoners.

Like ourselves, I replied; and they see only their own shadows, or the
shadows of one another, which the fire throws on the opposite wall of
the cave?

True, he said; how could they see anything but the shadows if they
were never allowed to move their heads?

And of the objects which are being carried in like manner they would
only see the shadows?

Yes, he said.

And if they were able to converse with one another, would they not
suppose that they were naming what was actually before them?

Very true.

And suppose further that the prison had an echo which came from
the other side, would they not be sure to fancy when one of the passers-
by spoke that the voice they heard came from the passing shadow?

No question, he replied.

To them, I said, the truth would be literally nothing but the shadows
of the images.

That is certain.

And now look again, and see what will naturally follow if the prisoners are released and disabused of their error. At first, when any of them is liberated and compelled suddenly to stand up and turn his neck round and walk and look towards the light, he will suffer sharp pains; the glare will distress him, and he will be unable to see the realities of which in his former state he had seen the shadows; and then conceive someone saying to him, that what he saw before was an illusion, but that now, when he is approaching nearer to being and his eye is turned towards more real existence, he has a clearer vision,—what will be his reply? And you may further imagine that his instructor is pointing to the objects as they pass and requiring him to name them,—will he not be perplexed? Will he not fancy that the shadows which he formerly saw are truer than the objects which are now shown to him?

Far truer.

And if he is compelled to look straight at the light, will he not have a pain in his eyes which will make him turn away to take refuge in the objects of vision which he can see, and which he will conceive to be in reality clearer than the things which are being shown to him?

True, he said.

And suppose once more, that he is reluctantly dragged up a steep and rugged ascent, and held fast until he is forced into the presence of the sun himself, is he not likely to be pained and irritated? When he approaches the light his eyes will be dazzled, and he will not be able to see anything at all of what are now called realities.

Not all in a moment, he said.

He will require to grow accustomed to the sight of the upper world. And first he will see the shadows best, next the reflections of men and other objects in the water, and then the objects themselves; then he will gaze upon the light of the moon and the stars and the spangled heaven; and he will see the sky and the stars by night better than the sun or the light of the sun by day.

Certainly.

Last of all he will be able to see the sun, and not mere reflections of him in the water, but he will see him in his own proper place, and not in another; and he will contemplate him as he is.

Certainly.

He will then proceed to argue that this is he who gives the season and the years, and is the guardian of all that is in the visible world, and in a certain way the cause of all things which he and his fellows have been accustomed to behold?

Clearly, he said, he would first see the sun and then reason about him.

And when he remembered his old habitation, and the wisdom of the den and his fellow-prisoners, do you not suppose that he would felicitate himself on the change, and pity them?

Certainly, he would.

And if they were in the habit of conferring honours among themselves on those who were quickest to observe the passing shadows and to remark which of them went before, and which followed after, and which were together; and who were therefore best able to draw conclusions as to the future, do you think that he would care for such honours and glories, or envy the possessors of them? Would he not say with Homer,

Better to be the poor servant of a poor master, and to endure anything, rather than think as they do and live after their manner?

Yes, he said, I think that he would rather suffer anything than entertain these false notions and live in this miserable manner.

Imagine once more, I said, such a one coming suddenly out of the sun to be replaced in his old situation; would he not be certain to have his eyes full of darkness?

To be sure, he said.

And if there were a contest, and he had to compete in measuring shadows with the prisoners who had never moved out of the den, while his sight was still weak, and before his eyes had become steady (and the time which would be needed to acquire this new habit of sight might be very considerable), would he not be ridiculous? Men would say of him that up he went and down he came without his eyes; and that it was better not even to think of ascending; and if anyone tried to loose another and lead him up to the light, let them only catch the offender and they would put him to death.

No question, he said.

This entire allegory, I said, you may now append, dear Glaucon, to the previous argument; the prison-house is the world of sight, the light of the fire is the sun, and you will not misapprehend me if you interpret the journey upwards to be ascent of the soul into the intellectual world according to my poor belief, which at your desire, I have expressed—whether rightly or wrongly God knows. But, whether true or false, my opinion is that in the world of knowledge the idea of good appears last of all, and is seen only with an effort; and when seen, is also inferred to be the universal author of all things beautiful and right, parent of light and of the lord of light in this visible world, and the immediate source of reason and truth in the intellectual; and that this is the power upon which he who would act rationally either in public or private life must have his eye fixed.

I agree, he said, as far as I am able to understand you.*

Like Glaucon, we may feel a little bewildered about the details, but the main idea is clear. The essential point is brought home by the return to the simile of the sun: the sun, representing the Good, blinds us until we get used to its light reflected in other things, but, once we have looked upon it, we understand that without its light we would never have been able to see these other things; we realize, in fact, that we have been looking upon it indirectly all the time.

The return of the released prisoners from the upper world (representing the world of the mind or true knowledge) back to the cave (the world of sense or mere belief) need not concern us here. We must remember that Socrates was discussing the education of those picked men in his state whose duty it would be to return from their contemplative studies to the practical work of governing their fellows. Socrates had no illusions about the reception that they would receive and the difficulties that they would have in acclimating themselves to practical matters.

Lest Plato's views should seem too narrowly intellectual or too unsympathetic to the good things in this world, we shall end our brief exposition of his Theory of Ideas by quoting another passage in a different context. As we have said, the Good of the *Republic* is to be identified with the Beautiful of the *Symposium*. The symposium, or banquet, in question was held in honor of the poet Agathon, who had won a prize at the dramatic festival on the previous day. Since most of the guests had drunk deeply on the actual night of the success, they decide to drink merely with moderation on this evening and, sending away the flute-girl to play to the women in the inner part of the house, they settle down to a kind of intellectual parlor game: each banqueter has to deliver a speech in praise of love. After speeches of varying flippancy and excellence, it comes to Socrates's turn. He, of course, cannot make a speech outright, but has to clear the ground first with his usual

* Plato, *Republic*, VII, 514a–517c.

method of question and answer—just to show how much off the track
the other speakers were. Then he tells them of a certain Mantinean
woman called Diotima and what she told him of love, love as the
motive force in the pursuit of perfection.

The *Republic* told us of the ascent to truth. If, like Keats, we look
upon truth from another point of view and call it beauty—if, that is to
say, we look at the glory of a thing's being what it is rather than the
fact that it is—we find ourselves drawn to that glory, or beauty, by love
(EROS).

Without love, in fact, knowledge itself would be impossible; for it
is love which attracts us to things and makes us want to know them,
and, when we know them, it is love which gives us joy in the knowledge.
Now, we saw that we reached the Good by proceeding from the truth
of particulars to the truth of universals, and then by ascending the
hierarchy of universals themselves, which take precedence in order of
their generality; since the pursuit of absolute Beauty is the same pursuit seen from a different point of view, it will naturally take the same
course. This is how Diotima described it to Socrates (after the same
hesitation at broaching a difficult theme that Socrates himself revealed
in the *Republic*):

These are the lesser mysteries of love, into which even you, Socrates,
may enter; to the greater and more hidden ones which are the crown of
these, and to which, if you pursue them in a right spirit, they will lead,
I know not whether you will be able to attain. But I will do my utmost
to inform you, and do you follow if you can. For he who would proceed
rightly in this matter should begin in youth to turn to beautiful forms;
and first, if his instructor guide him rightly, he should learn to love one
such form only—out of that he should create fair thoughts; and soon
he will himself perceive that the beauty of one form is truly related to
the beauty of another; and then if beauty in general is his pursuit, how
foolish would he be not to recognize that beauty in every form is one
and the same! And when he perceives this he will abate his violent love
of the one which he will despise and deem a small thing, and will become a lover of all beautiful forms; this will lead him on to consider
that the beauty of the mind is more honourable than the beauty of the
outward form. So that if a virtuous soul have but little comeliness, he
will be content to love and tend him, and will search out and bring to

the birth thoughts which may improve the young, until his beloved is compelled to contemplate and see the beauty of institutions and laws, and understand that all is of one kindred, and that personal beauty is only a trifle; and after laws and institutions he will lead him on to the sciences, that he may see their beauty, being not like a servant in love with the beauty of one youth or man or institution, himself a slave mean and calculating, but looking at the abundance of beauty and drawing towards the sea of beauty, and creating and beholding many fair and noble thoughts and notions in boundless love of wisdom; until at length he grows and waxes strong, and at last the vision is revealed to him of a single science, which is the science of beauty everywhere. To this I will proceed; please to give me your very best attention.

For he who has been instructed thus far in the things of love, and who has learned to see the beautiful in due order and succession, when he comes toward the end will suddenly perceive a nature of wondrous beauty—and this, Socrates, is that final cause of all our former toils, which in the first place is everlasting—not growing and decaying, or waxing and waning; in the next place not fair in one point of view and foul in another, or at one time or in one relation or at one place fair, at another time or in another relation or at another place foul, as if fair to some and foul to others, or in the likeness of a face or hands or any part of the bodily frame, or in any form of speech or knowledge, nor existing in any other being; as, for example, an animal, whether in earth or heaven, but beauty only, absolute, separate, simple, and everlasting, which without diminution and without increase, or any change, is imparted to the ever-growing and perishing beauties of all other things. He who under the influence of true love rising upward from these begins to see that beauty, is not far from the end. And the true order of going or being led by another to the things of love, is to use the beauties of earth as steps along which he mounts upwards for the sake of that other beauty, going from one to two, from two to all fair forms, and from fair forms to fair actions, and from fair actions to fair notions, until from fair notions he arrives at the notion of absolute beauty, and at last knows what the essence of beauty is.*

In discussing Plato, no less than Socrates, our first question must be: Is there an objective truth? We have already argued in the previous chapter that it is impossible to account for moral experience unless we assume an objective and absolute truth which can make absolute de-

---

* Plato, *Symposium*, 209e–211d (tr. Jowett).

mands on us. We would suggest a similar argument from our intellectual experience as a whole: just as moral experience makes no sense
if there is no right or wrong, so cognitive experience (the experience
of knowing) makes no sense if there is no true or false. We do not, be
it noted, wish to anticipate the different problem as to whether we can
be certain that we know; this so-called "problem of knowledge" has
been the main preoccupation of philosophers for the last three hundred years, and we shall examine it later on, together with Plato's own
views on the subject (Part III). What we are now asking is: Quite
apart from our ability to check the truth or falsehood of any statement,
does it make sense to use the words "true" or "false" if there is nothing
objective to which such a statement could apply? Some philosophers
say that "true" merely means "consistent": statements are true if they
are consistent with each other. But the obvious answer to that is that
one man may hold a series of consistent views and another a different
series equally consistent; can we really say that the first man's views
are no truer than the second man's, or even that there is no sense at
all in asking whether the one view is truer than the other? Differences
of opinion, in fact, suggest that there is something to differ about.
Without this any kind of discussion, any use of words, we might say, is
meaningless. The very attempt to prove the truth of the theory that
there is no objective truth is itself an absurdity.

Granted, then, that we agree that truth must be objective, our second
question must be: Is this to be found only in universal statements?
Does the statement: "Horses are animals" suggest a grasp of a fuller
kind of reality than the statement: "That is a horse"? Plato would say:
"Yes; because there is something inevitable and changeless about the
first statement, while the truth of the second is as transitory as the horse
to which it refers." Perhaps, before we go on any further, we ought to
make clear the distinction that we are making between "truth" and
"reality": we are using the word "true" as an epithet to be applied to
statements and "real" as an epithet to be applied to things; then, a
statement will be true (and objective) if it conforms to what is real.
A statement, of course, may be true but not objective—for example:
"Mermaids have tails like fish"; but it can be seen that this is a different kind of truth from the truth of the statement: "Horses are
animals." It is this latter kind of truth with which we are concerned

here. Does it refer to a higher kind of reality than the statement: "That is a horse"?

Assuming that it makes sense to talk about a "fuller" or "higher" kind of reality, most of us would still perhaps be rather suspicious of Plato's answer. We seem, in fact, to get our word "real" from the particulars that exist around us. Here we feel on safe ground; general statements can be notoriously misleading when, as we say, "we come to the actual facts of the case." Similarly, a person who is too fond of abstract thought, and so of making general statements, is sometimes criticized as being "out of touch with reality."

This last phrase is worth considering a moment. It implies that we shall not reach truth if our awareness of ordinary things becomes blurred. It implies that our approach has become, as we say, "merely academic," where the word "academic" does not hark back etymologically to Plato's Academy, but suggests an arid approach that is sometimes found in more modern dons or schoolmasters; it goes back, in fact, no further than our own adolescence when perhaps we were taught by some unenlightened teacher who had invented a little world of his own in which he used to amuse himself in the pretense of amusing us. Most people, then, feel that generalizations involve a certain loss of reality and that if we play the game of generalizing too eagerly, we shall lose reality altogether. We might put it this way: generalizations are true precisely in so far as they take into account the particulars to which they refer; for it is these particulars that in the first instance impress their reality upon us; the universal, so far from being more real, seems to borrow a kind of secondary reality from them. We shall say more of this in the next chapter; for this is just the point with which Aristotle begins.

We are now faced with something of a paradox: the particular is for us the real thing that arouses our interest and sets us thinking; but the moment we start thinking about it, we do so in terms of universals. Our minds seem quite incapable of treating a particular as a particular; we can understand it only in its relation to other particulars. Even if we make a particular statement like: "That is a brown horse," we have to use our former knowledge of colors and horses in order to make it; virtually we are saying: "That thing belongs both to the class of things that I have called horse and the class of things that I have called brown." Similarly, when I am introduced to a horse for the first time, I am virtually told: "When you see this kind of thing in the future, call it a horse"; and, as I see horses, as I accumulate knowledge of the species, I know more about every particular horse that I encounter. Thus if my horse is sick, I would prefer to call in a vet who has experience of horses. The particular introduces us to the universal, and knowledge of the universal brings us knowledge of the particular. Science studies the behavior of particulars, but in so doing it takes good care to discount any behavior that for any reason may be peculiar to the particular under observation. Science, in fact, is based on the hypothesis that the particular reveals the universal, and that relations between universals remain constant.

We might take this a stage further and say that all speech is based on the same hypothesis. It would be tempting even to say that the same is true of all thought. Yet, what are we to say about poetry? Poetry is speech, but it usually conveys its meaning by a direct form of suggestion through evocative words and images; in fact, it is not a bad definition of poetry to say that it is verse which you can understand but not analyze: if you put a piece of verse into prose—the medium of scientific analysis—and the prose exhausts all the meaning of the verse, then you can be sure that the verse is not poetry. Similarly with our ordinary thought from day to day: we often have thoughts that are difficult to convey in speech; it may because they are too vague, because we have not applied our minds to them with sufficient care; but it may also be because they are too deep, because we have something of the poet's insight but none of his special powers of expression. Such knowledge is often general, in a manner of speaking, but it does not take the form of a generalization; rather, it is a vista seen through the key-hole of the particular; in this way, for example, Blake was able "to see a world in a grain of sand."

Many philosophers, while admitting this kind of knowledge, treat it as exceptional. We would suggest that it is this attitude which has often led philosophy to fall into disrepute. A man engrossed in analysis comes to believe that all thought is analytical. He begins to work on the assumption that what cannot be reduced to a discursive, systematic form is not worth saying. So he produces a system which does violence to truth by trying to force it into a pattern which he can completely grasp and analyze. This is what we shall call "the systematic fallacy." It is a pity too that the word "reason" is used to describe both that faculty which distinguishes man from beast and that more limited faculty of discursive reasoning by which we argue stage by stage, building up logical connections between universals. Discursive reasoning can be seen in its barest form in mathematics: for example, take the simple inference "If $6x = 3$, then $x = \frac{1}{2}$"; this might be the final deduction of a series, all similar, if more complicated, in form. In fact any inference from one thing to another, whatever the subject of context, is a form of discursive reasoning.

We should argue that most of our intellectual activity, most of our consciousness, in fact, is only partly of this kind. Discursive thought is always interpenetrated by intuitive thought; we understand directly and indirectly at the same time. To revert to our old example (p. 4) of the animals that we see in a field: as these *things* (to use the vaguest word possible) impinge on our consciousness, we take in (intuitively) and classify (discursively) what we see; at no stage can we say that the process is purely intuitive or purely discursive, though we might call the beginning and the end, when we first turn our minds to the animals and then later grasp as a whole what we have seen, predominately intuitive, and the middle stages predominately discursive. In practice, of course, if the sight is familiar, all these stages are completed instantaneously; but this makes no difference to the essential procedure that is implicit in such instantaneous perception.

In the same way, if we contrast the approach of the mathematician with the approach of the poet, we can observe similar predominant, but incomplete, differences: the mathematician works for the most part discursively, but he must grasp intuitively the axioms from which he reasons and the logical necessity of each stage of that reasoning; the poet works for the most part intuitively, but he must observe elementary principles of grammar and logic, which are essentially discursive in form. The ordinary intellectual processes of most of us will fall somewhere between these extremes. Analysis is always an essential element in these processes, but it is only a means, not an end in itself. The end is a grasp of a reality that a more perfect mind would take in directly.

Plato was very much aware of this. His whole philosophy leads in the end to the grasp of the First Principle of things by the intuitive mind (NOUS). Moreover it is true, as Plato saw, that particulars are transitory in a sense in which universals are not. It is true that we can be exact and lucid about universals, whereas particulars are forever eluding us; although they seem to be the immediate object of our knowledge, we can never quite exhaust their meaning. It is also true that such intuition as we have of particulars is impressive chiefly because it seems to embrace something more than the particular. Whether we consider the poet or any other artist, it is the note of universality in his work that arouses our excitement; nobody would quote Blake if he saw only a grain of sand in a grain of sand.

Plato, we feel, was on the verge of a great discovery, but even he fell at least half way into the systematic fallacy. Although, as we have seen in discussing his use of myth (p. 33), he did not oversimplify what was complex and obscure, from the beginning he was misled by our habit of analysis: he found that we could talk about things only by talking about types of things; so he made these types themselves into things. Thus, he lost sight of the original thing, the particular with which he began, and found himself left with a whole set of new things which were no easier to explain. From the point of view of ordinary experience, he had invented a strange new world which threw little light on this one; from the point of view of pure metaphysics, not only, as we have seen, was it difficult for him to give a coherent account of the relation between the two worlds, but he had to face his original problem all over again and account for the relations between the Forms themselves: for the Forms were the particulars of the ideal world.

Plato makes acute the following dilemma. On the one hand, the object of knowledge is that which is. Whether acquired directly or indirectly, knowledge must ultimately signify a state in which the mind grasps that which has, in some sense, a reality of its own; you cannot, therefore, make the universal an ultimate object of knowledge unless you turn it into a special kind of particular; for universals as such are, by definition, abstractions. On the other hand, the mind is unsatisfied with that which is limited; it is always struggling to pass beyond into areas of more universal significance; but the particular is a particular precisely because it is limited to being that thing and not some other thing. It seems, then, that the mind is condemned to working on a reality that is inherently incapable of satisfying it. Worse even than this, it seems that there is a fundamental contradiction in the way the mind works: it ought to be grasping particulars, but in point of fact it seems always to be moving away from them. To put it in the language of the *Symposium*—and this language is of the greatest importance—the lover is unable to focus his vision on the object of his love; he is always gazing beyond into the distance.

4. A DIFFERENT APPROACH: ARISTOTLE'S REALISM

In many ways Plato marks the climax of what we might call typical Greek thought. That thought had begun in the land of Homer with something of the poet's sense of wonder. It took a slightly exotic turn in exile in the West, then came back to Greece and met the full impact of fifth-century humanism. This was especially true in Athens, where all her achievements in literature, art, science and government had left little room for any philosophy that looked to higher values in another world. Greek thought was then rescued by Socrates and set on its path once more, and was eventually crowned by Plato and adorned with all the riches that naturally fell to the new heir of Athenian culture.

After this, it was the turn of Aristotle, a biologist from Thrace. The Thracians were not recognized as Greeks by the rest, any more than were their neighbors in Macedonia. But Macedonia had already produced Philip, who, by the time of Plato's death, was already on the way to becoming the master of the highly cultured peoples who despised him. After Philip had completed his conquests in Greece and shown that he was no barbarian at heart but had profound respect for Greek culture and—at least in the case of Athens—for the Greek way of life, he was assassinated in middle age and succeeded in 336 B.C. by Alexander, a mere youth of barely twenty. Alexander was to conquer most of the world that the Greeks knew about and even places whose existence was new to them. He was no barbarian either; he had been educated by our Thracian biologist.

Aristotle (c. 384–322 B.C.) came to Athens as a young man and studied at the Academy under Plato for twenty years. He left to be Alexander's tutor when Plato died—Plato "whom," so he says, "bad men have not even the right to praise, and who showed in his teachings how to be happy and good at the same time." When Alexander succeeded to the throne of Macedon, Aristotle returned to Athens and founded the Lyceum. The Lyceum, in contrast with the broader basis of the Academy, concentrated more on research, particularly in the physical sciences. It heralded the new age of the specialist, when community life was being broken up and large empires were being built. There was still, however, much of the old Greek spirit at the Lyceum: its members, for example, were called "peripatetics" from their habit of walking about as they discoursed; the hardened specialist prefers to remain at his desk.

For all his devotion to Plato, Aristotle was not very happy with Plato's Theory of Ideas: the clumsiness of explaining one multitude of things by another and the vagueness of the relationship between the Forms and particulars worried his neat and exact mind. Moreover, as a biologist, he was deeply interested in the problem of change. As we saw (pp. 8–11), Heraclitus and Parmenides had raised this question in an acute form: If a thing becomes something else, what is it which changes? If, as we have said, grass becomes cow, how are we to identify what was once grass and is now cow? How are we to maintain the difference between change and substitution? Plato had answered that change occurs when one Form departs and another takes its place; thus, in our example, as the grass is consumed, the Form of cow takes over from the Form of grass. But this still does not explain what it is that is taken over; for, according to the Theory of Ideas, nothing exists where there is no Form to give it existence; grass, therefore, exists thanks to the Form of grass, but when that goes, nothing remains; if a different form gives existence to a new thing, there is nothing whatsoever to connect the new thing with the old. In other words, if you identify a thing with its specific nature, nothing is left when you remove that nature.

Aristotle met this difficulty by a distinction which is at the basis of all his most important philosophical thought—the distinction between potency (DYNAMIS) and act (ENTELECHEIA). A person or thing may be able to do something or to manifest certain qualities, although at any given moment he may not be putting this ability into effect; thus a man asleep has a potency for conscious thought, which is not the property of a stone; a man's ability to think, even though he is not using it, makes a positive difference to the kind of being that he is. In other words, the mere ability to do or be something is an objective difference and cannot be accounted for subjectively as though it were simply a trick of speech.

Now Aristotle used this distinction in two ways. Firstly, for a thing to change, it must have had the potency to undergo that particular kind of change: an acorn grows into an oak but not an elm; grass but not stones are eaten by cows. Change, therefore, is never mere chance substitution.

Secondly, we still have to solve the problem: what changes? This depends on the type of change. If there is no change of identity—if, for example, a green apple becomes red—it is the apple that changes. We shall describe in a moment the account that Aristotle gave of what is called "substance," the inner reality of things which constitutes their identity. The immediate problem of change does not arise so much with this "accidental" change of the apple as with "substantial" change —that is, when one thing becomes something else, as in our example of the cow eating grass. In such a case there must be some underlying identity which enables us to say: "*That* grass became *that* part of the cow." If there is no such identity, if we can only say: "Where there was grass, there is now cow," we are describing "substitution," not "change"; for there to be change, there must be something which changes, there must be some "substratum," something that underlies all substances like grass and cow and can become one or the other. This is what Aristotle calls "prime matter."

Now, prime matter is not a substance in the ordinary sense, because it underlies other substances; it has no nature of its own and, therefore, has no existence of its own; it is in fact merely that which is capable of becoming one substance or another; to use Aristotle's phrase, it is pure potency.

To sum up so far: substantial change is different from substitution for two reasons; firstly, the original thing must have the potency to become the new thing—water must be the kind of thing that can become steam; secondly, there must be a substratum that underlies the two substances; and, since substance is reality in its most fundamental form, this substratum has no existence of its own but is pure potency which needs some nature to actualize it. In both cases, therefore, Aristotle has made use of his distinction between potency and act.

It is, in fact, this distinction which has made it possible for him to answer Parmenides. Parmenides had said (vid. p. 10): "If anything is, it comes out of being or not-being." Aristotle denies this premise, on which Parmenides's whole position is based, by showing that the absolute distinction between being and not-being is an oversimplification. Aristotle has a more subtle approach to the problem of being: this will become clear in the account that he gives of particulars and universals. As a scientist, he was mainly concerned with observing particulars. So, in contrast to Plato, he built his philosophy on them. Now, every particular, every individual thing, has an identity of its own; thus, we speak of *that* cabbage or *this* bridge and give proper names to people, places and even things. This unique identity Aristotle calls "primary substance"; it is that which is "neither asserted of a subject nor present in a subject"; in other words, it is the thing itself—that in virtue of which it is, for example, *that* horse and no other. This terminology, then, allows for the reality of particulars and the distinction between them; it is this which identifies our apple which was once green and is now red.

With reference to universals, Aristotle uses the term "secondary substance," that which is "asserted of a subject, but not present in a subject"; thus "horse" can be asserted of individual horses—we say: "That is a horse," meaning: "That belongs to the species 'horse' "; but we do not identify "that" and "horse"—we do not identify the species with any individual member of it.

What is the significance of this language? Etymologically, "substance is derived from the Latin *substantia*, which means a "standing under"; *substantia* is the traditional translation of Aristotle's word (OUSIA), which is simply the noun from the Greek verb "to be." Thus, by any of these three words we mean the underlying reality of a thing as opposed to its "accidents" which, like the color of the apple, are incidental to it. Substance, therefore, is, as it were, the core of reality. It follows that when Aristotle uses the phrase "primary substance" to signify the identity of particulars, he is saying that reality is to be found, in the first instance, in those particulars. The universal or species, on the other hand, is still real; it is still a substance, but its substance is secondary; that is to say, it is in some way derived from primary substance.

Aristotle, therefore, agrees with Plato that universals are real, but does not agree that they exist separately. This, of course, is not to deny that the universal can "exist" separately in the mind: we can have an idea of "mermaid" by putting together the ideas of "woman" and "fish" although no mermaids exist; the existence of such a universal is subjective; it does not exist unless we think it. The objective universal, however, is quite different: as long as particular horses exist, the universal "horse" exists objectively—that is, quite independently of anyone's thinking it—and it is a reality which can be studied through observing the particular of which it is the species.

Aristotle, however, disagrees fundamentally with Plato in holding that if all the particulars of a universal cease to exist—if, for example, horses become extinct—then the universal or species dies with it: one particular is enough to give life to the universal, but if there is no particular, the universal has no source from which to derive its existence. For it is the essential doctrine of realism that *reality is to be found preeminently in what we perceive rather than in what we think.*

Now, we must not conceive of the Aristotelian universal as a kind of poor relation of the particular or as anything else on the same plane of reality. We must remember the playful irony of the Chinese philosopher when he said that there were three things in a field: a cow, a bull and a pair of animals. Just as "a pair" does not add to or subtract from the cow and bull but is a way of saying something about them, so the universal must not be conceived as existing *in addition* to particulars; rather, it isolates, as it were, a special kind of truth about them. It cannot be emphasized enough that the objectivity of universals, according to Aristotle's theory, is grounded in the particulars of which they are asserted. When, for example, the first black swan was found in Australia, the scientist knew that whiteness was not an inevitable characteristic of the universal "swan." Anything, therefore, that we say about the universal will be proved to be true or false by observation of the appropriate particulars.

Just as Aristotle answered Parmenides with his distinction between potency and act, so he answered Heraclitus with his theory of substance.

Heraclitus, it will be remembered, had denied any permanency in particulars with his statement that all things flow (*vid.* p. 8–9); Aristotle replies that this flux does indeed characterize the behavior of particulars, but does not affect the identity which underlies such behavior. He is, in fact, the first philosopher to give a coherent account of reality in support of the commonsense view that animals, plants and material things all have an identity that they keep over a period of time despite the ever-changing characteristics by which they make themselves known to our senses.

If we remember what we said about Socrates and Plato, the question immediately arises: If truth must be founded on reality, and if the source of reality is to be discovered in particulars, what are we to make of the fact that permanent truth is found only in relation to universals? To put it in another way, how are we to reconcile Aristotle's theory of the particular with his view that science is on the one hand the study of true reality and on the other is concerned with universals?

To understand the answer to this, we must go a little more deeply into his theory of primary substance. Primary substance, he held, was the union of what he called "matter" and "form." This brings us back to the terminology of change, and it is important to remember that Aristotle uses these words "matter" and "form" in a very special way:

a) matter, as we have seen, is that which is passive and potential; form is that which is active and actualizes. We might think of the radio set which "actualizes" the so-called sound waves and turns them into real sound, or, at least, makes them capable of being heard, whereas before they were only potentially so.

b) Again, form makes a thing what it is or gives it its nature; matter makes it that particular thing and no other or gives it its individuality; form in this case is more like the idea of the artist, and matter the paint in which he expresses it; the artist's idea determines the nature of the picture, and the paint receives the idea, as it were, and keeps it within a given space.

c) Lastly, matter is meaningless and opaque to the mind's eye; form has meaning and can be grasped by the mind: here, assuming that paint has no significance in isolation, we can keep our last analogy: what we understand in a picture is the idea that the artist put there.

Form, then, actualizes or gives reality to that which is potential; it gives a nature to that which has nothing but the possibility of becoming an individual of some kind; it gives meaning to that which is meaningless. Form, therefore, must be the meaningful reality which is the object of knowledge: thus, for example, it is the nature "cow" which makes cows what they are and it is the same nature which impresses itself upon our minds so that we distinguish "cow" from "horse." So form is not only the active principle in nature but also the active principle in knowledge: my mind is potential—like a blank sheet—until it is actualized by the various forms in the world outside with which it comes into contact. But the form of a thing is its nature, that which it has in common with other things of the same type. Thus in knowing the form we are knowing the universal.

It may seem that Aristotle is now leaning too much in the opposite direction; his realism may appear to be getting a little thin; he is getting very near to the Platonic view of the universal as that which is the true, intelligible reality. It is clear, however, that for him the universal, although it is the principle of existence, has in fact no existence except when it actualizes matter. In other words, the universal is immanent but not transcendent: it has no existence outside the matter which it informs. The universal is never more than an aspect of a thing already in existence. The union of matter and form is not the result of two separate entities coming together, but a way of describing the complexity of the particular as it in fact exists. This is the implication of Aristotle's term "secondary substance," which he sometimes uses to denote the form or universal. The universal is substantial; it exists. But its existence is secondary in the sense that it exists, not separately, but as an element of the particular. In short, the form of cow is the principle of existence for all cows; but, as such, it is a mere abstraction; for it cannot exist unless it is united with matter in particular cows.

With great subtlety, then, Aristotle worked out the relation of the particular to the universal. We must now consider the terms in which he examined its relation to its environment as a whole. He classified the explanation of things under the heading of four so-called "causes" ("causes" has become the accepted translation of the Greek, and we shall have to use it, but the word AITIA means something more like "explanation"; it has nothing to do with causality in the ordinary sense of the word). These four causes are called "formal," "material," "efficient" and "final." The formal cause of a thing is, as the name suggests, its form—its nature, that is, or essence: thus the form of a knife is the nature "knife" or "knifeness," as philosophers like to call it. The material cause is simply the stuff or matter (in the ordinary, not Aristotle's special sense of the word) out of which it is made; thus, the material cause of a knife might be steel. The efficient cause, the only one of the four which suggests our idea of causality, is the source of motion or change; thus, the knife-maker or cutler is responsible for changing the steel into a knife. Lastly, the final cause is the ultimate good or purpose of a thing; thus, the purpose of a knife is to cut.

The value of this method of classification is, I think, obvious. When we have defined a thing in terms of all four causes, we have given it a very full definition. In point of fact, these causes often overlap: the formal and efficient cause, for example, may be the same; this is true of fire: the man who lit the fire may be the efficient cause in the first instant, but, once under way, given the necessary tinder, fire itself produces new fire; its motion is at one with its nature.

Moreover, where the formal and efficient causes overlap, the final cause can often be included too; thus, the final cause of fire is "to burn," and this is hardly separable from the other two. To give another example, the final cause of an oak tree is simply to be a full-grown oak; but this is also its nature and what makes it grow, its formal and efficient cause. In natural things, therefore, the four causes tend to be reduced to two: the formal and material. In manufactured things, however, clear distinctions obtain: the formal cause of a house is its plan or lay-out in the mind of the architect; the material cause may be brick; the efficient cause is the builder; the final cause is "to be lived in."

Aristotle's classification by the four causes reveals his biological approach. Apart from its scientific neatness and thoroughness, it suggests a very definite attitude to the nature of things: everything is constructed with a view to its end; every natural thing carries within itself some principle of growth or development which, if there is no interference, will bring that thing to completeness. It follows that if we want to know the nature of a thing, we must ask: What is it for?

The reader will no doubt be reminded of Socrates's reaction to the theory of Anaxagoras that the world is the work of mind (*vid.* pp.

22–3); Aristotle himself came to much the same conclusion, but by a different route. Socrates, when reading Anaxagoras, saw in a flash that if the world is the work of mind, than it is possible to make sense of it; Aristotle, laboriously examining his biological specimens, discovered that every member of a species had in varying degrees of complexity an organization calculated to fulfill the end of that species, and he concluded that nothing but mind could be responsible for this nice adjustment between ends and means.

Many modern scientists, of course, would contend that Aristotle in his simplicity had got things upside down: they would say, for example, that a bird flies because it has wings, not that it has wings in order that it may fly; or that there is life on this earth amongst other reasons because the relative position of the sun is such as to nourish and not to destroy it, not that the sun is where it is in order that life on this earth may be maintained.

Scientifically, there is no way of deciding between the two views, but this is not surprising, since the problem belongs to philosophy, not science. Since the remarkable scientific discoveries of the nineteenth century and the bitter controversies that they raised, questions of this kind have been thought to be bound up with evolution. In point of fact, the theory of evolution—the theory that the bodies of all living things in this world have evolved from a single source by a natural process of selection—this theory, whether we include the bodies of men or not, is a scientific theory on which the scientist must judge. It is quite different from the question: Is this process blind, meaningless and due simply to chance, or is it an ingenious plan devised by a master mind? More scientific data, fresh discoveries may confirm or modify the theory of evolution, but it is difficult to see how they can throw any light on the second question. This question belongs to philosophy and is one which philosophy must judge. This is not, of course, to deny the right—or indeed the duty—of every man to make up his own mind on a matter of such fundamental importance; we merely argue that in doing so, a man must be quite clear as to the kind of question that he is considering and the kind of evidence that is relevant to it, particularly if he happens to be a specialist in another department of knowledge.

Remembering, then, that the theory of evolution is not much help either way, let us leave the question open for a moment. As it happened, Aristotle specialized in science and philosophy, and we may briefly give his own version of the Mind that he thought must exist if men and the rest of the world were to be explained.

As we have seen, Aristotle believed that if you examined the nature of a thing, you could detect the end for which it existed. Applying this to man, he found that intellect was his highest possession and concluded that man's end must be to use this intellect to its fullest capacity. Most of us are still grasping for truth; our intellects, that is to say, are only partly in act; in respect of the greater part of truth they are still in a state of potency; their end is to be fully in act, when the fullness of truth has actualized that potency. So the aim of human life is intellectual activity or contemplation. Since this is man's natural end, it will also be his happiness—provided, Aristotle adds characteristically—that he has sufficient material goods to free him from worries about his physical needs. This comfortable contemplation with which Aristotle identified man's ultimate happiness is technically known as "eudaimonism."

Aristotle seems unwilling to commit himself about the personal immortality of the human soul. He is not reluctant, however, to assert the existence of immaterial beings. He has discovered the end of human life, he has discovered the inner principle of the human species which corresponds to the principle of physical growth that he observed in the various species of plants, but he has not yet found an explanation of these species and principles in themselves. Now, in order to explain anything, you have to discover some higher principle from which it is derived; thus, for example, you explain the particular by the species. Moreover, when you have explained the species, you are left with the task of discovering a fresh explanation in terms of a yet higher principle; in fact, your first explanation is worthless unless it can be assumed that it has an explanation too. It follows that if anything is to be explained, everything that goes into the explanation must also be explained. Now, in your series of explanations you must stop somewhere: an infinite series of explanations simply shelves the question for ever; unless you come to an end somewhere, the very explanation with which you began has no validity.

Aristotle, therefore, had to find the ultimate Final Cause. We have already said that he thought of all reality in terms of potency and act;

potency meant limitation; in the natural order of this world, we rank things according to their freedom from limitation and their inherent ability to act. Thus, vegetables, with their immanent principle of growth, are higher than inanimate matter; animals, with their greater freedom of physical action, are higher than vegetables; and man, with his ability to initiate thought, and action depending on that thought, is highest of all.

Since, therefore, the scale rises as potency diminishes, our ultimate explanation must have no potency; it must be Pure Act. Now, act or being in its perfect form must be unlimited; it must be intellectual and have nothing to do with matter; so Pure Act is Pure Thought, the mode of existence of Unlimited Mind. But even an unlimited mind must have an object for its thought, and that object must itself be unlimited. Now, the only possible unlimited object for Unlimited Mind is Unlimited Mind itself. It follows that the Final Cause of all reality is Self-Contemplating Mind.

The reader familiar with books on Aristotle or even perhaps with the books of Aristotle himself may perhaps be raising an eyebrow at this account of his proof of the existence of Self-Contemplating Mind. I have used the word "explanation," where most writers use the word "mover" with a warning that it may be misleading. Without question, Aristotle himself uses the language of movement; his Self-Contemplating Mind, for example, is also described as the First Unmoved Mover. But Aristotle emphatically states that this First Mover is the final cause of the world, but not its efficient cause; for, to be the efficient cause of the world it would have to know it, but that would be to have an end outside itself and thus, in respect to this end, to be limited.

In Aristotle's view, then, the whole of nature, the whole of limited reality, in fact, is, as it were, moving towards its end, realizing its limited potentiality. Only Pure Act is unchanged, only the First Mover is unmoved, for change and movement imply potency. Since Pure Act is the Final Cause of all, the end to which the movement of all things tends, it can also be called the First Mover, as long as we understand movement in the Aristotelian sense of change from potency to act at the instigation of some final cause. In this sense, the meaning of "final cause" or "mover" seems to be most simply conveyed by the word "explanation." It is hoped, therefore, that I may be forgiven if, in order to avoid confusing the reader at the start, I used language which could be more readily understood without, as I believe, any sacrifice of Aristotle's essential meaning.

Since, then, Self-Contemplating Mind—to return to the third and most significant title of the Final Cause—is not the efficient cause of the movement of the world and other spheres, Aristotle argued that there must be intermediate powers who are the efficient causes of this movement. They are immaterial forms, who incidentally bridge the gap, as it were, between man and Self-Contemplating Mind in the hierarchical order of reality.

The isolation of this Mind has one other important consequence: since it knows nothing but itself, there can be no conscious relationship between it and the rest of reality; it follows that the movement of the latter towards it is simply an unconscious principle in the nature of things, like the development of a tree towards its natural fullness of growth. Plato's love of the Good or the Beautiful has no place in this scheme, and the reciprocity of the Christian love of God is further away still. Even in the Aristotelian theology it is still the biologist who speaks.

A short summary of any philosopher is bound to do him an injustice. We found that Plato was difficult to summarize because, while his thought is packed with stimulating suggestions and opens up any number of exciting lines of inquiry, many a problem is left unsolved and many a string is left untied; this, as we have indicated, may be a fault on the right side, but it makes it only too easy to oversimplify what he said. Aristotle is difficult to summarize for the opposite reason: he has written so much in a systematic form, his contribution to philosophy covers such a vast field, that when we try to convey the gist of his metaphysics in isolation from his logic, psychology, ethics and politics, quite apart from his scientific works, we are bound not only to reduce his stature but also to impoverish his thought.

It is hoped, however, that we have said enough about the two philosophers to show how very different their approaches were and to show

how much hangs in philosophy on the thinker's attitude at the start.
Almost all subsequent philosophers—at any rate until recent years—
have regarded themselves as Platonists or Aristotelians, as idealists or
realists developing the thought of their master. No doubt, since they
represent two distinct but complementary sides to human thought, the
really wise thing to do is to study both and hope that the two approaches can be reconciled in any view that we ultimately accept.

Both Plato and Aristotle, like the early Greek philosophers, saw that
any account of the universe must embrace it as a whole; they both saw
that this account must be based on the way we reason and behave in
ordinary life and must justify our habit of assuming absolute standards of truth in this reasoning and behavior; they both made a distinction, Plato's more absolute than Aristotle's, between the physical and
intellectual nature of man, and gave primacy to intellect. In a word,
they both considered that contemplation was the end of man, in which
he would find ultimate happiness.

When it comes to their actual account of reality, they differ profoundly. Aristotle's account of the material world solved several metaphysical problems and was perhaps very much more on the side of common sense than Plato's. On the other hand, Aristotle seems to be less
satisfactory in explaining the world as a whole; for example, he gives no
metaphysical reason for the permanent structure of his universals,
thanks to which the universal, rather than the particular, is the object
of science. It may be very sensible to say that the universal derives its
existence from the particular, but it is not at all easy to see why the
universal should then have a permanent quality which the particular
lacks.

Plato had a very clear idea of the world of Forms, but found it difficult to bring these Forms to earth, as it were, in this world; Aristotle
had a very clear idea of this world, but found it equally difficult to
attach it to that higher reality in which he too believed. If Aristotle
seems to be talking more about the world which we know, Plato seems
to give a very much better reason for the fact that it is intelligible at all.
The light of the Platonic sun may be rather blinding; in Aristotle's
world, the light is clear enough, but there is no accounting for it; his
universals, in fact, are like moons without a sun to shine on them.

Aristotle's greatest weakness, however, we have already touched upon. He seems to reduce human life to a biological process in which men and animals alike fulfill their destinies according to the inner principle that is within them; he leaves little room for the spontaneous activity of the person that seems to be at the roots of human nature. True, there is a kind of dignity and grandeur in the contemplation which Aristotle conceives to be the end of man, but there seems to be a profound difference between this lonely realization of intellectual capacity and the achievement of the Platonic soul when, driven along the hard path of perfection by love, it finally reaches its goal in an eternal union with the Good. Of course, the truth of a philosophy has nothing to do with its attractiveness; but, if Plato and Aristotle both claim to base their conclusions about the end of human life on their knowledge of human nature, we are entitled to ask which of them does greater justice to the potentialities that man has and to the kind of perfection which the best in man compels him to strive after.

For all that, history has not been kind to Aristotle. It is the luck of poets that every new reader can rediscover their works with wonderment as fresh as that of the first person who read them. The scientist, on the other hand, often wins greater admiration for the moment, but his discoveries are soon taken for granted, and few trouble to read his works after his death. The comparison can be roughly applied in the case of the two philosophers. Much of Aristotle's logic has passed into common speech; his very method, with its systematic approach and special terminology, has, for good or ill, proved the standard for almost all subsequent philosophy; but the *Republic*, the *Symposium* and many other words of Plato still have their public, whereas few read the *Metaphysics* or even the easier works of Aristotle.

Unquestionably our greatest debt to Aristotle is due to his insistence that philosophy should give a coherent account of the world as we know it in terms of our ordinary experience. It was this that led him to his greatest discoveries: he saw that we cannot help making statements in terms of individual things and so evolved his theory of substance; he saw that we must recognize the facts of change and so worked out the distinction between potency and act. This distinction in turn threw light on so much else: identifying matter with potency and form with act, he could reveal a structural beauty and coherence in the whole of nature, ranging from the shapeless bulk of inanimate matter that has little significance beyond its size, to the subtle intelligence of men that can leap over barriers of time and space. In a word, nothing has thrown so much light on the dynamic organization of nature as the Aristotelian paradox that limitation and potency are one.

5. EARLY CHRISTIAN THOUGHT AND AQUINAS'S THEORY OF BEING

It is quite common to hear people say that Plato and Aristotle believed in God. For a Christian, however, this statement can be misleading. Both philosophers, as we have seen, believed in an Ultimate that was infinite and absolute: for Plato, the Good gave intelligibility to the Forms and, through the Forms, to the rest of the world; for Aristotle, Self-Contemplating Mind was a kind of magnetic field to which all things were attracted, and the final source of their explanation. In both cases, this Ultimate was a principle to be grasped by the intellect; it was never a person to be loved with the fullness of the undivided soul. For both it was knowledge in which man's final happiness lay, a noble ideal but hardly satisfying in exactly that form. As Fr. D'Arcy wrote in *The Mind and Heart of Love:* "Knowledge is the soul's delight, its positive and personal bliss, but without the balancing desire to live in and by the life of another, this desire would be nothing but an enlightened selfishness. The two serve each other's ends, and bring it about that perfect love is mutual giving and taking, possessing and being possessed."*

Plato, one feels, saws the truth of this; he realized that man's soul could not reach the heights without love; but, despite the magnificence of the passage which we quoted from the *Symposium* (vid. pp. 45–6), one is always a little uncomfortable about it: we see what Plato means about ascending from the love of the individual to the love of institutions and laws, but we cannot help feeling that in such an ascent the

---

* London, Faber and Faber, p. 235.

lover would leave something behind that could never be replaced in the higher regions to which he is advancing; there is nobody now to return his love.

Aristotle, on the other hand, is perhaps more logical: he regards Self-Contemplating Mind as an object of desire, but he seems clearly to understand that this is not love in any true sense; for love, he says, must be reciprocal and between those on the same plane of reality. If Plato, therefore, does more justice to human nature, Aristotle is truer to the implications of his own system.

Human nature has been a more powerful force than logic; so it is not surprising that the Platonic tradition lived on whereas the Aristotelian system seemed to meet with very little immediate response. Thus, the seeds of Platonism remained active in Greece and Rome until they burst again into full flower with the Neo-Platonism of Plotinus, who was born in Egypt in about A.D. 203. There is no space here to do justice to his philosophy; suffice it to say that he regarded the world as an emanation that flowed necessarily from God and, while avoiding pantheism and keeping the personal immortality of the soul, he laid all the emphasis on direct union with God in that mystical experience of which we have already seen hints in Plato's *Symposium* and *Republic*.

Meanwhile, this mysticism had been anticipated by a historical event which had taken place two hundred years before, the Incarnation. For the Christian, the principle which the pagan philosophers were still trying to identify, that word or *logos* which would explain the universe, was made flesh. Before, it had seemed that the end of man had to be reached by the arid path of intellectual abstraction, and yet such an end did not fit in with what was known of human nature; it had appeared that man's very personality must be jettisoned along with his physical appetites and passions if any progress was to be made in that world of universals where individual distinctions had no place; it had also seemed that even if Infinite Being were found to be the ultimate end of man, that Being could have no object worthy of his contemplation and love except his own infinite Self. Now, God had taken on human flesh, a divine Person with a divine and human love, to bear witness to the love of the Father for man and to enable man, by living in Christ and becoming part of His Mystical Body, to share with Him the life of the Trinity.

Philosophy, it will be seen, has now yielded some of its position to theology; revelation has stepped in to complete what reason had left unexplained. If we are to understand the Christian philosophers, we must be clear as to the new role which they conceived philosophy to be playing: philosophy was the "handmaiden" of theology; she served her mistress by preparing the ground and clarifying the concepts by which the new theology was to be expounded. Philosophy, of course, was still the science of pure reason, whereas theology was the science of revelation; to insure clear thinking, it was essential rigidly to distinguish between the two. At the same time, the body of truth now available to man could be understood as a whole only in the light of both.

It might be thought that this left little room for speculation, but such was far from the case. Christian revelation was final, but only in the sense in which a seed is final when it is planted in the ground; it had to be developed by rational analysis and deduction. As for Christian philosophy, the phrase itself is misleading: by definition, philosophy cannot owe the force of its arguments to anything but reasoning itself; at the same time a philosopher who is also a Christian cannot help being guided by what faith tells him is true. The position is similar to the definition of dogma in terms of concepts borrowed from some particular school of philosophy. The doctrine, for example, that the consecrated host is the Body of Christ was defined as "transubstantiation," since substance was the current philosophical concept to denote the principle of identity; but the doctrine is in no way bound to the philosophy of which the concept of substance forms a part. Theology has to use the best tools that her handmaiden can offer at any given time; the finer the tools, the subtler the expression of the theology. In point of fact, the Christian philosophers took over the legacy of Greek philosophy, veering throughout the ages now to the idealism of Plato, now to the realism of Aristotle.

From what we have already said about the revival of Platonism, it was to be expected that early Christian philosophy would be Platonic in tone. St. Augustine (A.D. 354–90), for example, probably owed the more specifically intellectual element in his conversion to reading

Plotinus. Using Plato's terminology, and very much in his spirit, he held that the Forms were the ideas of God. There has been considerable controversy as to what exactly he meant by this; from his theology, however, it seems clear that he did not mean to suggest that when we know the Forms, we have a direct knowledge of God, but rather that the Forms were in a real sense dependent on God's ideas. In like manner, following Plato's simile of the sun, he held that it is only by a special God-given light that we can perceive the eternal truths; without this aid, the mind can perceive only what changes. This, however, is connected with the problem of knowledge, which we shall consider later (Part III).

In a similar spirit St. Anselm (1033–1109) attempted to prove the existence of God from our idea of God by what is known as the ontological argument; our idea of God, he argues, is of that than which no greater can be thought; now that which lacks existence cannot be that than which no greater can be thought; therefore God must exist. A contemporary monk tried to refute this argument on the grounds that it would be possible to prove the existence of the most beautiful island that we can conceive by the same process of reasoning The monk, however, had missed the point: Anselm was trying to prove the existence not of any particular thing, perfect of its type, but of Necessary Being, whose being is Its perfection; without Its being, one might say, It is nothing—not even an idea. The essence of God is to exist; it might seem, then, that the idea of God's essence must imply His existence, and that, if we have such an idea of Him, He must exist.

The answer, however, seems to be that even if we grant this definition, whereas it is certainly true that the *idea* of His essence implies the *idea* of His existence, yet this has no bearing on the *fact* of His existence, which belongs to a different order of reality altogether. In other words, to use our old example, a fact can no more be added to an idea than a cow and a bull can be added to a pair of animals.

However great the appeal of Plato, it might seem that it was in some ways more appropriate for a philosophy inspired by the Incarnation to be based more on the realism of Aristotle. Such at any rate was the view of St. Thomas Aquinas (1225–74). Born of an aristocratic Neapolitan family, educated by the Benedictines of Monte Cassino and then at the University of Naples, Aquinas decided to be a Dominican. His family objected, and he was kidnapped and imprisoned for nearly a year by one of his brothers. He had his way, however, became a Dominican friar and taught philosophy at the universities of Paris and Rome until his death at the Cistercian monastery of Fossanuova. Not yet fifty when he died, he had produced, in a prodigious literary output, a completely new synthesis of Christian philosophy and theology.

Substantially on the grounds that we have mentioned, he rejected Anselm's ontological argument and set out, in the manner of Aristotle, to prove the existence of God from our experience of the ordinary world around us. This fitted in with his belief that all our knowledge had first to be fed into our minds through the senses; since, then, God could not be seen, we could not know Him directly, but only through His effects. He produced five proofs on these lines, the so-called Five Ways.

The first proof is from movement in the sense of change from potency to act. Apart from certain refinements, it is substantially the same as the Aristotelian proof which we have already given (pp. 61–2): any movement can only be explained by a series of movers, the first of which must be itself unmoved; as we pointed out, you cannot explain any movement by an infinite series of movers, because the series cannot be conceived as a line produced to infinity, but rather as a structure which is built up of parts, in subordination to one another, that ultimately rest on a single foundation; without the foundation, the whole structure collapses. To use a common example, however many cars impart movement to each other in a freight train, the movement of the train as a whole on a flat surface is inexplicable if there is no engine to pull it.

Similarly, the Second Way sets out to prove the existence of God as Efficient Cause, from whom must have derived our existence, and the existence of the world we know. From the point of view of the argument, we might have had no first father—the human race might extend endlessly into a past that has no beginning—but its existence as a whole has still to be explained. The ultimate Maker or Creator is no less a logical necessity than is the ultimate Mover; just as the Mover must be unmoved, so the Creator must be uncreated. Where the first proof started from the movement or change that we observe in the world, the second proof starts from the actual existence of things. In both cases, the proof takes us back to a First Cause whose nature is radically different from the effect with which it began.

This brings us to the third proof which starts from the way in which we and things around us exist—the very nature, that is to say, of our being. This being is what is called "contingent": contingent beings happen to exist, but they might never have existed at all. As it is, their existence is transitory; they do not, in fact, contain within themselves the reason for their own existence. Since this is so, some other explanation must be found in a being which does contain the reason for its own existence, a being that is not contingent but necessary.

The Third Way is perhaps the most fundamental of the five; indeed, it goes to the very roots of the first two. Furthermore, I believe that the more simply it is expressed, the more cogent the conclusion is felt to be. There is no real need to talk about the impossibility of an infinite series; it is better simply to ponder on the nature of being as we know it: once we recognize the contingency of the effect, we must at the same time infer the necessity of the cause. It is like a shadow: the moment that we know a shadow for what it is, we infer the existence of a material thing and the light by which it is cast.

Some people, of course, simply shrug their shoulders and say: "I know these things around us come and go; perhaps there is no reason for it; perhaps it is all due to chance." As Aquinas says, if there were nothing but contingent being, it is difficult to see how anything could have come into being at all; possibilities can hardly actualize each other. But, however that may be, however we try to refine the argument, the issue seems to be very simple indeed: do we or do we not demand an explanation of the world as we know it? If we do not, if we hold that things just happened this way and that no more can be said, then, of course, argument is useless: it is idle to give a reason to a person who does not believe that a reason is possible.

It is important, however, to realize the radical hopelessness of such a position: if there is no final explanation of the world, then there can be no explanation of anything; if the freight train climbs a hill without an engine or any other source of motive power, then there is no reason to suppose that the couplings, for example, keep the train together; if the last car is uncoupled, there is no reason why that car should not go on climbing. We are reduced to this absurd position simply because there is no reason why any of the train should go on climbing at all; it is a ghost train to which reason cannot be applied. If, on the other hand, we do look for a reason in anything, however insignificant, we find that once we start looking for reasons we cannot stop until we find the ultimate reason of all. In other words, if we really look at contingent being, we cannot escape the shadow which Necessary Being has cast upon it.

The Fourth Way cannot claim the same merit of simplicity. It starts, not so much from any particular aspect of isolated natural objects, but rather from the pattern which those objects make in the hierarchy of nature. We see that some things are more perfect than others, whether we think in terms of goodness, nobility or truth. These attributes, good, noble and true, are not limited in themselves, but only in so far as the objects in which they are present are limited. The idea of goodness, for example, is not like the idea of red: "red" is limited to being red and not blue; but only by a misuse of words can we say that a thing is limited to being good and not bad, because "badness" is simply lack of "goodness." To put it in another way, "infinite goodness," whether we believe in its existence or not, is a possible phrase in a sense in which "infinite redness" is not.

According to Aquinas, different things can be good in varying degrees according to their position in the hierarchy of being; thus we can talk about a good apple, a good horse and a good man, but the goodness of a horse is always inferior to the goodness of man. It seems, then, that goodness is limited, not in itself, but by the limitation of the being that possesses it. Like everything else, however, it must have some ultimate explanation, which must itself be unlimited; for you cannot find the source of that which is intrinsically unlimited in that which is itself limited. The degrees of goodness, therefore, that we observe in things can only be explained by the existence of an infinite being who is infinitely good.

This argument implies the doctrine of analogy: that goodness as a whole proceeds from a single cause, but is present in good things and people not as it is present in the cause, which is infinite, but in a way appropriate to the respective natures of these things and people. Thus

the goodness of God is not the same as the goodness of man; the goodness of man is not even the same as the goodness of dogs; but, at the
same time, we are not using the word "good" equivocally, when we
apply it to God, man and dog. We are using it analogously: there is
a change of meaning, but it is not fundamental; to say that man is
better than dog is not like saying that light blue is lighter than a feather;
it is not, in other words, a mere pun.

There is a difficulty, however, if we leave the argument like this. It
seems possible to maintain that goodness is not a single quality even in
an analogous sense; but, much more simply, it merely indicates the
right relation between what a thing is and what it ought or is intended
to be. Thus "a good knife" means "a knife that cuts"—a knife, in other
words, that does its job; a good man is a man who does what is expected
of human nature. Here, it may seem, we are using the word "good" in
the same way in both cases; the use is neither analogous nor equivocal,
but univocal: that is, it has one meaning, merely indicating the right
performance of function.

The truth of the matter seems to be that ultimately we are evaluating
not levels of goodness so much as levels of being: if a thing is good
when it fulfills its function or nature, then this goodness can be rated
in terms of that nature which is fulfilled. In the Fourth Way, St.
Thomas rather loosely formulates the argument in terms of goodness,
truth, nobility and being, as though it applied in the same way to
each; but it is perhaps more accurate to say that we can detect an
analogy in the being of things which is reflected in our language about
truth, nobility and goodness, which are three fundamental ways of
talking about being.

We cannot here elaborate at length on the nature of this analogy,
but, briefly, it is closely bound up with unity and independence, which
are perhaps even more fundamental aspects of being. In terms of these
two aspects, a piece of rock, a cabbage, a dog and a man can be said to
form a hierarchy in ascending order; the unity of the cabbage comes
from an independent principle of life denied to the rock, which may be
hard to distinguish from the rock next to it; in the dog, this independent unity is greater and more highly developed than in the cabbage; in man it is raised to the level of conceptual thinking and free

will. Even within man himself the same distinction applies, in the sense that a good man will be more integrated, as we say; he will direct his activities harmoniously to a single end, whereas the bad man will lose his self-control and independence by being the slave to every chance desire.

Finally, by God we mean that Being who is so perfectly one that even his essence and existence are identical. We say, then, that a rock, a man and God "exist," but the meaning of the word has to be adjusted to meet each single case. It is not merely that one thing on the scale has a fuller kind of existence than the one below it; its very identity, its very claim to be called a "thing" or "being," is different. This then is roughly what is meant by "the analogy of being."

We conclude, therefore, that we experience in reality a coherent pattern wherein the existence of things has a value according to their nature. Moreover, this pattern of value is fundamental to all other values of which we are conscious; thus the life of a dog has some importance, but is not so important as the life of man. A dog's life, therefore, may properly be sacrificed on behalf of a man; it is the value of the end in view that determines our actions.

The first question, then, must be: Does this pattern make any sense if there is no fundamental value from which the rest are derived? It seems immediately clear that not only is it impossible to judge values except in relation to a common norm, but that the very existence of these values must be referred to a common source; otherwise the unity of the pattern as we know it would be inexplicable. This brings us to the second question: Is this common source absolute and infinite? Since it is a much more difficult question, it will have to be discussed at some length.

Let us, for a moment, compare standards of ordinary linear measurement: here we have a norm in, say, the foot rule; but when we say that one man is taller than another, this does not imply (although Plato seemed to think it did) that we are appealing ultimately to a standard of absolute length or tallness. In other words, the mere presence of a scale does not necessarily imply an absolute to which the scale must be referred. The case here, however, is different: we have to explain something much more fundamental than a scale of values; we have to explain *the* scale of values.

Moreover, we have to find not merely the norm by which the values are judged but, as we have said, the very source from which they come into being. As in the case of St. Anselm's ontological argument (*vid.* p. 70), the premises of this argument are unique, but there seems no need to employ the same methods of reasoning in order to reach our conclusion. Avoiding Anselm's approach, we could, like Socrates, argue from moral experience wherein we find that these values do in fact make absolute demands upon us; but that is a separate argument, which needs no such elaborate preamble as this.

As it is, we must adhere to the Thomist approach and keep the form of the first three ways: the various levels of being and the values that go with them must be explained as a whole, if any part is to be intelligible. Now, in looking for this ultimate explanation, we cannot stop at an imperfect being, who would necessarily possess these qualities imperfectly. Only Infinite Being with absolute goodness can be Its own explanation and not demand another in turn.

It may now be objected that all our ways are really forms of the same argument, which is expressed most succinctly in the third; the ultimate appeal is always, in some form or another, to the contingency of contingent being. From the point of view of bare logic, I think that this is true; but this is not to deny that each way not only gives a fresh reason for accepting the conclusion, but also throws more light on the conclusion that is accepted. It adds weight to the argument that we can begin not only from the movement of things, but also from the fact of their existence, from the nature of their being and from the perfections which we see imperfectly realized in and around us; it throws more light on the nature of God that he is proved to be not only First Mover, but also First Cause, Necessary Being and the Source of all perfection and value. In fact, it is only by a diversity of proofs that we get some faint idea of what we mean by God as the simple Cause of all.

It is for this reason that Aquinas ends, in the Fifth Way, with the so-called Teleological Argument. This argues quite simply from the complexity of nature and the law and order which underlies it. Today, when science has discovered so much about the mechanics of the universe, we are in a better position even than Aquinas to appreciate the subtlety by which this universe is organized. Indeed, the very methods of science presume that underlying this vast structure there are comparatively few principles, simple enough to be grasped by the human mind. There can be no science of chaos.

In inferring the existence of God from the reality that we experience, we have had to make a leap, as it were, from the contingent to the necessary or absolute. The reader may well be wondering whether such a leap is possible, whether the contingent mind of man is capable of realizing what is meant by any form of existence radically different from our own. How, in fact, can we know God?

Aquinas states quite clearly that we cannot know the divine nature in its fullness; it would be a contradiction in terms to suppose that the limited mind of man could contain the unlimited being of God. Moreover, the material on which we have to work is not God himself but the universe that God created; it is like trying to infer the mind of an artist from the pictures which he has painted; indeed, this comparison reveals the possibilities as well as the limitations of our knowledge. Some people who have no taste for poetry or music and are quite incapable of understanding a book on philosophy, may have their whole experience deepened and extended by a few paintings, although the artist has been able within the limitations of his medium only to hint at some idea that he wishes to impart; these people understand the medium of paint and therefore respond to the picture, although they would have looked quite blank if the artist had tried to convey his meaning to them by means of words. Similarly, we may be unable in the ordinary course of nature to have any intercourse with the divine Mind, but we can understand something of it in terms of the things around us which reflect that Mind in what is naturally intelligible to man.

Now, according to Aquinas, there are two ways in which we can have knowledge of God through his creation: by negation and by analogy. In the first case, we see various attributes and modes of behaviour which are peculiar to limited being, and are unthinkable in God. For example, since God is unlimited and absolute, he cannot be corporeal or com-

posed of parts; for matter is potency and parts must be potential in
the sense that they must be capable of being made one with the whole,
but, by definition, Absolute Being cannot include potency in Its nature.
Similarly, It cannot change, for change implies the potency to become
something else. Negative though it may be, this really does tell us
something about God: we have no experience of that which is unchanging, but our knowledge of change gives us a clue; we have no
experience of a being without parts, but the idea of perfect simplicity
is something more than a blank in our minds. We can continue in this
way, building up a coherent, if elusive, concept of what we mean by
God.

But as we proceed, we are probably making use of analogy at the
same time. God's being, as we have said, is inherently different from
ours—so much so that the very phrase "God's being" is inaccurate: God
simply *is*; indeed, in the Book of Exodus He Himself claims the title
"He Who Is." It follows that when we apply any attribute to God, even
negatively, we have to make the mental reservation that such qualities
in this case are not really qualities or attributes at all, but are included
in the simplicity of the eternal "I Am."

After all, we distinguish one quality or thing from another by its
very limitation; it is because it is limited to being *this* and not *that*
that we can give it a name (this is not quite true, as we have said, of
the so-called transcendentals like goodness, but these are intimately
bound up with the limitations of functions: a good pen is good in so
far as it is successful *as a pen*; the goodness of man is something higher,
because man is a higher kind of being. So, when applied to God, since
the quality is unlimited, it exists, as it were, without its identity or
separateness; it simply becomes merged in His being. For this being is
identical with His nature. Since it is His essence to exist, there cannot
be any distinctions within Him. It is only when God creates, it is only
when He gives expression to His nature in a limited medium, that He
can break up His own simplicity, as it were, into a series of incomplete
images.

We may perhaps understand this more clearly if we begin at the
other end: what do we mean when we say that God created the world?
Remember that the word "create" implies Necessary Being for the
cause and contingent being for the effect; for "created necessary being"

is a contradiction in terms, and contingent being cannot, by definition, be its own explanation.

Now, since the very identity of a contingent being takes the form of a distinction from something else, it follows that a single contingent being can have very little significance of its own. If God had created one such being with all the perfections of which contingent being is capable, His creation would have been of a much lower order than the creation which we know with its full diapason stretching from the purest spirit to the meanest and most shapeless slime. This creation is more perfect because the simple unity of the Infinite is most fully symbolized by the complex diversity of the finite organized into a coherent whole.

To return to our illustration from art, nothing reveals the creative imagination of the artist so well as a vast canvas in which every detail plays its proper part, subordinate to the grand conceptions of the whole. The effect of every detail, in fact, is to suggest the intensity of the artist's mind rather than the breadth, say, of his interest (although it may do this incidentally at the same time); each part should serve only to lead us on to the next, and, if we become so engrossed in the detail that we lose sight of the complete picture, most of our aesthetic appreciation will be lost. Similarly, we can best see God reflected in creation, if we remember that every detail, every new identity to which we come, is merely a boundary stone to show us where the next begins.

We should now be in a better position to see the light thrown on the problem of the One and the Many by the Christian emphasis on being, and especially on the idea of creation. For creation is the one link between necessary and contingent being which does not compromise the integrity of either; this marks Aquinas's great advance on Plato, who could find no satisfactory relation between the Forms and material reality. It is important to remember that creation is a perpetual link and not an isolated act with consequences that go on after the act is completed. It is not, in other words, like the fashioning of a statue out of stone, where the statue remains standing after the sculptor has finished with it; it is more like an electric current whose effects remain only as long as it is switched on. Logically, it is not even necessary for it to have a beginning, much less an end; essentially, it simply signifies the dependence of the one being on the other, which, from a logical point of view, could be timeless.

Since this dependence is not mutual, the Creator is transcendent and not in any way limited by what He has created; at the same time, since creation means the gift of being, the created Many are no mirage, but have a value of their own in virtue of what they are. Again, since this gift proceeds from an unchanging Intelligence, the Many may come and go, but the pattern of their existence remains the same; thus we have Aristotelian realism combined with a Platonic guarantee of the fixity of universals and the absolute objectivity of truth.

PART TWO
THE NATURE OF MAN

6. MAN IN HIMSELF

For Plato, it will be remembered, there was a sharp distinction between the material and spiritual world. The spiritual world, the world of the Forms, was the only true reality, and this world but a poor copy of it. It follows that for him man must be partly spiritual, and that it is this spiritual part which links him with the invisible world and enables him to know what is real or true.

It follows too that his soul is to be sharply distinguished from his body, which belongs to the visible world. The soul, in fact, is the principle of life, "the source of motion" or "self-initiating motion"; the body is inert and crass, a dead weight that only impedes the soul's freedom of activity. The soul is the source of intelligence and rational love; the body is the source of the irrational passions. Plato, in fact, agreed with the Orphics that the body is a tomb in which the soul is imprisoned: only death can put an end to this imprisonment, but the soul can live something of its own life in so far as it controls the physical appetites which distract it and becomes as independent as possible of bodily needs.

Thus Plato puts the following prayer in the mouth of Socrates: "Beloved Pan and all ye other gods who haunt this place, give me beauty in the inward soul and may the outward and inward man be at one. May I reckon the wise to be the wealthy, and may I have such a quantity of gold as none but the temperate can carry."* And we remember

* Plato, Phaedrus, 279b–c.

how Socrates did indeed attain this detachment (*vid. supra*, p. 16).

Such a philosophy, while it treats the body and soul as separate entities, at the same time implies that there is considerable interaction between the two. In man as we know him in this world, the characteristics of body and soul overlap, forming, as it were, a composite soul in which Plato distinguished three "parts" or "kinds": firstly, the Rational part, which is the truly spiritual element; secondly, the Spirited part, which is the source of self-respect, pride, ambition and the like; thirdly, the Passionate part, which is the source of the physical appetites.

Since only the first part belongs to the invisible and timeless world, that alone survives after death; but in this world, the second part is its natural ally in the difficult battle which it has to fight against the irrational disorderliness of the third part, which is likened to a violent and unmanageable beast; in modern terms, the Spirited part encourages the soul in the right emotional response to any given situation—it helps it to do "the decent thing," which corresponds with what is reasonable.

Although we shall not comment here on this psychology, it might be worth pointing out that the three leading psychologists in modern times have selected as the driving force in man three different characteristics, each of which might be ascribed to a different part of Plato's soul: Freud's Sex is clearly the most powerful appetite of the third part; Adler's "Will to Power" is at least one aspect of the second part; Jung's "Archetypes" are, if I understand him rightly, a kind of inherited memory-pattern—a tendency of the mind to form certain images— which can be compared with the implicit memory of the Forms which, Plato believed, the rational soul brought with it into this world (*vid. infra* p. 127—we may note that neither Jung nor Plato wished to suggest that we have any innate ideas of which we are *explicitly* conscious). It would be grossly superficial to press this comparison too far, but it may show that the Platonic psychology is not lightly to be dismissed, and suggest to the reader certain lines of comparison that are worth pursuing.

In contrast with the dualism, or two-world view, of Plato, Aristotle's biological approach may be expected to pay more respect to the physical in man. For him, the body was no accidental encumbrance which tantalized the soul, but something complementary to it: applying his theory of matter and form (*vid*. pp. 57–8), he held that the soul was the act (ENTELECHEIA) of the body, the form which gave being to the potency of matter, the principle of life whereby it moved and grew. Thus body and soul form a single substance; no human act is exclusively physical or mental; the soul is not degraded by being joined with the body, but rather this union is merely a higher application of that natural law by which all things in the physical universe exist.

The soul, then, is a higher kind of form; it confers not only existence, as the form of rock gives existence to particular rocks, but also life; and this life itself may be higher or lower according as it is found in men, animals, or plants. Thus there are three types of soul: the *nutritive*, which enables things to assimilate food and reproduce; the *sensitive*, which is the source of sense-perception, desire, and the ability to move from one place to another; the *rational*, which confers the ability to think and act from conscious motive. Each of the higher forms of soul includes those beneath it; thus the animals have something in common with the plants, and men have something in common with both. Thus we have in Aristotle a characteristically biological table in contrast to Plato's division on a psychological basis.

Aristotle, therefore, avoids one serious difficulty which Plato never really solved: how to account for the interaction between the spiritual and the material. For Aristotle, the two combine to make a single substance, and it is the substance which acts. This not only avoids the logical difficulty, but is much more consistent with experience: it always seems true to say that *I* know, act and feel on a plane that is at once physical and spiritual; my body and soul unite in a single act that is mine. I have no experience of purely spiritual or intellectual action; even when I think, my brain gets tired; if parts of my brain are removed, I cannot think at all. Similarly with physical actions: if there are purely reflex actions of the body, I cannot call them *my* acts in any full sense of the word; on the other hand all conscious "physical" actions and experiences—and probably many that are unconscious—are at the same time spiritual, as the very word "conscious" suggests. Thus, for example, we distinguish mental from physical pain, but we know that in fact no pain is exclusively physical; and even mental distress, although it may not include physical pain, does at least exclude all sense of physical well-being.

Once we accept the spiritual element in man, we are faced with problems about death: is this event purely physical or not? Both Plato and Aristotle found it difficult to believe that the rational principle in man, which they regarded as a kind of link with unchanging Truth, was subject to the same laws of disintegration as his body. The immortality of the soul was indeed the whole implication of Plato's philosophy: the soul, entombed within the body, was living an unnatural life and had at least the opportunity of gaining its freedom on the death of the body, provided that it had not polluted itself with too much physical preoccupation in this life; if it had, it would be born again in another body, and so on until it had proved itself fit to live in the true world of the Forms.

Even if we reject Plato's dualistic philosophy, his arguments for the immortality of the soul still have their force. Perhaps his greatest contribution to philosophy consists in revealing those aspects of human thought and behavior which are irreconcilable with any materialistic account of man. He realized, of course, that to prove that man has a soul is not to prove that he has an immortal soul. In fact, he would never have claimed to have proved the second point as cogently as the first.

The subject is dealt with most fully in the Phaedo, where his main arguments for immortality are based on the nature of the soul itself: it is not composite like the body, and only what is composite can disintegrate; at the same time, it is the principle of life within man and, as such, is incompatible with death, just as something hot like fire is incompatible with something cold like snow. This, of course, as Plato points out, only proves that the word "dead" cannot be applied to the soul as it can be to the body; you cannot talk about a "dead soul." The soul cannot disintegrate or "admit of the form of death"; if it does cease to exist, then it must simply be annihilated—literally reduced to nothing.

Such a possibility was rejected by Plato because he believed that every soul carried with it evidence that it had already existed in the world of Forms; the Platonic economy, therefore, on the spiritual plane had something in common with what physical scientists call "the conservation of energy"; in other words, if you reject the possibility of continuous creation—if, that is, you reject the theory that some Power is ever creating anew what is being annihilated—then the world must cease to exist unless what appears to be annihilated in fact continues to exist in some other form; just as manure nourishes new life, so the soul of a dead body must pass into one newly conceived.

Now, we may not accept this particular conclusion, but the evidence on which it is based is of the greatest importance; it is the same evidence which led Plato to believe in the Forms: we have ideas of perfection—absolute straightness, absolute good, perfect man and so on—but no perfection of any kind exists in this world; perfection does not exist here, but how is it that we are constantly aware of the fact?

Moreover, it is not simply a question of observation: perfection is an ideal for which men can constantly be found to strive; in fact, nothing short of perfection, we feel, can satisfy any of us; perfection is felt to be our end. In other words, we have a fundamental urge to break through the barriers of this imperfect and temporal world; this urge is so much part of our nature that it is inconceivable that it should be incapable of fulfilment. If this world, then, is the kind of place where anything makes sense, then the immortality of the soul must be assumed if we are to make any sense of man.

However cogent this argument is in itself, we must admit that the conception of survival after death is easier for the idealist than the realist: if you begin with the difficult task of living in two worlds at once, it is easy enough to conceive that some day you will live in only one; but if you really belong to this world, how can a part of you go off and live in another? In Aristotelian terms, if man is a substance composed of matter and form, how can the substance remain when the matter has decomposed? Aristotle never really solved the problem, and, in any case, his thought on this subject is too obscure to pursue at the moment. Briefly, however, his conclusion seems to be this: the intellectual principle in man is partly active and partly passive; the Active Intellect abstracts an idea, the Passive Intellect absorbs it; the Active Intellect, however, "comes from without"; it is not really part of the individual substance; and it is this alone which is immortal.

So, whatever Aristotle meant by the Active Intellect, he does not seem to have believed in any personal immortality. Plato certainly believed in the immortality of the individual soul, but even here we may ask whether this constitutes personal immortality: if, after passing through the waters of forgetfulness, as Plato picturesquely puts it, the same soul is born again in another body, in what sense can the person be said to survive? Leibnitz, a German philosopher of the late seventeenth and the early eighteenth century, put it neatly enough: "Of what use would it be to you, sir, to become king of China on condition of forgetting that you have been? Would it not be the same as if God at the same time that he destroyed you, created a king in China?" The truth of the matter seems to be that beneath this paradoxical question of human immortality there lies the fundamental paradox of human personality, to which neither Platonic idealism nor Aristotelian realism did sufficient justice.

Once again, as we pass from Greek to Christian thought, we must try to appreciate the revolutionary implications of the Incarnation and all that followed from it. For the orthodox Christian, the Son of God had not entered into a body in any Platonic sense, but "was made man." Moreover, the Incarnation was not a temporary expedient, but a final and irrevocable act; God became Man for eternity; as Man He was born and as Man He rose from the dead; as Man He retains in heaven that same body which He had on earth—a body, that is to say, which is the same in substance as that which was born of the Virgin Mary, whatever its accidental differences may be. Thus to the early Christians, the central Christian dogma was not so much the immortality of the soul as the resurrection of the body. However difficult the doctrine might be, it was at least consistent: if Aristotle had left no room for love in the human ideal, Plato had left no room for the personality from which love must spring and upon which love must be directed. Again, Plato's heaven and Aristotle's earth had to be reconciled by Christian philosophy.

As we should expect, Aquinas accepted Aristotle's theory that the soul is the form of the body and that the two make up a single substance; but, having accepted it, he too had to face the same difficulty: how can the form continue when the substance is destroyed? Now, it must be remembered, first of all, that both philosophers believed in the existence of pure forms or purely spiritual beings—what Aristotle called "Intelligences" and Aquinas "Angels." These forms were substances in themselves; so that there was no difficulty in believing that forms could exist without matter; in fact, the form is always the principle of life. On the other hand, in the order below the pure forms—the order, that is, of humanity—where form combines with matter to make a single substance, it would seem that the form cannot be complete without the matter. Aquinas admits this, but argues that the form can still exist without the matter, however incompletely. His argument might be paraphrased as follows:

1. Substances are known by their acts, and all acts must be the acts of substances. Now, by means of our intellects we can know the nature of corporeal things; but "knowing" implies the ability to override the limitations of the material, which a body cannot do; therefore, the intellect must be incorporeal substance. (We might note, in passing, that animals do not possess this ability to know; so there is no question of the immortality of animal souls.)

2. This intellect is blinded by the pure intelligible—we have no direct knowledge of forms or essences—but open to the intelligibility involved in matter; in other words, we cannot know reality by a direct intuition of the mind, but only with the help of the senses; therefore, the incorporeal substance of the intellect is incomplete without a body.

3. At the same time, since the soul is the principle of life for the body, its own life is not stopped by the corruption of the body. So the soul without the body is life without the means of acting fully.

So far, then, Aquinas has saved the immortality of the soul, but, like Plato, only at a cost; it is not the immortality of the complete human being. At this point, the doctrine of the resurrection of the body comes in as at once a help and a stumbling block.

It is obviously a help in that we can keep the Aristotelian theory of man and the Christian doctrine of immortality, which both Plato and Aristotle seemed to want but could not account for, if we can say that the body survives death no less than the soul. Here, we must remember that to Aristotle "matter" is simply potency or limitation; it has none of those spatial or tangible qualities with which we associate it; so that it is possible, according to this definition, to believe in an incorruptible body, identical in substance with, but different in its accidents from, the corruptible body with which we are familiar in this world (for the distinction vid. p. 55).

The doctrine of the resurrection of our bodies is a stumbling-block because the doctrine states that we do not regain our bodies until the end of the world. Thus it seems that until the Last Day the souls of the dead live on in an incomplete state. This is difficult to understand, but contains no logical impossibility. The real difficulty becomes apparent only in the light of what Aristotle and Aquinas have to say about matter as the principle of individuation.

According to this theory, which is bound up with their whole conception of matter and form, what distinguishes, for example, one cow from another is not the form—the nature of "cow" which is common to them both—but that particular amount of matter to which the form of this particular cow has given being (what Aquinas calls *materia quantitate quadam signata*, "matter which has the seal of a certain quantity set upon it"). Now we can see the difficulty: how can individual souls exist as such when parted from the very matter which divides them into individuals? Aquinas too sees the difficulty; his answer takes us deeper into his idea of substance.

Substance, as we have said, is precisely that inner reality which constitutes a thing's identity; it is the subject of which anything else to do with it is predicated. Now, substantiality is conferred not by matter but by form. So it seems that we have two separate principles of identity: quantitative matter, the principle of individuation, which distinguishes the particulars within the species, and substance-conferring form, the principle of individuality, by which a particular thing exists as that particular thing.

In point of fact, however, these two principles are not independent, but can be explained only in the light of each other: in anything material, whether animate or inanimate, although the form confers substantiality, the substance itself is composed of matter and form; it follows that once the substance exists, it can never be understood except in terms of both aspects. So that when the form is temporarily divorced from the matter, it is still to be distinguished as the form of *that* matter. Similarly, to use a very rough analogy, when a man's wife has died, he remains in a certain sense a married man, but his identity as a husband cannot be understood apart from the wife who is dead. Thus matter remains the principle of individuation even for the soul immediately after death; the soul is distinguished, as it were, by the mark which its matter has left upon it.

Individuation and individuality can be understood in this way of all substances that arise from the union of matter and form—in other words, of all material objects. But, as we have said, a human being is "one" in a very special sense: he has personality. Boethius (A.D. 480– 524), who marks the transition from Roman philosophy to the systematic Christian philosophy known as Scholasticism, had defined the human person as "an individual substance of a rational nature." Reason implies freedom of will; a rational creature is one capable of acting for a purpose, and in so far as his acts are consistently purposeful, he is more rational and thus has greater claims to be called a person; so it is the great dignity of man that he has what we might call a "self-creative" power: what he becomes is, in a sense, in his own hands. Thus human persons are, in Professor Gilson's phrase, "autonomous sources of spontaneous activity."

Now, the rational principle in man is the soul, and the soul is none other than the form which confers substantiality. In the human being, therefore, personality and the principle of individuality are due to the same cause. Perhaps it would be simpler to say that where the form is a rational soul, individuality is raised to the level of personality; the new principle of unity transforms the old. At the same time, whether we look upon these principles as two or one, we must remember that they still imply within themselves a subsidiary unity, as it were, of material individuation. To put it in more homely language, whether in this world or the next, whether before or after the Day of Judgment when our bodies are restored, we still love, think and feel in a manner peculiar to creatures that are composed of matter and spirit.

According to Aquinas—and indeed all Christian thought—personality is a value which transcends all other values in the world. As Professor Gilson says, where "everything is suspended from the creative act of a personal God," personality is "the mark of being at the very summit of its perfection." In this spirit, Aquinas holds that nature looks primarily to the good of the species where the individuals are corruptible, but to the individuals where they are incorruptible; every person, therefore, has a unique and absolute worth. The consequences of this belief in the sphere of ethics and politics are, as we shall see, incalculable.

Before we leave man in himself, however, something must be said of the modern theories which deny that man is a spiritual being in the sense in which we have been using the phrase. These theories may roughly be summarized under the nineteenth century title of behaviorism, although some more modern philosophers whose views are similar would not wish to be called behaviorists. Behaviorism emerged as a by-product of the scientific advances of the last century and in its more modern form is part of the positivist attack on metaphysics, which we shall discuss later (pp. 182 f.).

In its original form, then, behaviorism held that all so-called "mental" events (thoughts, passions, acts of memory and so on) consist simply in physical events or changes in our bodily constitution, which it was hoped that scientists might be able to observe and classify. According to this theory, there is no mental or emotional activity distinct from its so-called manifestations: a man is angry, for example, when blood rushes to his face, he gesticulates in an excitable manner, and numerous other physical changes take place. The point is that however numerous these changes may be, all, in principle, are capable of observation; this does not necessarily mean that they will in fact be observed, but to observe them is a possible ideal for the scientist; whereas the soul and intellect of the earlier philosophers was by definition beyond the range of any such observation.

Behaviorism seems to be involved in a vicious circle. For according to its own premises, every philosophy must simply be the result of certain physical stimuli within the brain of the philosopher who expounds it; it is therefore meaningless to say that one philosophy is truer than another: we cannot say that behaviorism is truer than Platonism or any other philosophy; we can only say that behaviorists are differently constituted from Platonists.

Behaviorism is important because of its historical association with the new science of psychology. Many psychologists have in fact tended to be behaviorists, and—which is quite a different thing—experimental psychology can be described, in a loose sense of the word, as a "behavioristic" technique. To take the last point first, the experimental psychologist, by definition, is concerned to observe and tabulate human reactions to various sets of circumstances (and, of course, animal reactions in so far as they be considered relevant to the human study). Clearly, there is nothing philosophically significant in this (although, of course, his private views on the nature of man may subconsciously affect his experiments and the conclusions that he draws from them).

The first point is more intricate. The biologist, as biologist, is entitled to regard the human organism with which he is concerned as coming completely within the range of his own experimental science. But since the psychologist is concerned with man as a whole, he cannot regard his own science as similar in kind to biology and the other experimental sciences, unless he accepts behaviorism as philosophically true. If he does not adhere to behaviorism, he must, if he is to be consistent, regard psychology as a different kind of science from the others; its subject matter will extend beyond the material.

Clearly, the historical connection between behaviorism and psychology has been due to the psychologist's hope—natural enough in itself—that if his science takes a parallel course to the others, it will meet with equal success. But if our objections to behaviorism as a philosophy are well founded, behavioristic psychology, in the full sense of the phrase, is scientifically unsound: its major premise is based on a false analogy between itself and the other sciences.

7. THE NATURE OF HUMAN ACTION

Having attempted to discover what kind of thing man is, we naturally go on to inquire what sort of aim or ultimate object such a thing might be expected to have, and, with this aim in view, how we should expect him to act in any particular instance.

Aristotle's whole approach to ethics, the particular branch of philosophy which deals with moral behavior, is on the lines of what we might roughly call common sense. He points out that ethics is not an exact science, because, although general principles can be laid down, in the last resort the rightness of an action depends on the circumstances. He held that the basic principle of right action—the good for man— can at least be partly deduced from the nature of man, but that the application of this principle had to be learned by analyzing those actions which we ordinarily accept to be virtuous. His approach was teleological; in other words, he thought that the good of man must be identical with his end; for, if this were not so, the world—at least as far as man is concerned—would be meaningless, and all philosophical speculation vain.

Now Aristotle points out that some ends are subordinate to others: we may take medicine to make us sleep; we want to sleep to maintain our health, and so on. Here, we are asking: What is man's ultimate end or good? It seemed to him that the generally accepted end of life was happiness. In what, therefore, he goes on to ask, does happiness consist? It is not pleasure; for that is transitory. It is not honor; for that depends on the giver. It is not even moral virtue; for that can exist with inactivity and misery (clearly, Aristotle's whole metaphysic demanded that happiness be an act; potentiality could not be an end). Happiness, therefore, he says, must consist in the exercise throughout life of that activity peculiar to man—namely, of reason in accordance with virtue. He added that this is possible only for those who have at least a modicum of external goods: the mind is not free to act unless the body is adequately satisfied.

Aristotle now goes on to say that the highest form of rational activity is contemplation, in which the intellect grasps and rejoices in ultimate truth. For contemplation is the highest activity of man's highest faculty and is most complete when directed upon the highest form of reality. In the *Eudemian Ethics*, Aristotle calls this "the worship and contemplation of God." By "God," he presumably means the Self-Contemplating Mind of the Metaphysics (*vid. supra* p. 62), but on such points he tends to be vague.

However this may be, there is essential agreement between Aristotle and Plato that the highest thing that man can do is to contemplate the highest form of reality—what Plato called "The Good"; they also agreed that this contemplation would give him the greatest happiness. For Plato, the idealist, this vision was only possible in another world, where the pure light of spirit would be free from the opaque mass of matter. For Aristotle, the realist, man was essentially a creature of this world, and he must be content with the greatest happiness that this world can give; thus Aristotle's ideal is "the composite life" (SYNTHETOS BIOS), where such contemplation as is possible for man on earth is combined with adequate material resources. This "Eudaimonism," as it is called, was truly the life that Aristotle mapped out for himself, the life of the university professor without the responsibilities of administration. At the same time, he seemed to recognize that this was only a compromise and should itself include a yet higher ideal, "activity according to complete virtue," whereby we should strive as far as possible to overcome the limitations of human nature and cultivate exclusively the divine element in us by pure contemplation. Thus we might "lay hold on eternal life" and find true happiness.

It seems, therefore, that although Aristotle's common sense told him that too much could not be expected of this world, he shared Plato's idealism enough to believe that this much would never satisfy. Indeed, a century before his birth, the Athenian dramatists had written many a

variation on the theme that human life inevitably falls short of the
ideals to which human nature will always aspire; in modern times
Rupert Brooke echoes their cry:

How can
We, being gods, win joy or peace, being man?

The "composite life," therefore, was not the final answer; it was the
practical answer of the biologist who ignored the paradox at the roots
of man's being; the metaphysician saw that this answer would not do,
but could only point to a higher ideal without holding out any hope of
its realization.

For a more complacent optimism, we have to jump the centuries to
the England of Queen Victoria. John Stuart Mill (1806–73), it is true,
owed much of his thought to the Greek philosopher Epicurus (c. 342–
270 B.C.), but there was a positive spirit about Mill's utilitarianism and
its "Greatest Happiness Principle" which was far removed from Epicurus's negative emphasis on serenity of soul, achieved by avoiding all
occasions of pain.

Mill was brought up as strictly as any child of his time in the atmosphere and precepts of rationalism. His father, James Mill, a man
of humble origin from Angus, had not taken advantage of his licence
to preach in the Church of Scotland, but moved to London, where he
lived by his pen, until a book on India gave him entry into the India
Office. If James Mill had exchanged faith in God for faith in human
reason, he preached his new faith as dryly as he might have preached
his old. His son, who began Greek at the age of four, was taught that
sentiment and emotion were the greatest barriers to human happiness:
if men could be kept to the narrow path of reason, human life would
be a much more satisfactory experience. The precocious son followed
his father into India House. Not surprisingly, at the age of twenty, he
had a nervous breakdown; there seemed nothing in life worth working
for. The ultimate effect, however, of this illness was salutary: the
younger Mill learnt that happiness was not to be won by seeking it for
its own sake; even emotion had its place in life; poetry, music and the
other arts had values which the rationalist could not entirely analyze.

The East India Company was abolished in 1857, and he retired from the India Office on a substantial pension early the following year. He divided the rest of his life between Blackheath in London and Avignon in the South of France; for three years (1865–8) he was a Member of Parliament. Thus he was always a practical man of affairs, never the merely academic thinker. Of all philosophers who have based their rule of action on pleasure of some form or other, Mill is perhaps the best known and most convincing; so it will be worth considering his system in some detail.

His father's friend, Jeremy Bentham (1748–1832), had already introduced the maxim that "It is the greatest happiness of the greatest number that is the measure of right and wrong"; but Bentham, like Epicurus, had laid considerable emphasis on absence of pain; and on the positive side (unlike Epicurus, who carefully distinguished intellectual pleasures) had treated all pleasures as alike in kind, if different in degree. So for Bentham, moral judgment simply consisted in weighing the various amounts of pleasure which were likely to result from the various possible courses of action and choosing the largest. For Mill, it was not so simple as that: pleasures are different in kind, and some people are capable of much higher pleasures than others: "A being," he says, "of higher faculties requires more to make him happy, is capable probably of more acute suffering, and is certainly accessible to it at more points than one of an inferior type; but in spite of these liabilities, he can never really wish to sink into what he feels to be a lower grade of existence." In another passage, he says:

"If I am asked, what I mean by difference of quality in pleasures, or what makes one pleasure more valuable than another, merely as a pleasure, except its being greater in amount, there is but one possible answer. Of two pleasures, if there be one to which all or almost all who have experience of both give a decided preference, irrespective of any moral obligation to prefer it, that is the more desirable pleasure. If one of the two is, by those who are completely acquainted with both, placed so far above the other that they prefer it, even though knowing it to be attended with a greater amount of discontent, and would not resign it for any quantity of the other pleasure which their nature is capable of, we are justified in ascribing to the preferred enjoyment a superiority in quality, so far outweighing quantity as to render it, in comparison, of small account. Now it is an unquestionable fact that those who are equally acquainted with, and equally capable of appreciating and enjoying both, do give a most marked preference to the manner of existence which employs their higher faculties."*

Mill, then, agrees with Aristotle to this extent: that happiness in fact consists in the employment of our highest faculties and that these are intellectual.

For proof of his system, Mill appeals to the general consensus of opinion:

"The only proof capable of being given that an object is visible, is that people actually see it. The only proof that a sound is audible, is that people hear it; and so of the other sources of our experience. In like manner, I apprehend, the sole evidence that it is possible to produce that anything is desirable, is that people do actually desire it. If the end which the utilitarian doctrine proposes to itself were not, in theory and practice, acknowledged to be an end, nothing could ever convince any person that it was so."†

He goes on to say that "desiring a thing and finding it pleasant, aversion to it and thinking of it as painful, are phenomena entirely inseparable, or rather two parts of the same phenomenon . . . to desire anything, except in proportion as the idea of it is pleasant, is a physical and metaphysical impossibility."‡

Mill's argument, then, is essentially empirical; it is, in other words, an argument from experience. Let us for a moment examine it in that light. It is true, of course, that we desire only what is pleasant, but this is not to say that we *will* only what is pleasant. Consider a common, if comparatively trivial, example of moral conflict: shall I get up or have a few more minutes in bed? (assuming that there is a moral reason for getting up); in such a case, I may choose to get up, although I *desire* to stay in bed; if I so *desired* to get up, there would be no moral conflict. In other words, moral questions arise precisely on those occasions when our desires are not at one with our sense of duty.

Moreover, this verbal ambiguity in Mill conceals an empirical fact of some importance: however much we may desire our own pleasure,

---

* *Utilitarianism*, ch. II.   † *Utilitarianism*, ch. IV.   ‡ *ibid.*

we do not normally feel it our duty to promote it. For example, if a person denies himself pleasure, we may think him foolish, but it would be absurd to call him a rogue. On the contrary, if a person denied himself considerable pleasure in order to give some quite small pleasure to a friend, should we not admire him for it?

It might be thought that we do in fact feel it our duty to give pleasure to others; but even this is not always so. Suppose a dangerous lunatic were drowning; it would surely not be my duty to save him, if it were likely that he would kill me as soon as I brought him to the bank? In such a case, as in many others, I know that I have a right to preserve my own life. Thus although selfishness is never a duty, the rights of the agent as a person may be an important consideration in moral action. These rights are quite independent of any sum of happiness or pleasure that may be produced by one action or another.

This brings us to our second point: do we in the ultimate analysis decide moral problems by a process of calculation? Let us say that by stealing five pounds from my wealthy but parsimonious friend Smith, who would not even notice the loss, I can give considerable pleasure to my impoverished friend Jones; would it then be my duty to make the transfer? There is no law in this country or, one might venture to say, in any other that would recognize such an obligation. Once again personal rights—in this case the rights of property—have decided the issue quite independently of any pleasure involved.

Similarly, we may feel that an obligation to keep a promise is more binding than that of giving pleasure to others. If I have solemnly promised Robinson to keep a secret about his private life, it is my duty not to tell it to Davidson, however little harm it might do to the former and however much pleasure it might give to the latter—quite apart from the additional pleasure it might give to me to tell it to him.

The truth is that promises have an intrinsic value of their own which demands our respect, whatever the amount of pleasure that may be involved. This too may have some connection with personal rights: the person to whom we make a promise has a right to expect that we shall keep it. In fact, it is generally recognized that a promise may be broken only when we can be sure that this person would allow it, or more especially, when it is to his interests that we should do so. Thus a doctor might reasonably withhold the truth from a patient, despite a promise to the contrary, when the knowledge of the truth might endanger that patient's health.

Utilitarianism, therefore, will not stand the test of experience. It is true that most of us desire pleasure and all of us desire happiness, but this desire is constantly being checked by the presence of other values in the world which have no obvious or immediate connection with either. In fact, the vast majority of moral conflicts arise precisely in such circumstances. Conversely, when we do act out of consideration for our own pleasure or happiness, we may feel that our action is reasonable and good, but we do not feel that it is done out of a sense of obligation. One might go further and say that the idea of obligation has slipped out of Mill's theory altogether; in trying to explain moral duty, he has explained it away.

This raises another point (for which I am indebted to Sir David Ross's *Foundation of Ethics*). Some moral theories, notably Kant's (which we shall discuss very shortly), explain rightness in terms of the intrinsic nature of the act itself; in other words the burning question must be: Did I have the right *attitude* when I did this; was I sincere? Others explain rightness in terms of the consequences of the act. This, clearly, is what Mill is trying to do. But with these "consequence" theories, a further distinction has to be made: do they suggest that the consequence in question (in Mill's case, the greatest happiness of the greatest number) is the essence of rightness or merely its ground? In other words, to apply the question to Mill, is he *defining* right in terms of the Greatest Happiness Principle, or is he leaving right as an indefinable term and saying that if we use the Greatest Happiness Principle as our criterion, we shall in fact be acting rightly?

Mill, of course, does not explicitly make this distinction, but he certainly seems to imply that he is actually defining rightness. He seems to suggest that the Greatest Happiness Principle speaks for itself; since it is self-apparent, there is no need to appeal to any obligation outside it; the very enunciation of the principle reveals its demands upon us. If this is so, as we have shown earlier in this book (p. 30), it is a mere tautology to say "It is our duty to promote the greatest happiness of the greatest number"; for we have already defined duty as "the promotion of the greatest happiness of the greatest number." This is what we meant by saying that the idea of obligation has slipped out of Mill's theory.

On the other hand, it may be that, if pressed, Mill would have said that he was merely illustrating the ground of rightness and not attempting to define its essence. This saves the theory from being a mere tautology, but would hardly make it any the more convincing. As we have already said, frequently our moral experience and behavior are independent of any calculation of happiness and pleasure. Many duties that we recognize, like promise-keeping, respect for our parents, respect for the individual as a person, may involve the happiness of our neighbour, but they also seem to involve something even more fundamental; they make their own demands upon us, which we do not see fit to ignore simply because happiness can be given to a greater number of people if we do so.

It was this fundamental and apparently indefinable demand upon us that impressed the German philosopher, Immanuel Kant (1724–1804). Kant was the son of a master harness-maker of Königsberg, the capital of the Duchy of Prussia and the cultural center of East Germany. Pietism, an intensive form of Lutheranism, was strong in that area, and Kant's parents were its devoted adherents. When Kant showed a great aptitude for learning, he was sent to the *Collegium Fredericanum*, popularly known as the "pietist school." In fact, the externals of religion made such demands on the pupils of that college that Kant seems to have left with a dislike of all forms of institutional religion, although he always had a firm belief in God and remained a man of high moral integrity with a gentle and kindly disposition.

Bent on an academic career, he at first acted as a private tutor, until in 1754 he became a lecturer at his own university. In 1770 he was appointed its Professor of Logic and Metaphysics. His life was devoted partly to teaching his students at Königsberg to think and partly to preparing for the world a new philosophical synthesis, the main part of which we shall discuss in Part III. Although Kant died two years before Mill was born, we have decided to treat Kant's ethical theory after Mill's because it is at once deeper and more difficult. Of course,

Utilitarianism in some form or another is as old as philosophy itself, but Kant seems to take us a step nearer to the understanding of moral obligation.

In contrast to Mill's empiricism, he held that ethics, the science of behavior, must be based upon metaphysics, the science of ultimate reality. Although our particular duties at any given points of time may vary according to circumstances, the idea of duty itself is one which lies outside any temporal considerations; its demand is absolute. In this he was at one with Socrates, as we have already seen (Part I, Chapter I).

Kant felt this absolute demand of duty so forcibly that he not only thought it wrong to try to explain it in terms of anything else (as Mill explained duty in terms of happiness), but also held that you debased the very conception of morality if you tried to treat the demands of duty as the demands made by some reality external to the will of the person who experienced those demands (even though that external reality be absolute like the Good of Plato or God as understood by Aquinas). This is not to say that Kant did not believe in God; in fact, he held that His existence could be deduced from the absoluteness of the moral demands of which we are speaking. For Kant, as we shall see, the moral law was rooted in the rational order of the universe; and this rational order must itself have the sanction of Absolute Being who, as it were, sets the seal of absoluteness on the whole structure of that reality which our moral experience implies. This will perhaps become clearer if we give a brief summary of Kant's theory.

Kant begins his *Metaphysic of Morals* by saying, "Nothing can possibly be conceived in the world, or even out of it, which can be called good without qualification, except a Good Will." "A Good Will," he continues, "is good not because of what it performs or effects . . . but simply by virtue of the volition." He argues this point, as Socrates might have done (cf. his criticism of Anaxagoras—pp. 22–3), on the grounds that this alone makes sense of nature's purpose in making us as we are: "In a being which has reason and a will, if the proper object of nature were its *conservation*, its *welfare*, in a word, its *happiness*, then nature would have hit upon a very bad arrangement in selecting the reason of the creature to carry out this purpose."* Instinct, he goes on to say, would have done it very much better. "In fact, we find that

* *Op. cit.*, s. 1.

the more a cultivated reason applies itself with deliberate purpose to the enjoyment of life and happiness, so much more does the man fail of true satisfaction."

Actions, therefore, must be done from duty. Moreover, "an action done from duty derives its moral worth, *not from the purpose* which is to be attained by it, but from the maxim by which iti s determined."*

Since "duty is the necessity of acting from respect for the law," this maxim can be explained as follows: "I am never to act otherwise than so that I could also will that my maxim should become a universal law."

This is the core of Kant's ethics. It is based on two principles: on the one hand, nature is rational as a whole; therefore, what is rational for me must be rational for everybody; so my duty must also be the duty of everybody else who finds himself in similar circumstances; on the other hand, I must act on the principle which I find in my own rational nature; for if I act for the sake of something outside myself, I shall need a further principle obliging me to act according to the first principle and so on *ad infinitum*. Thus conscience always serves us with a "categorical imperative"; we feel it our duty to do a thing because the action is good in itself, not because it will lead to some other good.

Clearly, in a philosophy where "the good will" has such a unique position, the human person must have a special value: "rational beings," in fact, "are called *persons*, because their very nature points them out as ends in themselves."† The categorical imperative, therefore, although it proceeds from the self, is not self-centered; it takes all humanity into account.

Kant expands the imperative as follows: "So act as to treat humanity, whether in thine own person or in that of any other, in every case as an end withal, never as means only."‡ Thus rational beings as a body make up "a kingdom of ends," and every will, when it acts, is legislating for this kingdom; that is why the agent must always be able to will that his maxim should become a universal law. In so legislating, therefore, he will not only respect all other persons as ends in themselves, but also "endeavour, as far as within him lies, to forward the end of others. For the ends of any subject which is an end in himself, ought as far as

---

* *Ibid.*   † *Op. cit.*, s. 2.   ‡ *Ibid.*, s. 2.

possible to be my ends also, if that conception is to have its *full* effect with me."*

Kant, then, would not agree with Mill that happiness is an end in itself, but he would no doubt agree that often in practice the categorical imperative takes the form of a command to increase the happiness of others. Yet it would not take this form where the interests or rights of any individual were compromised; for every individual must be regarded as an end in himself. Thus, many of the objections that we raised to Mill's theory do not apply to Kant's position. It would not be my duty to save the lunatic at the risk of my own life, for I am an end in myself; it would not be my duty to assist the impoverished Jones by stealing from the wealthy Smith, for Smith is an end in himself; I must keep my promise to Robinson, for Robinson is an end in himself; again, it might be the duty of a doctor to tell a lie when it is in the interests of his patient to do so, for that patient is an end in himself.

We saw that Aristotle, true to his scientific calling, approached moral problems from the point of view of common sense. Kant, no less characteristically, argues in terms of pure logic; he argues "a priori," as we say; he argues, that is, from a basic principle to conclusions deduced from that principle. Now we have already given the two main principles from which Kant deduces his categorical imperative (p. 103). The first principle—"If nature is rational, then what is rational for me must be rational for everybody"—is sound enough; what of the second? Is it true that if I act for the sake of something outside myself, I shall need a further principle on which to base my choice of this external good, and so on in an infinite regress?

It is only too easy for these questions to become academic and divorced from the very experience which we are trying to analyze. Let us revert to our example of getting up in the morning (*vid.* p. 98). We have already seen that "desire" and "choice" are not synonymous; but this word "choice" is itself ambiguous. When I do get up, I may *choose* the brown suit rather than the blue, but the act of "choosing" to get up in the first place is something quite different. Here, we do not have to look around for motives as we do in the case of choosing

---

* I *loc. cit.*

the suit (e.g., whether it is a cold or a warm day, which suit goes better with our clean pair of shoes, etc.); the whole point is that the motive is already there: a demand is being made upon us whether we like it or not; the question is not whether I shall "choose" this course or that, but whether I shall "choose" at all. To act wrongly in a moral situation is not to act at all—in the full sense in which a person may be said to act; it is a failure to make one of those acts of will out of which personality is formed (cf. p. 91). We all know what it is to make such moral decisions, even though they may be difficult to analyze and, when good habits are already established, are made almost unconsciously.

No question, then, of moral action arises at all except in the context of some particular circumstances: it may be that I am in a responsible position and have a duty to correct an injustice; it may be that I am tempted to buy a luxury which I cannot afford; it may be—in the much broader context of my life as a whole—that I have to decide how best to make use of the particular talents with which I have been gifted. In every case, something external makes a demand on me; it may be the demands of justice; it may be the demands of my wife and family for a reasonable standard of living before I spend money on luxuries; it may be some vaguer demand, which I experience but cannot analyze, that my talents should not be wasted. In every case, the circumstances make the demand, and I act or fail to act in response.

This seems to be the exact opposite of what Kant is saying. According to him, *I* am the legislator; I make the demand. True, I legislate in accordance with some objective principle of reason; but the fact remains that, according to Kant, some particular act is my duty, not because it is in accordance with reason in itself, but because I have so legislated that it is so.

Kant regards reason as in some way shaping its own material; for him, the reason gives precepts to the will as the appetites give desires to the senses; but, as T. K. Abbott says in his introduction to his edition of Kant's ethical works: "Reason is not our own in the sense in which our appetites or sensations are our own; it is not under our own control; it bears the stamp of universality and authority." It is the privilege of a free intelligence, therefore, not to legislate for itself, as Kant thought, but to recognize the validity of the moral law and accept it for its own sake. The link between the individual will and the universality of moral obligation is not in any mysterious "kingdom of ends"—and here Kant does seem to turn from logic to mystique—but quite simply in the apprehension of a universal truth by a particular faculty of reason.

This does not compromise our freedom, but rather establishes it. When we are confronted by some problem in mathematics, our reason seems limited and confined until we manage to work it out; only then—when the logical implications contained in the problem have been revealed to our minds—do we feel that sense of freedom which comes from mastery of the truth. Similarly, a person acting according to what Aristotle called "the rules of right reason" attains to the fullest freedom in the moral sphere; for he is acting according to the laws of his being. In the same way, to use another analogy, a train runs smoothly when it keeps to the rails; for it is designed precisely to run in this way. In short, an external moral law no more restricts the freedom of a rational being than the railway lines restrict the freedom of the train. At the same time, there is an essential difference between the "freedom" of the animal, which instinctively acts according to the laws of its being, and the freedom of man, who accepts such laws for their own sake.

So Kant misses the point when he says that if nature intended us to according to an external law, she would have arranged for us to act by instinct rather than reason. True, if we acted purely from instinct, we would not break the law as we do now, but we could not act for the sake of the law, which Kant rightly saw was so important. The essence of freedom, then, lies not in being able to make laws for oneself, but in being able to recognize the law of our nature for the good thing that it is and—more important still—proving our recognition by action upon it. It must be admitted, however, that to be fair to Kant we would have to examine his whole theory in much greater detail; so much here depends on the special status which he ascribes to the human will and the limited powers which he allows the human intellect.

In discussing the nature of human action, it seemed appropriate to quote two philosophers who approached the problems of ethics from diametrically opposite ends, Mill arguing from experience, Kant from the principle of moral freedom. We have endeavored to meet them on their own ground, and, curiously enough, this is where they are most vulnerable. Mill does not distinguish the sense of obligation from those very desires which are most often found in conflict with it; Kant does not appreciate that the logic of a demand originating in oneself is much more difficult to explain than the demand of an external principle whose validity we recognize and respect for its own sake.

At this point philosophy and religion meet. Kant, as we have seen, believed in God, but he was anxious to produce a rational system that relied as little as possible on any ideas—like that of Infinite Being—which could not be fully understood by the human mind. We have already commented on this kind of approach (vid. supra p. 22): it is right that we should try to analyze as much as we can of reality, but it is foolish either to begin, like the rationalist, on the presumption that we can analyze it all, or, like Kant, to ignore what we cannot analyze and imagine that a coherent and self-supporting system can be evolved with what remains.

Moral experience takes us into the very heart of reality. It is the theme of the greatest plays and novels. It is at once simple and almost hopelessly complex: most of us know what we mean by right and wrong until we attempt to put it into words. When we make the attempt, it seems that we must either stop short of the truth, like Mill and Kant, or step beyond the limits of analytical reasoning like the saints. This is not to suggest that we must plunge into mystery without knowing what we are about, but rather that we can only explain what is within our grasp by recognizing that there is much which is beyond it.

It is not surprising, therefore, that Thomas Aquinas, who was both philosopher and saint, made no attempt to evolve an ethical system distinct from the revelation which he believed the Church of Christ to possess. Indeed, if his belief in the incarnation of Christ profoundly affected his approach to Aristotelian metaphysics, it completely transformed his approach to Aristotelian ethics. Christ had said: "I am the way, and the truth, and the life," (John xiv. 6); and the moral experience was now no less than the experience of Christ within the soul.

Since this is a book on philosophy and not theology, it would be out of place to pursue this particular point any further; but it would perhaps be equally inappropriate to finish this chapter without a brief look at the general views of Aquinas on the problems which we have been discussing, since he is the most prominent example of a philosopher whose thought was inspired by the Christian revelation.

Aquinas agreed with Socrates and Plato in deriving the absoluteness of moral values from infinite being. He also held that man could find no satisfaction in his own contingent self, and could not realize the potentialities of that self unless he recognized his dependence on God. In this last point, he went further than Plato because of his conception of God as Creator: for Plato, all goodness was derived from the Good; but for Aquinas, all being is for ever—in one timeless creative act— derived from God.

Since God, then, is at once our Creator and our End, man moves towards his natural end just in so far as he performs the will of God. God, however, is no whimsical tyrant; Aquinas, like Kant, believed that the rational character of the whole structure of the universe was derived from God as ultimate Truth; therefore, the rational and the will of God are identical. So our freedom is not compromised; for as rational beings we are most free when we accept what is rational for its own sake. If Kant had enjoyed a more profound insight into the contingency of created being, he would surely have seen that it is a very much better reason to accept a law because it is God's than because it is one's own.

We have already seen that Aquinas does not in any way detract from the dignity of human nature. On the one hand, man is utterly dependent upon God; but, on the other hand, man is made in the image of God. It follows that in the concrete experience of daily life, nothing makes so much demand on our respect as do the dignity and rights of the human person. Christ himself repeated again and again that we serve God most effectively by serving our neighbor. On this point, therefore, any Christian philosophy will be much more in the spirit of Kant than in that of Mill. For, although the happiness of one's neighbor is a major aim of Christian charity, that happiness should never be won at the expense of the fundamental rights of a third party.

On the subject of happiness in itself, Aquinas would perhaps be more on the side of Mill than of Kant. There is something impersonal about Kant's world of rigorous logic; the word "happiness" does not appear often in his writings. Aquinas, however, held that we were created to be happy, and that happiness consisted ultimately in the contemplation of God. Moreover, he saw that it is unreal to treat happiness as though it were a value separate from the activity which makes you happy. Happiness comes from doing what is worthwhile. It is a commonplace that the man who pursues happiness in the void, so to speak, never finds it.

Mill said that we always desire pleasure; Aquinas said that we always desire the good. Psychologically and philosophically, the difference is profound, though the application may often be very similar. Mill is thinking of man as a bundle of instincts, believing that some instincts when satisfied bring deeper pleasure than others; Aquinas is thinking of him as a rational being, who always has a reason for his actions, even though it may be a bad reason. Socrates may not be right in saying that virtue is knowledge, but as we have seen (p. 25 seq.), virtue is the fulfilment of the rational creature, while vice is the distortion of his nature.

The ideal of natural law, therefore, plays an important part in Thomist—and indeed in all Christian—ethics. What is right is always rational for man, considering the kind of being that he is and the end for which he was created. If a flower is allowed to grow according to the laws of its being, it will reach fulfilment in the bloom that crowns its growth; so man, by obeying the laws of his being, will reach fulfilment in the happiness that crowns his highest activity.

8. MAN AND SOCIETY

The influence of philosophy on history is a subject too vast for us to consider here; but it is hoped that this chapter will suggest at least its influence on modern Europe. In fact, if we consider the history of Europe since the French Revolution, the remarkable—and indeed tragic—lesson that we learn is just how great this influence has been.

The modern "ideology" hardly deserves the name of philosophy; but it has philosophical antecedents, and the very completeness of its application to the whole of human life has something in common with the approach of traditional metaphysics. But with this superficial resemblance the comparison must end. Aristotle after all was careful to emphasize that politics was not an exact science. Plato indeed may have been guilty of too systematic an approach (vid. p. 50), but fundamentally he was true to the spirit of Socrates; he was always trying to bring the truth to light, not to impose a system of ideas from without; "midwifery" had not yet given place to indoctrination.

Obviously, the history of political thought would demand a book in itself, and this chapter is no attempt at a substitute. On the other hand, if we are discussing the nature of man, we must say something of his place in society. To introduce, therefore, the theories of Hegel and Marx at this point has two advantages: it is relevant to our theme and at the same time particularly relevant to the historical circumstances in which we live.

Wherever his philosophy may ultimately have led, nobody could accuse Hegel (1770–1831) of trying to produce a popular "ideology." With Teutonic thoroughness and industry, he built up, on an entirely new logic of his own, what is perhaps the most complex system that has ever been devised. Unfortunately, complexity often means obscurity, and Hegel's case is no exception: "Only one man ever understood me," he complained on his deathbed, "and he did not understand me either." We cannot hope to do anything like justice to Hegel's system in this book; we shall attempt only to suggest the kind of way in which he thought—particularly in connection with those ideas which had such a profound effect on Karl Marx.

Hegel was born at Stuttgart of uppei-middle-class parents and led an academic life, holding professorships in various German universities until in 1818 he succeeded to the chair of philosophy in Berlin, the most important in Germany. In his youth, he and Schelling, another distinguished philosopher, were fellow students; and although Hegel spoke contemptuously of him in after years, Schelling had a powerful influence on his thought.

Hegel, like most philosophers, began with a quite simple truth: the history of philosophy—and indeed the history of the world as a whole—consisted very largely in the exclusive assertions of conflicting attitudes. We have seen, for example, how in the very beginning the more or less empirical, quasi-scientific approach of the Milesians was followed by the abstract, mystical approach of the Pythagoreans; we saw how the Absolute Unity of Parmenides gave way to the multifarious relativity of the Sophists; we saw how the idealism of Plato was succeeded by the realism of Aristotle, and that all subsequent philosophies have tended to veer towards the one direction or the other. A case could also be made, on Hegelian lines, that truth has often in fact emerged from a comparison between these conflicting positions. This can well be accounted for by the limitations and fallibility of the human mind, which has to reach its goal by devious and painful means. Hegel, however, had more confidence in human powers of reasoning and argued that there must be an inherent contradiction in reality itself.

Now, Hegel was an idealist—an idealist even more extreme than Plato. For him, therefore, this reality was hidden in the abstract world of thought; the real was what could be grasped by the mind, not what could be perceived by the senses. Like Kant, therefore, he argues by a deductive process from the fundamental principles of his logic. This logic was based on a paradoxical identity of Being and Not-Being: unlimited Being in the abstract could not be distinguished from Nothing; for, to be anything in particular, it would have to be limited. It would be absurd to argue from this that nothing exists; rather it was true to say that existence is found somewhere between these two absolute contradictions of Being and Not-Being. We can take an example from light: in pure light—light without color or shadow—we should be unable to see anything; similarly, in pure darkness, we should be unable to see anything; we can see, then, not in pure light or in pure darkness, but in a combination of the two. In the same way, everything that exists is a combination of Being and Not-Being.

Clearly, on such principles, it is impossible to believe in the existence of Absolute Being as such; for such a being would be equivalent to Nothing. On the other hand, Hegel was an idealist, and all idealists must ultimately think in terms of some ideal Absolute. It is not clear what exactly Hegel conceived the nature of this Absolute to be; perhaps he did not pretend to know. At any rate, he believed that the Absolute manifested itself in nature. Hegel, we must notice, was not simply a pantheist; he did not believe that Nature is God. Nature is rather the external manifestation of the Absolute Intelligence which uses the world as a kind of chess-board on which it works out its own problems—in which, we might say, it discovers its own essence.

The Hegelian Idea, then—for here he used the Platonic terminology—was Thought in an active form. It was the supreme experimenter, working out in history all possible manifestations of itself. The pattern of history, therefore, has the characteristics of the pattern of thought. "Contradiction," he says in the Encyclopaedia of Philosophical Sciences, "is the very moving principle of the world." The pattern, in fact, takes the form of a "thesis," followed by an "antithesis," and out of these two emerges a "synthesis," which is the new thesis in the next phase. Hegel worked out this "dialectic," as the pattern is called, in its application to religion, history, law and philosophy respectively.

Of these applications, the Philosophy of History has had by far the most influence and calls for a special word of comment. Now, the Hegelian dialectic suggested that each pair of contradictories—each thesis and antithesis—were truths which implied each other as well as being contradictory to each other; they, in fact, combined to produce some higher truth. It follows that each term in the process (whether thesis or antithesis) is of less importance than the synthesis, and the synthesis itself, as the new thesis, is subordinate to the new synthesis, and so on.

We can visualize this schematically as a number of increasingly large circles which are ever being embraced by yet larger circles. Apply this to the concrete facts of history, and we find that the smallest unit is man and the largest the State; in order for the State to be formed, it must pass from family to horde, from horde to tribe, and from tribe to state. Moreover, it is a dialectical process—a process through the contradictions of strife. Groups assimilate each other by force and form larger groups. "War," he says, "is not an accident," but an element "whereby the ideal character of the particular receives its right and reality."* It follows that the most important class within the State is the military class, "the class of universality," as Hegel calls it.†

Thus, each state represents some idea, and the military class within the state personifies that idea as a living force which meets some contradictory idea (also personified in a military class) in bloody combat and forges a new synthesis in the fire of war. By such means the Absolute's self-knowledge evolves. As Professor Gilson puts it: "If the realization of the Idea is the march of God through the world, the path of the Hegelian God is strewn with ruins."‡

Clearly, in this terrible philosophy, the individual counts for little. At the first encounter with some other individual, he is swept up into a group wherein he must surrender his individuality in the interests of the Absolute's self-knowledge. We know something of the effects of such ruthless mysticism. It was no coincidence that Hegel came from a land that would one day acclaim Adolf Hitler as its leader.

Hegel had come from Bavaria, but Karl Marx (1818–83) was born in Prussia. Racially, he was of distinguished Jewish descent, but his

* Loewenberg, *Hegel Selections*, p. 464.   † *Ibid*. p. 465.
‡ *The Unity of Philosophical Experience*, London, 1955, p. 250.

father had turned Protestant, and Karl was baptized a Christian. At an early age, he denounced both the religion and the class into which he had been born. At the age of twenty-four, he edited a paper which was suppressed in the following year, and soon he had to leave his country for Paris, the fountainhead of European revolution. He was not allowed to live there for long, and spent the last thirty-four years of his life in England. Hegel, by far the greater and more dynamic philosopher of the two, had moved up by steady academic stages from Stuttgart to Berlin: Marx, after a restless and rootless life, was buried in the cemetery at Highgate.

In Paris, Marx met Friedrich Engels (1820–95), with whom he was to collaborate for the rest of his life. In fact, the famous *Communist Manifesto*, which appeared in 1847, was their joint work. There is something of the same ambiguity in discussing Marx and Engels as there is in discussing Socrates and Plato; it is not always possible to assess their respective contributions. For our purposes, therefore, we shall follow the common practice of discussing their combined product under the simple name of "Marxism."

Marx was inspired by the dynamic force of the Hegelian dialectic; but where Hegel believed that all true reality was spirit, Marx believed that nothing existed except matter. This, first of all, is why Marx's chief interest was in Hegel's philosophy of history, which, we are apt to forget, was only a part—albeit a central part—of Hegel's system. History is concrete and factual—or at least it is easy to think of it as such—and, as every historian knows, there are no limits to the number of patterns which these facts can be shown to make. Marx, therefore, had no difficulty in taking over the dialectical idealism of Hegel and, after turning it inside out, producing the dialectical materialism which is the central theme of his philosophy.

Both Hegel and Marx saw the collective whole as a higher form of reality than the individual, and thought such collective units increased in importance as they increased in size. Hegel's collective unit, whatever its external manifestation, was always in essence an idea; but the unit of Marx, the materialist, is a given state of society—and a state of society conceived in economic terms.

For Marx, therefore, the progress of history proceeds through a series of conflicts of one state of society with another. Basically, these conflicts are between economic forces, and each conflict is solved in a new synthesis that takes the form of an economy which is an advance on the previous two. This inevitable progress, he thought, would ultimately end in an ideal state of society, where economic tension ceased to exist—a state of society, in other words, where all men had an equal share of material possessions. To illustrate his theory, Marx began with the feudal system of the Middle Ages: then, the class in power was represented by the landlords and guild-masters; but the system of production changed from handicraft to manufacture, and the bourgeoisie emerged on top; with the discovery of steampower and the use of machinery on a large scale, there emerged a new class, the proletariat, the people who produced nothing but their own children, as this grim term suggests. It was only a matter of time before we should have the dictatorship of the proletariat, and after that the millennium.

According to Marxism, the economic factor is not merely the predominant force among many, but it is the essential basis of all other historical forces. As Engels puts it: "All the social, political, and intellectual relations, all religions and legal systems, all the theoretical outlooks which emerge in the course of history . . . are derived from the material conditions of life."* Religion, for example, is simply the outcome of imperfect modes of production, which leave human needs unsatisfied; this dissatisfaction causes man to "project," as the psychologists now term it, another world where his needs will be satisfied; this is what Marx meant by calling religion "the opium of the people." In the millennium of universal satisfaction, religion will have no place; drugs are wasted on those who have no pain to relieve.

Marxism, then, essentially belongs to the scientific optimism of the nineteenth century: every human problem was ultimately a material problem, and it was only a question of time before science would have sufficient control over matter for all problems to be solved. This outlook is no longer so prevalent as it used to be. It is beyond the scope of this book to discuss the cynical opportunism which passes under the name of Marxism today; suffice it to say that Stalin seems to have had no illusions about the dictatorship of the proletariat, let alone the millennium that was to follow; nobody quite knows what his successors

* *Ludwig Feuerbach*, p. 93.

think, but there have been no signs of Messianic idealism up to date.

It seems that now, at least the Western half of the world is reacting against the collectivism that was a nineteenth-century theory and a twentieth-century fact; the modern philosophy of Existentialism, which we shall discuss in Chapter 12 of Part IV, reveals this reaction in its most extreme form. But we still have our welfare states, trade unions and rigid party systems; the collectivist controversy is still very much in the air. Some of the problems are matters of principle; many are simply difficulties of practical application; but, however that may be, it would help if we could get our principles clear.

It was Aristotle who first defined man as a "political animal." By this he wished to convey the characteristically Greek idea that man at his best lives in a "*polis*," a small, organic community. "He who is unable to live in society," he says, "or who has no need because he is sufficient for himself, must be either a beast or a god."* In other words, it is natural for man to be born into a family, and for families to combine together into some form of political unity. If we believe in a rational universe and the validity of some form of natural law, the overwhelming evidence of history suggests that the family in the first place and the tribe or state in the second place are unities indispensable to the right living of human life. Some kind of "world-government" is, of course, conceivable, but only as the apex of a pyramid built up out of smaller organisms among which the state, at least in a modified form, would have its place.

So far, the individualists and the collectivists need have no cause for disagreement; but the real question is whether the whole exists for the individual or the individual for the whole. Has the whole some law of its own which entitles it to swallow up the individuals within it and work exclusively for the fulfilment of its own end? Clearly, we cannot answer this question in the affirmative unless we believe in pantheism or some kind of Hegelian modification of it. On this point, Marx, who rejected Hegel's idealism, is inconsistent; for what is there in Marxism which makes it obligatory or even advantageous for a man to assist the progressive course of history and usher in a millennium which he will not live to enjoy?

* Pol., 1253a, 27–9.

It would be unfair to attempt a detailed criticism of Hegel without first giving a more detailed account of his theory; but surely we have seen enough to suggest that there is a fundamental fault in his general approach. Hegel, of all people, is guilty of the "systematic fallacy" to which we referred in discussing Plato (*vid*. p. 50); not only does he erect a vast framework of abstract thought which has no obvious connection with reality, but he bases this very framework on the paradox of a logical contradiction—the kind of paradox which brought all philosophy into disrepute after the time of Parmenides and has driven metaphysics from the universities today.

Finally, Hegel tried to force the pattern of actual events into the mold which his abstractions had prepared for it. This set a precedent for the leaders of mass movements which was to cause terrible suffering in the world; this enabled Hitler and Stalin to pose as figures of destiny who would lead their followers to the glory prepared for them by the inevitable logic of history.

As F. J. Sheed points out in his book, *Communism and Man*,* Engels let the cat out of the bag in *Ludwig Feuerbach:* "But while in all earlier periods the investigation of these driving forces of history was almost impossible—on account of the complicated and concealed interconnection between them and their effects—our present period has so far simplified these interconnections that the riddle could be solved." As Mr. Sheed says: "The economic interpretation of history is to be applied with confidence to the most recent period of history; for the rest it is an act of faith" (p. 51). Hegel himself provides examples of the superficial form which such arguments from history can take.

In the *Phenomenology of Mind* he argues that Christian optimism was a reaction from pagan despair. As an instance of pagan despair, he quotes Greek comedy as ridiculing the ideas of Greek tragedy and thus revealing an even more tragic attitude of mind. Apparently, he was content to ignore the historical fact that they grew up side by side, both reflecting at the beginning the idealism and at the end the disillusionment of contemporary Athens, during the course of the fifth century B.C., which saw her rise and fall. At the same time, he seems to have

* London and New York, Sheed and Ward, 1938.

taken no account of Judaism, the most direct historical antecedent of Christianity, which itself had all the optimism of a Messianic creed. It seems, then, that we must turn from the profitless mystique of searching the crystal of history for some sign by which to live, and examine things as they are in the light of the actual values which they are found to possess. Following our argument in the last chapter, this means that we should focus rather on the human person as that which has more dignity and value than anything else of which we are immediately aware. Thus, society, as a collection of such persons, will always be a worthy end for which to work, but it will never be an end in itself for which men must surrender that very personality which alone gives dignity to the society to which they belong.

To this extent, as we have said, we can welcome as a healthy reaction the individualism of modern French philosophers (*vid.* Part IV, Chapter 12). But, in our view, when we focus on the person, our line of vision does not stop there. In the mind and conscience of mortal man, we are forced, with Plato and Aristotle, to recognize unchanging values beyond, and independent of, man and history. Since society, then, exists for man and helps him to fulfill his end, the laws of society must ultimately be framed in the light of that end which it is its function to serve.

PART THREE

THE PROBLEM OF KNOWLEDGE

9. SOME PROBLEMS OF PERCEPTION

1. Our Ideas and Their Source

The end of the Middle Ages had seen the visionary spirit of the great scholastic philosophers decline into the sophistic quibbling of pedants who played a rather complicated form of chess with their Latin tags, the original meanings of which had lost their lustre with indiscriminate use and abuse. Moreover, a new spirit was in the air: as we approach Descartes, we move into the world of Copernicus and Galileo, of Kepler and Roger Bacon—a world excited by the first important discoveries of physical science since the long-forgotten days of the Greeks.

In the world of medicine today, if a new drug is discovered, there is a tendency for doctors to prescribe it for every kind of ailment; much the same thing happens in the world of philosophy. Every new age has its own spirit; the new panacea is applied to every kind of problem: in the seventeenth century, there was a tendency to submit everything to the discipline of mathematics—the science that was enabling the calculations of the physicists to bear so much fruit. In this spirit, René Descartes (1591–1650), after an apocalyptic dream which inspired him with a mystical fervor to found a new, scientific philosophy, determined to assert no truth but what he could clearly and distinctly apprehend, and to build up on such a basis a metaphysical system whose logic would be as unimpeachable as Euclid's.

Descartes was born of an old, landed family of La Haye, a small town in the province of Touraine. He was educated at the Jesuit college of

La Flèche, and then, after four more years in Paris, in the spirit of discovery of which we have spoken, he joined the army to see the world. Indeed, enlistment on such terms allowed considerable scope for private enterprise in those days, when a soldier could hire his services to whatever duke happened to be campaigning in the land of his choice. Descartes's soldering was much more eclectic than his philosophy and, as soldier and tourist, he had soon covered most of Europe.

In the midst of these peregrinations, at Ulm in the month of November 1619, Descartes had his dream: the Spirit of Truth, he said, wanted to open for him "the treasure of all the sciences." The next day, he vowed a pilgrimage to Loretto. It was not, however, until ten years later that he finally settled down to his philosophy, choosing to live in Amsterdam where, as he claimed, he could think with a cool head; for in Italy and France, he could only produce phantasies of the brain.

In the same religious spirit, Descartes wrote his most important work under the title of *Meditations*. Here he preaches the duty of doubt: "My reason convinces me that I ought not the less carefully to withhold belief from what is not entirely certain and indubitable, than from what is manifestly false." Now, he continues: "All that I have, up to this moment, accepted as possessed of the highest truth and certainty, I received either from or through the senses." He has observed, however, "that these [senses] sometimes mislead us; and it is the part of prudence not to place absolute confidence in that by which we have even once been deceived."* In the second Meditation he gives his celebrated example of such deception:

Take this piece of wax; it is quite fresh, having been but recently taken from the bee-hive; it has not yet lost the sweetness of the honey it contained; it still retains somewhat of the odour of the flowers from which it was gathered; its colour, figure, size, are apparent [to the sight]; it is hard, cold, easily handled; and sounds when struck upon with the finger. In fine, all that contributes to make a body as distinctly known as possible, is found in the one before us. But, while I am speaking, let it be placed near the fire—what remained of the taste exhales, the smell evaporates, the colour changes, its figure is destroyed, its size increases, it becomes liquid, it grows hot, it can hardly be handled, and, although struck upon, emits no sound. Does the same wax still remain after this

---

* *Meditations*, i; I have used John Veitch's translation of 1899.

change? It must be admitted that it does remain; no one doubts it, or judges otherwise. What, then, was it I knew with so much distinctness in the-piece of wax? Assuredly, it could be nothing that I observed with the senses, since all the things that fell under taste, smell, sight, touch, and hearing are changed, and yet the same wax remains.

We shall return in a moment to the problems about sense perception which Descartes here raises. Meanwhile, we must briefly note how he went on from here—how he came to adopt what was known from then on as the Cartesian approach to reality.

Since he found that the senses were unreliable, he began by shutting out the external world and concentrating on his own thoughts; thus, by concentrating only on what he knew for certain, he hoped to build up his impregnable system. The first truth that struck him was stated in the famous formula: *Cogito ergo sum* ("I think, therefore I am"); in other words, by the very act of reflection I recognize my selfhood or identity.

From here, Descartes went on to prove the existence of God by his own version of the ontological argument, which we have already discussed in connection with St. Anselm (*vid.* p. 70), adding that: "I should not . . . have the idea of an infinite substance, seeing I am a finite being, unless it were given me by some substance in reality infinite."*

Besides the ideas of self and God, there was another set of ideas which Descartes believed to be innate or born in men without any reference to the outside world's being required—the truths of mathematics; for, he said, "I am able to form in thought an innumerable variety of figures with regard to which it cannot be supposed that they were objects of sense."† The rest of our ideas came to us from the outside world, but not all of these had that mark of certainty upon them which was the characteristic of innate ideas.

This is where Descartes's problem begins. It is not merely that our senses can play tricks on us—in some conditions we may "see" mirages, pink elephants, spots before the eyes, and countless other phenomena whose actual existence is doubtful—but even in the course of normal sensation, there are some curious features: railway lines appear to converge; houses and other objects appear to grow smaller as we go away

---

* *Meditations*, iii.   † *Meditations*, v.

from them; hills look quite different in size and shape as the light varies.

And then, on top of all this, scientists tell us that what we think that we perceive in the external world bears little relation to what actually exists: chairs and tables are really whirling masses of atoms; the rose is not red in itself, but only gives off certain light rays which give us the sensation of red; the gramophone itself does not make a noise, but only disturbs the molecules of air in such a way that if our eardrums are brought into contact with this disturbance, we have a sensation of noise —if, in fact, a gramophone plays in the desert with none to hear it, there is no noise at all. As we shall see, this is a picture which is by no means philosophically acceptable, but at first sight it does seem to be implied by what the scientist has to say.

Descartes may not have seen all these problems quite in this way; but science was beginning to raise such difficulties, and, in any case, there were problems enough in our ordinary experience, such as he illustrates in the example of the wax. Descartes had satisfied himself that he had proved the existence of God. Now, it was unthinkable that God should deceive us. It followed that when I have a clear and distinct idea of anything, that idea must be true. Let us now see how the passage about the wax continues:

"It was perhaps what I now think, viz., that this wax was neither the sweetness of honey, the pleasant odour of flowers, the whiteness, the figure, nor the sound, but only a body that a little before appeared to me conspicuous under these forms, and which is now perceived under others. But, to speak precisely, what is it that I imagine when I think of it in this way? Let it be attentively considered, and, retrenching all that does not belong to the wax, let us see what remains. There certainly remains nothing, except something extended, flexible, and moveable. But what is meant by flexible and moveable? Is it not that I imagine that the piece of wax, being round, is capable of becoming square, or of passing from a square into a triangular figure? Assuredly such is not the case, because I conceive that it admits of an infinity of similar changes; and I am, moreover, unable to compass this infinity by imagination, and consequently this conception which I have of the wax is not the product of the faculty of the imagination. But what now is this extension? Is it not also unknown? for it becomes greater when the wax is melted, greater when it is boiled, and greater still when the heat increases; and I should not conceive [clearly and] according to truth, the wax as it is, if I did not suppose that the piece we are considering admitted even of a wider variety of extension than I ever imagined. I must, therefore, admit that I cannot even comprehend by imagination what the piece of wax is, and that it is the mind alone (*mens*, Lat., *entendement*, F.) which perceives it. I speak of one piece in particular; for as to wax in general, this is still more evident. But what is the piece of wax that can be perceived only by the [understanding] or mind? It is certainly the same which I see, touch, imagine; and, in fine, it is the same which, from the beginning, I believed it to be. But (and this it is of moment to observe) the perception of it is neither an act of sight, of touch, nor of imagination, and never was either of these, though it might formerly seem so, but is simply an intuition (*inspectio*) of the mind, which may be imperfect and confused, as it formerly was, or very clear and distinct, as it is at present, according as the attention is more or less directed to the elements which it contains, and of which it is composed."*

Thus, Descartes believed that he had succeeded in removing, as it were, all the sensible qualities from the wax and arriving at an intellectual perception of its true nature. Ultimately, therefore, he knew the external world by sifting with his mind the data given by his senses and arriving at a distinct idea whose veracity was guaranteed by God.

It will be noticed, however, that his account is essentially dualistic; the *cogito* assumes a mind working in a void without any assistance from the senses, and his account of perception implies two separate operations—of the senses, on the one hand, and of the mind, on the other. He is now faced with Plato's difficulty of explaining how the senses and the mind interact on each other—and in this age of scientific reasoning, an answer in clear terms would be demanded.

His answer, in fact, gives his whole position away: when we perceive anything, he said, there are two stages in the process: firstly, our sense organs are modified (thus, for example, there is an image on my retina when I perceive anything with the organ of sight); secondly, this modification produces an intellectual image; but—and this is the significant point—the first stage is transferred into the second by the pineal gland.

---

* *Meditations*, ii. Veitch's translation is from the Latin text with some additions (printed in square brackets) from an emended French text.

So, ironically enough, Descartes's idealism ends in crude materialism; thought is reduced to a kind of glandular secretion. Having excluded the external world, he has to resort to such an unlikely theory in order to bring it back. The lesson has its value.

There is, of course, much of more positive value in Descartes's analysis, to which we shall return later (vid. p. 132). Meanwhile, let us turn from the hard logic of France to the commonsense, empirical approach of the Englishman, John Locke (1632–1704). He was born at Wrington in Somerset, the son, like Descartes, of a lawyer. He was educated at Westminster School and Christ Church College, Oxford, where he was elected to a Senior Studentship in 1659; in the following year, he became lecturer in Greek and subsequently Reader in Rhetoric and Censor of Moral Philosophy. A don, however, was normally expected to take Holy Orders, a vocation which did not appeal to him; and, in any event, he had turned his attention to medicine. Eventually, in 1674, he took his degree of Doctor of Medicine, and very soon became engaged in politics. Politics in the reign of Charles II no doubt had its fascinating side; but in 1683, after his patron, Shaftesbury, had stood his trial for high treason, Locke found it safer to leave Oxford for Holland, where, in a more peaceful atmosphere, he applied himself to writing philosophy, until he came back to England with William of Orange.

On the continent, Locke had caught something of the Cartesian enthusiasm; he, too, wished to bring philosophy into line with the methods and discoveries of physical science. In fact, Locke followed the empirical approach of the scientists, where Descartes had used the a priori methods of mathematics. Locke believed that a child's mind at birth is a complete blank, a "tabula rasa," as he calls it. All our ideas subsequently come from experience, whether by "sensation," wherein things imprint their images on our minds, or by "reflection," wherein the mind reflects on its own operations and forms ideas of knowing, believing, doubting, willing and so on. These are what he calls "simple ideas"; by further mental operations—abstraction, comparison and "compounding" (as the idea "mermaid," for example, is compounded of the ideas of "fish" and "girl")—we form "complex ideas," all of which can be traced to simple ideas derived from experience.

Locke's definition of "idea" is highly significant: "Whatsoever the mind perceives in itself, or is the immediate object of perception, thought, or understanding, that I call *idea*; and the power to produce any idea in our mind, I call *quality* of the subject wherein that power is."* In other words, the mind perceives ideas, and ideas are images produced through our senses by the qualities of physical objects; thus, when I see a red ball, the qualities of redness and roundness produce in my mind a picture that is round and red, and it is the perception of this image that is meant when I say that I see the ball.

This theory of representative ideas owes its origin to the approach adopted by Descartes, despite his own belief in an apparently intuitive *inspectio mentis* at the final stage of perception; it was the direct outcome of his dualistic view of self as a spirit trying to get in touch with the material world by means of the clumsy weapons of sense. For all his realism, Locke seems to have accepted the position without question. It was a theory that was to have momentous consequences for philosophy, as we shall see in the next chapter. For the moment, however, we must take stock of some of the other ground that we have covered.

The main difference that we have noted between Descartes and Locke lies not so much in their explanations of the nature of our ideas as of their source. Locke rejected the suggestion that any of our ideas are innate; but for Descartes, this was the basis on which his whole system rested. The theory of innate ideas goes back to Plato; it was essential to his doctrine that the soul, between one incarnation and another, should have some sort of contact with the world of Forms. Since this world of ours was but a copy of that ideal world, material objects reminded us of their ideal prototypes, so that all universal ideas were to be ascribed to acts of "recollection." How else, he asks, can we account for ideas like "straightness," when material things, at best, are only approximately straight? If we did not already have an idea of perfect straightness, we could not even account for the fact that we know that material things are not perfectly straight. In a dialogue called

* An *Essay Concerning Human Understanding*, bk. 11, ch. viii, para. 8.

the *Meno*, he represents Socrates as illustrating this doctrine of "recollection" by calling in an ignorant slave-boy and going through a theorem of geometry with him: the boy, who knew no geometry, is coaxed into making the required demonstration himself—not without, it must be added, many leading questions from Socrates; Socrates alleges that he is merely reminding the boy of truths that he had forgotten.

Plato, therefore, held the theory of innate ideas in a much more complete form than Descartes. I do not think, however, that it is necessary to appeal to the text of the *Meno* to show that the slave's answers to Socrates's questions do not prove that the slave already knew the answers, but that rational beings, to a greater or lesser degree, are capable of recognizing truth when it is pointed out to them. In the light of subsequent scepticism, however, this proof is more important than it might seem. It is indeed worth remembering that all forms of instruction and argument—even philosophical argument—presume that there is common ground between the parties concerned.

Now, if, like Aristotle and Locke, or even Descartes, we take a realist view of the external world, it is natural to suppose that our knowledge of reality comes from that external world, which we believe to be, in the fullest sense, real. Common sense also suggests that we do in fact perceive reality through our senses, and that this perception—whether direct or indirect in the first instance—leaves us with ideas corresponding in some way to what we have perceived. It seems impossible to conceive of our forming any new ideas which are not made up out of the raw material of experience. What then are we to say to Descartes's theory that we have a limited number of innate ideas?

The idea of self need not present much difficulty to the empiricist: necessarily, it is unique, in that it is the same self that has the idea and which is the object of the idea. Owing to these unique conditions, it is neither innate nor ascribable to an external source: as soon as we begin to act as rational beings, we become conscious of ourselves as so acting.

What we might say, however, is that any such rational action presupposes an external reality on which to act; it is very doubtful whether "I think" means anything, if we do not presume an object of thought; and we would say that it is a psychological fact that the idea of self comes comparatively late in the history of a child's rational life; it comes from his catching himself, as it were, in the act of perceiving external things and at the same time making a distinction between those external things and himself. In this sense, the idea of self, so far from being innate, is subsequent to at least some ideas drawn from outside.

If we were right in what we said about the existence of God (p. 77 seq.), similar points could be made about the idea of God. Firstly, this idea is unique; for, unless we accept the ontological argument, we cannot say that it comes from introspection, like the idea of self; nor do we perceive God directly, like objects of the external world: secondly, we cannot form the idea, as some people seem to think, simply by putting together all that we know; a finite sum, however large, gets no nearer to the infinite. It does not help to say that we take the word "finite" and add a negative prefix, because the idea "finite" already presupposes the idea "infinite," just as the idea "wet" presupposes the idea "dry."

The answer seems to be that there is a certain idea of incompleteness which goes with our perception of material things that gives us the ideas of "finite" and "infinite." In other words, like the idea of self, it takes its origin from the way we perceive external reality, and not from any separate act of abstraction or compounding; on the other hand, of course, this incompleteness is an objective "quality"—if we may use the word of what is after all a unique characteristic—which is perceived in external objects and indeed in ourselves. Needless to say, the word "infinite" is not used in this context in the mathematician's sense of "endless" (as we talk of an "infinite series"), but as denoting positive perfection; we deliberately use the word in a vague sense: to decide exactly what we mean by it would take us back again to the proofs for the existence of God.

Descartes's belief that mathematical ideas are also innate raises rather a different type of question; since it is chiefly of importance to mathematicians, we shall not say much about it here, except to suggest that the "innumerable variety of figures," of which he speaks, are simply modifications of the lines and curves which we see in the world about us; similarly, there seems to be no reason why the idea of number should not be abstracted from particulars.

On the other hand, Descartes may have been thinking not merely of the mathematical ideas themselves, but also of the absoluteness with which mathematical truths are argued and expressed: the mathematician is concerned with absolute straightness, roundness, triangularity and so on, and—what obviously appealed so much to Descartes—these truths have themselves a timeless and absolute character, which cannot be said of ordinary empirical knowledge. In other words, we still have the problem of Plato's straight stick.

As we have said (p. 75), there is no question of proving (as Plato tried to prove) the existence of absolute straightness, as Aquinas claimed to prove the existence of Absolute Being. Because we think of straight lines in terms of an absolute standard of straightness, there is no reason to suppose that this standard actually exists somewhere; we merely extend the scale, as it were, until we reach the idea of perfect straightness. In the same way, all mathematical figures—triangle, circle and so on—are ideal concepts from which all particularity and irregularity have been abstracted. There still remains, however, a different question to be solved: granted that ideas of absolute straightness and the like are the fruits of mental operations of a particular kind, how do we account for the fact that we perform such operations at all?

This brings us to a final point about our mental operations which, obvious though it may be, does not seem to have received sufficient recognition in discussions of this kind (although Locke in his own way deals with it in some detail). As we have tried to show, it seems unlikely that any of our ideas are innate, in the sense that we can form them independently of our experience of the external world; but there do seem to be certain innate habits of mind which cannot be accounted for by any automatic operation of external things upon us. I am not here concerned with the habit of forming abstractions—we shall discuss this in the next chapter—but with three other habits which give rise to ideas which are sometimes thought to be innate.

The first is this tendency, of which we have been speaking, to apply the standards of perfection in so many different contexts: mathematics does it by making convenient abstractions whose relations can be described in absolute terms (we might note, incidentally, that such abstractions are by no means irrelevant to the actual world; a football field, for example, can be marked out with the help of Pythagoras's theorem about the square on the hypotenuse); artists do it by aspiring to a perfection of beauty and form which they know they cannot reach; all of us do it by aspiring to counsels of perfection at least at some stage in our lives, and—perhaps more frequently—measuring the achievements of others by such standards. This brings us back to what we said of Greek drama and to our quotation from Rupert Brooke (p. 96); Thomas Carlyle has his own way of making the same point in *Sartor Resartus*, where Teufelsdröckh says: "Man's unhappiness, as I construe, comes of his Greatness; it is because there is an Infinite in him, which with all his cunning he cannot quite bury under the Finite." It seems, then, that although the idea of perfection may not be innate, the habit of mind which causes such an idea to be formed is innate and very frequently manifested in widely different contexts.

The second innate habit of mind is one in which we have been indulging throughout this book—the habit of asserting some things to be true and others false. Much labor has been spent in modern times in trying to explain exactly what we mean by such assertions. We shall say something of this later (*vid.* p. 156), but it is very doubtful whether the idea of truth—if we may for the moment describe it as such—can be analyzed in terms of anything other than itself. All of us, however, like Plato's slave in the *Meno*, can recognize at least some truths when we see them, and when we say that they are true, we have no doubt as to what we mean.

The third innate habit of mind is the similar custom of applying the terms "right" and "wrong" to what we call "moral actions." We have said much of this (*vid.* esp. pp. 30, 105–6) and we do not wish to labor the point here. If it is true, as we have claimed (p. 30), that it is impossible to give the idea of "right" to a person who does not already possess it, then at least our ability to make the distinction between right and wrong must be innate, but it still seems likely that we cannot in fact make the distinction until we experience actions which, as it were, elicit it from us.

We would say, then, that in general the scholastic tag "*nihil in intellectu nisi prius in sensu*" ("nothing is in the intellect unless it is first in the senses") is correct; it is correct, that is, of all fully formed ideas. But, at the same time, we cannot account for the formation of these ideas unless we accept as innate the three fundamental habits of mind of which we have spoken. It also follows, of course, that if our minds are proper instruments of knowledge—if, that is, we can think at all with any confidence—then these habits must themselves signify something about the reality on which they work.

2. Primary and Secondary Qualities

Having concluded, then, that Locke is right in ascribing the source of our ideas to the external world, it is now time to consider his account of perception in more detail. Locke makes a distinction which is found in Aristotle and implied by Descartes's account of his perception of the wax—a distinction between what he called Primary and Secondary Qualities: Descartes, it will be remembered, had been disturbed by the fact that when the wax was melted, its taste, smell, color, figure and sound (when tapped) were no longer the same as before, although commonsense suggested that it was the same piece of wax. These qualities, with the exception of figure, Locke calls secondary; the primary qualities are solidity, extension, figure, motion or rest, and number.

Science was beginning to give an account of secondary qualities which upset the simple assumptions of common sense: it was not merely that the wax, when melted, changed color, but that the color itself was an effect produced (as we know now) by the action on the retina of the light rays given off by the wax. Secondary qualities, therefore, Locke argued, "in truth are nothing in the objects themselves, but powers to produce various sensations in us by their primary qualities."* Primary qualities, on the other hand, "are such as are utterly inseparable from the body, in what estate soever it be; such as, in all the alterations and changes it suffers . . . it constantly keeps; and such as sense constantly finds in every particle of matter which has bulk enough to be perceived, and the mind finds inseparable from every particle of matter, though less than to make itself singly be perceived by our senses: v.g., take a grain of wheat, divide it into two parts; each

* *Essay*, bk. 11, ch. VIII, para. 10.

part has still solidity, extension, figure, and mobility; divide it again, and it still retains the same qualities; and so divide it on, till the parts become insensible; they must retain still each of them all those qualities."*

It is primary qualities, then, which safeguard the objective validity of our knowledge; here we can be certain that we are seeing what really exists. In a word, our ideas of primary qualities are true resemblances of the original, while our ideas of secondary qualities are merely sensations produced in us by the original in virtue of certain powers that it has. Of secondary qualities Locke says: "Take away the sensation of them; let not the eyes see light or colours, nor the ears hear sounds; let the palate not taste, nor the nose smell; and all colours, tastes, odours, and sounds, as they are such particular ideas, vanish and cease, and are reduced to their causes, i.e., bulk, figure, and motion of parts."†

To complete Locke's account, we must mention a third class of qualities, called "powers," which function in much the same way as secondary qualities; he refers to "the power that is in any body, by reason of the particular constitution of its primary qualities, to make such a change in the bulk, figure, texture, and motion of another body, as to make it operate on our senses differently from what it did before. Thus the sun has a power to make wax white, and fire, to make lead fluid."‡ The main difference, he says, between powers and secondary qualities is that while secondary qualities are thought by the ordinary man to resemble our ideas of them, no such mistake is made with powers: "We look upon the whiteness and softness as produced in the wax, not as qualities in the sun, but effects produced by powers in it."§

A detailed discussion of this theory would take us deep into the technicalities of psychology, which would be beyond the scope of this book. Locke has, however, raised general questions about the nature of sense-perception which cannot go unanswered. Before we proceed, it would be as well to remember firstly that Locke's theory of primary and secondary qualities is bound up with his theory of representative ideas, and

* *Ibid.*, para. 9.   ‡ *Ibid.*, para. 23.
† *Ibid.*, para. 17.   § *Ibid.*, para. 24.

secondly that a very similar distinction was made by Aristotle, who implied a much more direct theory of perception.

Aristotle uses the terms "Special" and "Common Sensibles"—the special sensibles (e.g., color, sound, etc.) being peculiar to one sense, the common sensibles (movement and rest, number and unity, shape and size) being common at least to the senses of sight and touch. According to Aristotle, there was also a third object of perception which was a concomitant of the special sensible: if, he said, you see a white object which is the son of Diares, you also perceive the son of Diares; in other words, you perceive not only the color, but the thing which is colored; perception is here direct. Leaving aside the last point, to which we shall return later (*vid.* pp. 156–7), it is interesting to note that for Aristotle, the special sensibles, or Locke's secondary qualities, are almost completely reliable, whereas it is the common sensibles, or primary qualities, which mislead us: the parallel railway lines or the size of the sun may be deceptive, but a red rose does not cease to be red as we get nearer to it. It is the exact opposite of Locke's view.

Without going into the question whether it is proper to describe motion or rest, for example, as qualities at all, we can perhaps agree that there is some point in this distinction which Locke and Aristotle make: at least we can say that scientific accounts of matter have raised problems about the objectivity of secondary qualities which are at any rate different from any problems that might be raised about primary qualities. In the next chapter, we shall discuss Berkeley's difficulties about primary qualities; meanwhile let us consider this question of secondary qualities, which has an important bearing on our whole attitude to problems of this kind.

What in fact does the claim of the scientist amount to? He can give us an account, such as we have no reason to dispute, of what happens when we see "red" or hear a low note; he can explain that the light rays given off by the flower were such as to make us see red and not blue, or that the vibrations caused by the beating of a drum were such as to make us hear a low rather than a high note. But to explain *how* we hear or see is not at all the same thing as to explain *what* we hear or see.

The physicist, quite rightly, is talking in terms of the abstractions of his own particular science. In point of fact, as Aristotle implies, the phrase "to see red" is in itself an abstraction; we never literally see red, but we see a red flower or a red letter-box; but since the physicist is concerned only with the mechanics of the act and not the act itself, he makes a convenient abstraction. To a great extent, we all look at things from different points of view; we all make unconscious abstractions of our own. Thus a horse, for example, will look quite different to a biologist, an ordinary man, a jockey and an artist; these various people will have different things to say about the horse, but there is no reason why they should not all be true.

This is not to suggest that there is no problem, but only that it must be understood in the right terms. Clearly, if a gramophone is playing in the desert, there is nothing taking place which can be described as "hearing a noise," but there is a disturbance of the molecules of air according to a certain pattern. This pattern we may compare to a musical score: there is a real sense in which the gramophone is playing music, just as there is a real sense in which the pattern of the score is musical; in fact, a skilled musician, by reading the score, can "hear" the music without actually playing it. To this extent, therefore, it is merely a matter of terms whether we choose to call "noise" a sound heard or a pattern capable of being heard.

But one important point remains: the skilled musician would not be able to "hear" the music from the score, unless he had already heard other music in the ordinary way; a person deaf from birth would not know what it would be like to hear the gramophone; it follows that in either use of the word "noise," we have in mind the quality of sound as we have experienced it, and this quality cannot be described in mathematical terms of pitch, volume, etc., or in any other terms. Therefore, if it is inadequate to describe this quality in terms of moving patterns of molecules, it is equally inadequate to describe it in terms of vibrating eardrums; the molecules and the eardrums are merely means whereby we have an experience that can only be described as hearing the gramophone.

In all philosophical questions, but particularly with this problem of knowledge, it is of the utmost importance to cling to these fundamental facts of experience which it is so easy to believe explained away by this scientific demonstration or that philosophical theory; and at no time has this been more important than today, when the functions of scientific and philosophical reasoning have become so confused. In the nature of things, science can have nothing to say about the quality of those experiences which we call "hearing" and "seeing"; but this is no reason either why philosophers should not attempt to clarify our ideas on the subject, or why, in so doing, they should not make use of scientific discoveries which may be quite valid in their own context.

10. THE LANDSLIDE OF DOUBT

1. Locke's Theory of Universals and Substance

"The word *universal* is used by philosophers to denote general concepts like 'cow,' 'grass,' 'man,' etc., as distinct from *particulars* like 'that cow,' 'this grass,' and 'the man that I met yesterday.' Philosophers have disagreed as to how far universal concepts correspond to something real and independent of our thought, and how far the universal is just a name for a somewhat arbitrary collection of particulars—a name which our thought has devised for its own convenience. This is the so-called problem of universals. In Part 1 we saw the importance which the Greeks attached to this problem, though they approached it from a slightly different angle. In fact their solution to this problem colored their whole outlook. We called Plato an idealist because he thought that universals—the Forms or Ideas of his system—were the true reality, but did not exist in this world; we called Aristotle a realist because he thought that all reality was embodied in the particular. Aristotle was also a realist in the wider sense that he thought that all our statements about the particular referred to aspects of it that had a real, objective existence. We saw in the last chapter how Locke disagreed with this view in the case of secondary qualities; in this chapter, we shall see how Locke's disagreement was very much wider than this, how Berkeley substituted an idealism of his own, and how their combined efforts led to the scepticism of Hume, who, in a sense, carried the thought of Locke and Berkeley to rather startling conclusions.

137

The question of universals was still very much alive in the Middle Ages. Thomas Aquinas and the main stream of scholasticism had followed Aristotle; however, William of Ockham (c. 1290–1349), coming right at the end of the scholastic period, had attacked the whole Aristotelian theory of universals by saying that only individual things exist—that "an existing universal" is a contradiction in terms; universals are simply terms which signify individual things; they are objective in the sense that they stand for particulars, but subjective in the sense that they do not themselves exist outside the mind; in short, they are not part of reality, but the productions of the mind necessary to the knowledge of reality. This is called conceptualism: the universal is a concept; it exists in the mind and has an objective reference to things in the external world which are in fact similar but have no common nature.

In the seventeenth century, the more extreme view, known as nominalism, was adopted by another Englishman, Thomas Hobbes (1588–1679), the author of Leviathan. The Leviathan is one of the great English works of philosophy and has left its mark on European thought; but its importance lies chiefly in the sphere of political philosophy, which is beyond the scope of this book. We shall have to content ourselves with one brief quotation which will show Hobbes's theory that universals are nothing but names that signify a number of objects which the mind has found it convenient to lump together in a more or less arbitrary manner: "This word universal is never the name of anything existent in nature, nor of any idea or phantasm formed in the mind, but always the name of some word or name, so that when a living creature, a stone, a spirit, or any other thing is said to be universal, it is not to be understood that any man, stone, etc., ever was or can be universal, but only that these words are universal names, i.e. names common to many things, and the concepts corresponding to them are of singular animals or images or phantasms of other things."* Once again, we see the influence of seventeenth century mathematics: "By reasoning," he says, "I understand computation. . . . So all reasoning is reduced to the two operations of the mind, addition and subtraction."† In short, Hobbes looked upon reality as a collection of digits,

---

* De Corpore, ii, 9.   † Ibid., i, 2.

and knowledge as the understanding of the mathematical relations between them.

Locke's view was less naïve. He begins by recognizing that the use of universals is fundamental to all language: "All things that exist being particulars, it may perhaps be thought reasonable that words, which ought to be conformed to things, should be so too, I mean in their signification: but yet we find quite the contrary. The far greatest part of words, that make all languages, are general terms: which has not been the effect of neglect or chance, but of reason and necessity."*
It is most important to note that this "reason and necessity" does not, according to Locke, spring from the nature of reality, but from the need "to abridge discourse." But this raises the question of "how general terms come to be made." "For," he asks, "since all things that exist are only particulars, how come we by general terms, or where find we those general natures they are supposed to stand for?" "Words," he answers, "become general by being made the signs of general ideas: and ideas become general by separating from them the circumstances of time and place, and any other ideas that may determine them to this or that particular existence."†

The views expressed in this last sentence are not peculiar to conceptualism or nominalism; the important question is: "What do these universals stand for?" "It is plain," Locke continues, "by what has been said, that *general* and *particular* belong not to the real existence of things; but are the inventions and creatures of the understanding, made by it for its own use, and concern only signs, whether words or ideas . . . but universality belongs not to things themselves, which are all of them particular in their existence."‡

But he is still at pains to avoid the extremist view of Hobbes: "I would not here be thought to forget," he says, "much less to deny, that nature, in the production of things, makes several of them alike; there is nothing more obvious, especially in the races of animals, and all things propagated by seed. But yet, I think we may say, the sorting of them under names is the workmanship of the understanding, taking occasion, from the similitude it observes amongst them, to make abstract general ideas, and set them up in the mind with names annexed

* *Essay*, bk. iii, ch. 3, para. 1.   † *Ibid.*, para. 6.   ‡ *Ibid.*, para. 11.

to them, as patterns or forms (for in that sense the word form has a very proper signification), to which, as particular things existing are found to agree, so they come to be of that species, have that denomination, or are put into that *classi.*"*

This is an important modification of Hobbes. Locke recognizes that there must be a "similitude," as he calls it, for it to be possible to apply a universal term at all; a universal, in other words, must have some foundation in reality. At this point, he makes an important distinction between what he calls "real and nominal essence"; "real essences" are the inner constitutions of things as they truly exist; "nominal essences" are simply those collections of attributes to which we happen to give a name: real essences are hidden and unknown; nominal essences are vague and dependent on the mind that forms them. Locke comes to this view because experience shows that one so-called essence tails off into another; biologists, for example, may gives names to different species, but sooner or later some specimen will be found that overlaps the distinctions which have been made, so that they have to adjust their terminology; if the species were real essences, this could not happen.

It would be difficult to deny the force of this argument, but the conclusion need not be so drastic as Locke thinks. A surveyor, for example, may make a rough map of an area and later, as he comes to know more about the place in question, may adjust his original outline and fill in more details. This does not destroy the validity of the outline: it always had a certain foundation in reality, and that was all the surveyor wished to claim for it. Similarly, the important question about our abstractions is whether they have any basis in reality; even the most extreme realist would not claim that they are always accurate and precise.

If the reader cares to study the relevant passage for himself,† he will see that Locke is far from consistent. The only solution for him would seem to be to make the distinction between real and nominal essence to mark a difference of degree rather than kind: thus the nominal essence would merely signify that we have an imperfect knowledge of the real essence; but it must be confessed that this does not seem to have been Locke's intention. It does, however, seem to have been his

* *Ibid.,* para. 13.   † *Essay,* bk. iii, ch. iii.

intention to suggest that a nominal essence denotes a collection of real attributes, however arbitrary the selection may have been. To this extent, Locke is not a nominalist.

There is a similar vagueness about Locke's treatment of the allied problem of substance. Substance was, of course, the ground anchor of Aristotelian realism; so it is very much bound up with the nominalist issue. Aristotle's substance was a metaphysical entity—not a quality that could be detected by physical science.

Both Descartes and Locke kept the idea, but they differed from Aristotle and from each other in their use of it. For Descartes, extension was the all-important quality of physical things and was in itself sufficient to account for their separateness; since matter existed, material substance had to be supposed, but there was no need to postulate more than one material substance: the difference between one material thing and another was mathematical, not substantial.

For Locke, substance was a complex, not a simple, idea: "The mind being, as I have declared, furnished with a great number of the simple ideas conveyed in by the senses, as they are found in exterior things, or by reflection on its own operations, takes notice also, that a certain number of these simple ideas go constantly together; which being presumed to belong to one thing, and words being suited to common apprehensions, and made use of for quick dispatch, are called, so united in one subject, by one name; which, by inadvertancy, we are apt afterwards to talk of and consider as one simple idea, which indeed is a complication of many ideas together: because, as I have said, not imagining how these simple ideas can subsist by themselves, we accustom ourselves to suppose some *substratum* wherein they do subsist, and from which they do result, which therefore we call *substance*."*

This appears to be a rejection of substance as a real entity, but such does not seem to be Locke's intention. He is anxious to uphold the commonsense view that each thing has a separate existence and unity of its own, but denies that we know the thing in any way except by

* Bk. 11. ch. xxiii, Para. 1.

the collection of ideas which we have made of it. The idea of substance, then, has some basis in logic, but, at best, it is a mysterious "I-know-not-what."

Thus his views on substance and essence are very similar: they are entities which we cannot know in themselves, while our ideas of them, though not objective, have a certain linguistic convenience. At the same time, our linguistic habits are not arbitrary tricks: our ideas are always at least prompted by what we find in the world outside.

Locke, in fact, was faced with a dilemma, and he does not seem entirely happy about its solution. The dilemma was this: he was committed to the view, firstly, that we begin life with a blank mind and, secondly, that the mind passively receives the sense-impressions which fill in the blank; but, although we do not have any sense-impression of substance or essence, he was too much of an empiricist to deny that we do think of things as unities in no arbitrary sense and as having properties about which even scientists can make confident statements—statements which are, moreover, confirmed by their experiments.

In short, while the theory of representative ideas was an attempt to apply scientific methods of reasoning to metaphysics, it could not account for the very truths on which science itself was based. Moreover, there were, as Berkeley saw, other difficulties about this theory, and it is time to consider what he made of them.

2. Berkeley

George Berkeley (1685–1753) was born near Thomastown in County Kilkenny. At the age of fifteen, he entered Trinity College, Dublin, and was elected to a fellowship there in 1707. Having taken orders, he held various ecclesiastical appointments in Ireland until he was made Bishop of Cloyne in 1734. His life was uneventful, apart from a project to found a great missionary college in Bermuda, of which he was to be principal: having persuaded Walpole to promise a Government grant of £20,000, in 1728 he left his Deanery in Ireland and sailed for America; when he arrived, he found that powers of persuasion lose their force at a distance: nothing more was heard of the grant, and he was compelled to return.

As early as 1705, Berkeley had formed a society at Trinity to discuss the New Philosophy, as it was called: Locke's *Essay*, combined with the exciting discoveries of Newton and Boyle, had done for Britain what Descartes had done for the Continent: empiricism, always psychologically attractive to Englishmen, had found its home; but it was given an unpredictable twist by the young Irish don.

Berkeley took up the obvious objections to representative ideas: firstly, nobody had explained how matter can operate on spirit; secondly, if we know only the idea, which is by definition a mere representation, how do we know that the "real" thing exists at all? Berkeley accepted the current definition of ideas as "the immediate objects of the understanding,"* and concluded that nothing does in fact exist apart from ideas and the spiritual beings that have them; in other words, matter, as an independent reality, is a myth. This is how he states his position in his most famous book, *The Principles of Human Knowledge* (published in 1710):

Sec. 3. That neither our thoughts, nor passions, nor ideas formed by the imagination, exist without the mind, is what everybody will allow. And to me it is no less evident that the various sensations or ideas imprinted on the sense, however blended or combin'd together (that is whatever objects they compose) cannot exist otherwise than in a mind perceiving them. I think an intuitive knowledge may be obtain'd of this, by any one that shall attend to what is meant by the term *exist* when apply'd to sensible things. The table I write on, I say, exists, *i.e.* I see and feel it, and if I were out of my study I shou'd say it existed, meaning thereby that if I was in my study I might perceive it, or that some other spirit actually does perceive it. There was an odor, *i.e.* it was smelt; there was a sound, *i.e.* it was heard; a colour or figure and it was perceiv'd by sight or touch. This is all that I can understand by these and the like expressions. For as to what is said of the absolute existence of unthinking things without any relation to their being perceiv'd, that is to me perfectly unintelligible. Their *esse* is *percipi*, nor is it possible they should have any existence, out of the minds or thinking things which perceive them.

* *Dialogues*, p. 272.

Sec. 4. It is indeed an opinion strangely prevailing amongst men, that houses, mountains, rivers, and in a word all sensible objects have an existence natural or real, distinct from their being perceiv'd by the understanding. But with how great an assurance and acquiescence soever, this principle may be entertained in the world: yet whoever shall find in his heart to call it in question may, if I mistake not, perceive it to involve a manifest contradiction. For what are the foremention'd objects but the things we perceive by sense, and what do we perceive besides our own ideas or sensations, and is it not plainly.repugnant that any one of these or any combination of them shou'd exist unperceiv'd?

Berkeley was at great pains to assert that he did not deny any of the usual assumptions of common sense. He admitted, for example, that real fire was different from our idea of fire, but denied that this destroyed his argument: real pain is also different from our idea of it; but nobody suggests that pain exists independently of the person who suffers it.

His theory is based on the argument that an idea can only be like another idea: "If you can but conceive it possible," he says, "for one extended, moveable substance, or in general, for any idea or any thing like an idea to exist otherwise than in a mind perceiving it, I shall readily give up the cause."

Following Locke's theory of substance as a collection of attributes, Berkeley held that an object was simply a collection of ideas:

Smelling furnishes me with odours; the palate with tastes, and hearing conveys sounds to the mind in all their variety of tone and composition. And as several of these are observ'd to accompany each other, they come to be marked by one name, and so to be reputed as one thing. Thus, for example, a certain colour, taste, smell, figure and consistence have been observ'd to go together, are accounted one distinct thing, signified by the name *apple*.*

Later in the book, he clarifies this further:

As to what philosophers say of subject and mode, that seems very groundless and unintelligible. For instance, in this proposition, a die is hard, extended and square, they will have it that the word *die* denotes

---

* *Ibid.*, s. 1.

a subject or substance, distinct from the hardness, extension, and figure which are predicated of it, and in which they exist. This I can't comprehend: to me a die seems to be nothing distinct from those things which are termed its modes or accidents. And to say that a die is hard, extended and square, is not to attribute those qualities to a subject distinct from and supporting them, but only an explication of the meaning of the word *die*.*

On the other hand, my ideas are not purely subjective; they do not depend on me; I perceive them, whether I wish to or not. It follows, he says, that there must be another spirit that produces them. Moreover, my ideas are consistent and uniform, so it must be a good spirit. In short, in place of the traditional belief that God created the external world, Berkeley substituted the theory that God creates the ideas that we call "the world"; since, he thought, the creation of ideas was all that God needed to fulfil his purpose, it was foolish to suppose that he would go to the unnecessary lengths of creating an external world to correspond with those ideas. Thus, the commonsense distinction between "real" and "unreal" was explained:

"The ideas," he says, "imprinted on the senses by the Author of nature are called *real things*, and those excited in the imagination being less regular, vivid and constant, are more properly termed *ideas*, or *images of things*, which they copy and represent."†

Now, it follows from this that so-called scientific laws do not denote relations between things that necessarily follow from the constitution of those things, but relations between ideas which are guaranteed by the fact that God maintains our ideas according to a certain pattern. If we apply Plato's allegory of the cave (q.v., p. 40), scientists are doing what the prisoners were doing—namely, discovering the pattern which the shadows make on the wall—but, in this case, there would be no puppets: the shadows would be created directly by God. Thus, the chemical formula, H_2O, according to Berkeley's system, does not describe the constitution of water, but only the ideas associated with it in the divine economy. Berkeley, therefore, cannot accept the ordinary meaning of cause and effect: "The connexion of ideas," he says, "does

---

* *Ibid.*, s. 49. †*Ibid.*, s. 33.

not imply the relation of cause and effect, but only of a mark or sign with the thing signified. The fire which I see, is not the cause of the pain I suffer upon my approaching it, but the mark that forewarns me of it. In like manner the noise that I hear is not the effect of this or that motion, or collision of the ambient bodies, but the sign thereof."* This part of Berkeley's theory was developed by Hume with important consequences.

Once again, we must remind the reader that Berkeley's fundamental doctrine that *esse* is equivalent to *percipi* was not meant to imply a view of the world as a kind of disjointed and jerky cinematograph; the objects of perception did not come and go according as men perceived them or not: the fire in the grate, to use Berkeley's own illustration, still burned when people were out of the room, because it was still being perceived by God.

The essential fact, as Berkeley says himself, was that he was denying material substance: "I do not argue against the existence of any one thing that we can apprehend, either by sense or reflexion. That the things I see with my eyes and touch with my hands do exist, really exist, I make not the least question. The only thing whose existence we deny, is that which philosophers call matter or corporeal substance."† A little later, he expands this: "If the word *substance* be taken in the vulgar sense, for a combination of sensible qualities, such as extension, solidity, weight, etc., this we cannot be accused of taking away. But if it be taken in a philosophic sense, for the support of accidents or qualities without the mind: then, indeed, I acknowledge that we take it away, if one may be said to take away that which never had any existence, not even in the imagination.‡

Needless to say, Berkeley's theory of universals was no more realist than his theory of particulars: the universal did not stand for any common quality of particulars, but merely referred to any one particular of a given number. We associate certain particular ideas and give them a common name simply because God has chosen to present them in a connected way. Thus, Locke's dilemma is sidestepped; without giving universals a special kind of being or entity, Berkeley accounts for their

* S. 65.   † Sec. 35.   ‡ Sec. 37.

validity in the same way as he accounts for the validity of particulars: both are guaranteed by God.

On the other hand, Berkeley is most insistent that we should distinguish spirit from idea: "That an *idea* which is inactive, and the existence whereof consists in being perceiv'd, shou'd be the image or likeness of an agent subsisting by itself, seems to need no other refutation, then barely attending to what is meant by those words."* We do not, therefore, have an *idea* of spirit in Berkeley's sense of *image*, but we have what he calls a *notion* of it; the notion of other spirits is by analogy based on the notion of self. We know other spirits, he says, "by their operations, or the ideas by them excited in us."†

It must be remembered, however, that it is Berkeley's basic contention that only ideas can be the object of knowledge. When it comes, therefore, to our knowledge of each other, he is in a dilemma: either he must admit other forms of knowledge or commit himself to solipsism—the view that we can know nothing at all outside ourselves and our own ideas, not even other people. In point of fact, he chooses the first alternative, but this in turn produces a new dilemma: this knowledge by means of a notion must either be direct in the realist sense or indirect like representative ideas. As we have seen, he seems to prefer the latter alternative: we know other spirits by a notion of them based on the analogy of self.

But this raises three further difficulties: firstly, the very notion of "otherness" is difficult to account for on Berkeley's theory; secondly, we might apply to this theory Berkeley's own objection to the theory of representative ideas—the impossibility of knowing that anything lies beyond our notion; thirdly, his answer that we know others by their operations seems to indicate some idea, or notion, of cause and effect, which he had so roundly rejected.

In fact, Berkeley's attempt to explain away the ideas of cause and effect was to have serious repercussions which we shall discuss later. For the moment, we may say that the good spirit who, according to Berkeley, furnishes us with our ideas, seems at great pains to mislead us with notions like "otherness," "externality" and "space." Protest as he may,

* S. 137.   † S. 145.

Berkeley cannot convince us that his is the world of common sense; but his theory remains a very important criticism of Descartes and Locke. Meanwhile, let us take criticism a good step further and return to Hume.

3. Hume

David Hume (1711–76) was born in Edinburgh, the son of the laird of Ninewells in Berwickshire. Apart from the fact that he attended Edinburgh University, little is know of his early education; he tells us, however, that he "was seized very early with a passion for literature, which has been the ruling passion of my life, and the great source of my enjoyments . . . I found an insurmountable aversion to everything but the pursuits of philosophy and general learning."

Despite this somewhat restricted outlook in youth, his subsequent career was not unlike Locke's—a basically academic diet seasoned by an occasional incursus into affairs of state. After leaving the university, he made the usual retreat into foreign parts and, by a curious coincidence, spent three years at La Flèche, where Descartes, over a hundred years before, had been taught by the Jesuits. On his return to Scotland, he found that his heterodox views did not recommend him to the elders of his university, and he applied in vain for the Chair of Ethics and Pneumatic Philosophy. With equal lack of success, he failed in the humbler office of tutor to the insane Marquis of Annandale. He seems, however, to have been looked on with more favor by General St. Clair: in 1746 he was appointed secretary to the general's force, which had assembled to invade Canada, but contented itself with a raid on the coast of France; two years after this, he went on diplomatic missions to Vienna and Turin. In later life, he was to hold appointments as *Chargé d'Affaires* at the British Embassy in Paris and Under-Secretary at the Foreign Office. Meanwhile, he wrote most of his philosophical works before he was forty, and after that turned to writing history and essays; his *History of England* won him most fame during his lifetime.

One can live on one's imagination in Ireland, but in Scotland they tend to be more hard-headed. As we turn from Berkeley to Hume, we cannot but be conscious of this change of atmosphere. This is not to belittle Berkeley's logic, or even to extol Hume's, but merely to indicate how philosophers so often differ from each other not so much on the merits of the logic with which they build their systems as on their attitude at the start.

It may already have struck the reader that unless you accept the ontological argument, the existence of God in Berkeley's system can be accepted only on faith; Hume refused to make the act of faith, and the whole Berkeleyan edifice fell. But though the edifice fell, there remained the bricks of the old system—the sense-impressions which constituted our knowledge. Hume began to take up these bricks and heave them at the metaphysicians. We shall briefly state his argument as it is given in the most important of his philosophical works, A *Treatise on Human Nature.*

Hume recognized the logic of his position. If he rejected Berkeley's God, he was left with a purely atomic world of disconnected sense-impressions. For Berkeley, God had guaranteed the coherence of these impressions, but Hume could allow no such guarantee. He had to explain, therefore, how we come to form ideas not merely of universals, but also of particulars—how, in other words, we come to arrange our momentary impressions in such a way as to talk about chairs, tables and even people. His explanation takes us to the foundation of his whole system—the theory of the Association of Ideas. This theory has had a great influence on subsequent philosophy.

Firstly, Hume states that all simple ideas come from simple impressions; in fact, the only difference between ideas and impressions "consists in the degrees of force and liveliness, with which they strike upon the mind."* All other ideas are formed through association—association in terms of resemblance, contiguity in time or place, or cause and effect. Since Hume is working on the basis of extreme empiricism, he does not, of course, allow any objective validity to these forms of association; they merely denote a tendency of the mind. This is what he says:

* *Treatise*, bk. 1, pt. 1, s. i.

As all simple ideas may be separated by the imagination, and may be united again in what form it pleases, nothing would be more unaccountable than the operations of that faculty, were it not guided by some universal principles, which render it, in some measure, uniform with itself in all times and places. Were ideas entirely loose and unconnected, chance alone would join them; and it is impossible the same simple ideas should fall regularly into complex ones (as they commonly do), without some bond of union among them, some associating quality, by which one idea naturally introduces another. This uniting principle among ideas is not to be considered as an inseparable connection; for that has been already excluded from the imagination: nor yet are we to conclude that without it the mind cannot join two ideas; for nothing is more free than that faculty: but we are only to regard it as a gentle force, which commonly prevails, and is the cause why, among other things, languages so nearly correspond to each other; Nature, in a manner, pointing out to every one those simple ideas, which are most proper to be united into a complex one.*

A little further down, he emphasizes that he makes no attempt to explain why we associate ideas as we do:

These are, therefore, the principles of union or cohesion among our simple ideas, and in the imagination supply the place of that inseparable connection, by which they are united in our memory. Here is a kind of *attraction*, which in the mental world will be found to have as extraordinary effects as in the natural, and to show itself in as many and as various forms. Its effects are everywhere conspicuous; but, as to its causes, they are mostly unknown, and must be resolved into original qualities of human nature, which I pretend not to explain. Nothing is more requisite for a true philosopher, than to restrain the intemperate desire of searching into causes; and, having established any doctrine upon a sufficient number of experiments, rest contented with that, when he sees a further examination would lead him into obscure and uncertain speculations. In that case his enquiry would be much better employed in examining the effects than the causes of his principle.†

Despite this agnosticism, Hume realizes that in view of his claim that all ideas are distinct and separable, he must give some account of the way in which we form at least a certain class of abstract ideas: he must

* Ibid., s. 4.   † Ibid.

explain how we make distinctions of reason—distinctions, that is, which exist in our minds but not in the objects concerned. Thus, we may distinguish the shape of a globe of marble from the marble itself—a distinction, to use the scholastic jargon of the time, between the figure and the body figured. He argues that the very number of possible distinctions suggests the arbitrariness of their nature: the distinctions that we do in fact make with regard to any object depend entirely on what other similar objects we happen to have come across:

It is certain that the mind would never have dreamed of distinguishing a figure from the body figured, as being in reality neither distinguishable, nor different, nor separable, did it not observe, that even in this simplicity there might be contained many different resemblances and relations. Thus, when a globe of white marble is presented, we receive only the impression of a white colour disposed in a certain form, nor are we able to separate and distinguish the colour from the form. But observing afterwards a globe of black marble and cube of white, and comparing them with our former object, we find two separate resemblances, in what formerly seemed, and really is, perfectly inseparable. After a little more practice of this kind, we begin to distinguish the figure from the colour by a *distinction of reason;* that is, we consider the figure and colour together, since they are, in effect, the same and undistinguishable; but still view them in different aspects, according to the resemblances of which they are susceptible. When we would consider only the figure of the globe of white marble, we form in reality an idea both of the figure and colour, but tacitly carry our eye to its resemblance with the globe of black marble: and in the same manner, when we would consider its colour only, we turn our view to its resemblance with the cube of white marble. By this means we accompany our ideas with a kind of reflection, of which custom renders us, in a great measure, insensible. A person who desires us to consider the figure of a globe of white marble without thinking on its colour, desires an impossibility; but his meaning is, that we should consider the colour and figure together, but still keep in our eye the resemblance to the globe of black marble, or that to any other globe of whatever colour or substance.*

The word "substance," at the end of this quotation, simply refers, of course, to the material out of which the thing is made. Needless to

* *Ibid.,* s. 7.

say, entities like metaphysical substance have no place in Hume's philosophy. Particular things can be understood only in terms of the impressions which they make upon us; they are merely collections of ideas. To take a simple example: I see brown and white patches roughly in the shape of a rectangle supported by four perpendiculars, smell a certain odor and hear mooing sounds in the same area, lump all these contiguous impressions together and call the collection "cow." I cannot tell whether this unity exists outside my mind. Substance, therefore is a myth:

I would fain ask those philosophers who found so much of their reasonings on the distinction of substance and accident, and imagine we have ideas of each, whether the idea of *substance* be derived from the impressions of sensation or reflection? If it be conveyed to us by our senses, I ask, by which of them, and after what manner? If it be perceived by the eyes, it must be a colour; if by the ears, a sound; if by the palate, a taste; and so of the other senses. But I believe none will assert, that substance is either a colour, or sound, or taste. The idea of substance must, therefore, be derived from an impression of reflection, if it really exist. But the impressions of reflection resolve themselves into our passions and emotions; none of which can possibly represent a substance. We have, therefore, no idea of substance, distinct from that of a collection of particular qualities, nor have we any other meaning when we either talk or reason concerning it.*

In any event, by Hume's time, as we have seen, the idea of substance had already become rather thin; he merely dealt the final blow.

More original and of far-reaching importance was his attack on the traditional conception of causality. This attack follows lines similar to his attack on substance: the idea of causality, he says, comes from the association of pairs of ideas. The two in a pair are repeatedly found to be contiguous in time and place, the so-called cause always preceding the so-called effect. Having said this much about it, in Hume's view we can give no further account of causality: "Having thus discovered or supposed the two relations of *contiguity* and *succession* to be essential to causes and effects, I find I am stopped short, and can proceed no further in considering any single instance of cause and effect."† In

---

* *Ibid.*, s. 6.   † *Ibid.*, pt. iii, s. 2.

another passage, he offers the following definition: "A cause is an object precedent and contiguous to another, and so united with it that the idea of the one determines the mind to form the idea of the other, and the impression of the one to form a more lively idea of the idea of the other."*

Closely connected with the idea of cause are the ideas of necessity, power and production: there is often thought to be a certain necessary connection between cause and effect, which includes the idea that there is a certain power in the cause which produces the effect. All these ideas Hume explains away in a similar manner. He argues, for example, that the proposition, "whatever has a beginning has also a cause of existence," is not intuitively certain:

We can never demonstrate the necessity of a cause to every new existence, or new modification of existence, without showing at the same time the impossibility there is, that anything can ever begin to exist without some productive principle; and where the latter proposition cannot be proved, we must despair of ever being able to prove the former. Now that the latter proposition is utterly incapable of a demonstrative proof, we may satisfy ourselves by considering, that as all distinct ideas are separable from each other, and as the ideas of cause and effect are evidently distinct, it will be easy for us to conceive any object to be non-existent this moment, and existent the next, without conjoining to it the distinct idea of a cause or productive principle. The separation therefore of the idea of a cause from that of a beginning of existence, is plainly possible for the imagination; and consequently the actual separation of these objects is so far possible, that it implies no contradiction or absurdity; and is therefore incapable of being refuted by any reasoning from mere ideas, without which it is impossible to demonstrate the necessity of a cause.†

So also, the idea of power, like the idea of necessity, is simply the result of a psychological trick: "For after we have observed the resemblance in a sufficient number of instances, we immediately feel a determination of the mind to pass from one object to its usual attendant, and to conceive it in a stronger light upon account of that relation. This determination is only the effect of the resemblance; and, there-

---

* *Ibid.*, s. 14.   † *Ibid.*, s. 3.

fore, must be the same with power or efficacy, whose idea is derived from the resemblance."* In short, since all genuine ideas are impressions, we cannot have a genuine idea of a relation; therefore, the relation of cause and effect must be discarded with the rest: "The repetition of perfectly similar instances can never *alone* give rise to an original idea, different from what is to be found in any particular instance, as has been observed, and as evidently follows from our fundamental principle, *that all ideas are copied from impressions.*"†

Of course, once you accept the fundamental premise, which we have just quoted in italics, these and many other rather startling conclusions must follow. That is the most important point about the argument. If we think that in fact we all have an idea of cause and effect which *means* more than Hume is able to allow, then we are entitled—and indeed forced—to reject his premise. We shall examine this premise on its own merits later (pp. 156–7); in Part IV (pp. 194 seq.) we shall also re-examine the whole problem of causality in its modern context; meanwhile, let us consider another consequence of Hume's reasoning—the impossibility of any contact with the external world.

Hume, as we have already seen, always had, as it were, the courage of his own logic: since all knowledge was made up out of impressions, it followed that we can never get beyond them; we are incapable, he thought, of telling whether anything external exists. "To reflect on anything simply," he says, "and to reflect on it as existent, are nothing different from each other . . . Whatever we conceive, we conceive to be existent."‡

Now, [he continues in another paragraph] since nothing is ever present to the mind but perceptions, and since all ideas are derived from something antecedently present to the mind; it follows, that it is impossible for us so much as to conceive or form an idea of anything specifically different from ideas and impressions. Let us fix our attention out of ourselves as much as possible; let us chase our imagination to the heavens, or to the utmost limits of the universe; we never really advance a step beyond ourselves, nor can we conceive any kind of existence, but those perceptions, which have appeared in that narrow com-

* *Ibid.*, s. 14.   † *Ibid.*   ‡ *Ibid.*, pt. ii, s. 6.

pass. This is the universe of the imagination, nor have we any idea but what is here produced.*

It is now pertinent to ask what we mean by "true" and "false"; if, at least as far as my perception is concerned, there is no distinction between existence and non-existence, how do I come to say, for example, that there is in fact no pink rat under the table, although I thought that I saw one?

Or again, what makes Hume say that his philosophy is true and Berkeley's false? He answers that belief and assent depend on vivacity of memory: "All probable reasoning is nothing but a species of sensation. 'Tis not solely in poetry and music, we must follow our taste and sentiment, but likewise in philosophy. When I am convinced of any principle, 'tis only an idea which strikes more strongly upon me."† Ultimately, then, we cannot give reasons for our assertions; we can only make them: "Nature, by an absolute and uncontrollable necessity, has determined us to judge as well as to breathe and feel."‡

It would seem, then, that my only anchor in this sea of shifting impressions is my knowledge of myself, but Hume will not allow us even that. For my idea of self does not come from a simple impression; if it did, it would have to be the same; as it is, I am only aware of myself in my perceptions, but:

All these are different, and distinguishable, and separable from each other, and may be separately considered, and may exist separately, and have no need of anything to support their existence. After what manner therefore do they belong to self, and how are they connected with it? For my part, when I enter most intimately into what I call myself, I always stumble on some particular perception or other, of heat or cold, light or shade, love or hatred, pain or pleasure. I can never catch myself at any time without a perception, and never can observe anything but the perception. When my perceptions are removed for any time, as by sound sleep, so long am I insensible of myself, and may truly be said not to exist. And were all my perceptions removed by death, and could I neither think, nor feel, nor see, nor love, nor hate, after the dissolution of my body, I should be entirely annihilated, nor do I conceive what is further requisite to make me a perfect nonentity.§

* *Ibid.* † *Treatise*, pt. iii, s. 8. ‡ *Treatise*, pt. iv, s. 1.
§ *Ibid.*, s. 6.

So "self" denotes merely a bundle of perceptions; as Hume puts it, "They are the successive perceptions only which constitute the mind."

To take the last point first: although we have already agreed that the self is not an object of perception in the sense in which the cat is, we do in fact know ourselves in our actions. All that Hume's argument proves is that we do not know ourselves in any other way; and, of course, it is not to be expected that we should. It would be highly paradoxical to suggest that the self could detach itself and know itself as it knows the cat.

At the same time, words like "responsibility," "guilt," "memory," etc., make no sense unless the idea of self is assumed: it would be il-logical, for example, to punish a "person" now for an offence done yesterday, unless we believed that the person who is to be punished is the same as the person who committed the offence. Again, words like "friendship," "love," "hatred," etc., imply the existence of other selves as much as of our own.

In fact, if Hume is right, most of human thought and language is nonsensical—and this is to condemn an empiricist on his own ground. The truth is that Hume himself makes wide use of the concept "self" in his writing, using it apparently in the ordinary sense. It is only when he comes to examine it in the light of his own theory of impressions that he begins to doubt it. What, then, is wrong with this theory?

Firstly, it is worth noting that even if we accept Hume's approach of trying to register our moments of consciousness—as a physicist might register electrical discharges on a dial—and of trying to build up a kind of scientific "model" from the data thus discovered, we find that this very data will not bear close examination. For the data is meant to consist of impressions, and, of these impressions, those that have a high degree of "force and liveliness" are to be called ideas.

Professor Ryle, in his recent book, *The Concept of Mind*, has shown this distinction to be quite meaningless: when Hume talks of the "live-liness" of an impression, "lively" must either mean "vivid and lifelike" or "acute and intense"; but, to take the first sense, it is easy to show that an impression—which, in Hume's view, does not represent any-thing apart from itself—cannot be more or less lifelike: as Professor Ryle puts it: "One doll can be more lifelike than another, but a baby cannot be lifelike or unlifelike."* On the other hand, if we take the second sense of "acute and intense," it may be possible to talk of some impressions, or sensations, being more acute than others, but an acute sensation is quite different from an idea: an idea of a loud noise is itself neither loud nor soft. In other words, ideas and impressions are not the sort of things that you can put side by side and compare; they belong to different spheres altogether.

This brings us to our second point—that Hume has got his psychological data upside down: we do not in fact have a series of impressions, lump them together and call them "cow." The process is rather the reverse: we first see a cow and then, if we choose to do so, begin to divide it up into its respective properties. True, we may hear a mooing sound and infer that there is a cow in the neighborhood, or we may see a brown tail behind the hedge and infer that it is attached to a cow behind the hedge, but all this implies that we first know what we mean by a complete cow. Of course, if we have not seen a cow before, we may know the meaning of "cow" merely because a friend has told us its characteristics; but again this implies that either the friend or somebody else at some stage has seen a cow and enumerated its characteristics at the same time; this last person may even have given it its name.

Hume is responsible for the fallacy, which is still current in some circles today, that sense impressions are the material with which our knowledge is pieced together, whereas in fact they are abstractions which physicists and psychologists find it convenient to make for their own specialized lines of investigation. It was this fallacy that led Hume to confuse ideas and impressions. It is, however, precisely upon this false distinction that his whole argument rests; once it is exposed, Hume is left with no explanation of how we come to form any of our ideas, let alone the ideas of cause and substance.

On Hume's own grounds, however, it makes no sense to ask whether his views are right or wrong; all that we can say is that they strike us with more or less vivacity. In the last resort, then, Hume adopted a position which should be described more as an attitude of mind than as a philosophy—a fundamental scepticism which made him turn from

* *The Concept of Mind*, p. 250.

philosophical speculation to the writing of history. It would be profitable just to turn back for a moment and recall how it came about that Hume was forced into this policy of despair.

As the heading of this chapter suggests, when Descartes, in the interests of truth and certainty, first shut his eyes and pronounced his *cogito*, he set the precedent for that attitude of doubt which was to grow under Locke and Berkeley and reach its climax in the hopeless paradoxes of Hume. The *cogito* itself, as we have suggested, was a false abstraction: there is no act which corresponds to "I think"; I must think of something; in other words, the act of thought or perception presupposes two terms, myself and the external world. Descartes was like a man standing on one leg on the supposition that the less you stand on, the less there is to give way; there is no wonder that philosophy lost its balance.

At the same time, it is instructive to see exactly *how* this happened. Once the *cogito* had been uttered, it was inevitable that problems should gather around sense-perception. If you divide matter and spirit, it is not quite so difficult to see how the mind might work without the senses as it is to see how the senses might work without the mind; moreover, the mechanism of our sense organs was a fascinating question for a world that was beginning to learn a great deal about the behavior of matter.

Thus, for all his mathematical bias, Descartes was more interested in the wax than in his innate ideas; but he longed to be able to explain his perception of the wax with the same exactness with which Euclid had explained his theorems. Locke's theory of representative ideas follows the same division of matter and spirit that Descartes made, and his theory of passive perception uses the kind of mechanistic terms which the physicists were employing. Reversing the Aristotelian conception, he thought of matter as active and mind as passive: matter left its impression on mind, as the wind leaves its mark on sand. Thus, in the theory of primary and secondary qualities, primary qualities were reduced to a form of physical energy, for which "quality" was no longer an appropriate term. This was an instance where the physicists's interest in material behavior was confused with the philosopher's interest in material things. Berkeley completed the confusion by treating the whole material world as simply a form of behavior—in this case, the purposeful behavior of God. Hume, who could see the behavior but not the purpose, accepted the technique, but rejected the premises.

Descartes, Locke and Berkeley had all presupposed that within man there was some spirit which, as it were, lurked behind all this confusion of sense perception—the very spirit, in fact, which was trying to find some coherence in the misleading data with which it was being furnished; but by now it had become established that all that the philosophers had to work on were the so-called data of sense-perception.

Locke had interpreted these data as representative ideas, and Berkeley as ideas and nothing else; Hume was merely accepting the logical consequences when he made a further dissection and left us with a chaos of bare impressions. Professor Ryle calls the Cartesian idea of man "the dogma of the ghost in the machine"; on this analogy, Hume had exorcised the ghost, but at the same time left the parts of the machine on the bench in some confusion.

However, whatever we may think of Hume's philosophy, he undoubtedly succeeded in showing up the absurdities to which the Cartesion approach was bound to lead. To do him justice, it is probably true to say that he regarded himself primarily as a destructive critic, who would make philosophers think out their most cherished axioms again. Whether deliberately or not, the moral which Hume points is that there is a certain attitude of doubt which is neither scientific nor of value to philosophy: it is not scientific, because it does violence to our reason, and it is of no value to philosophy because it starts a landslide which, in the nature of things, can leave us no ground on which to stand.

11. THE RECONSTRUCTION OF KANT

The benign professor of Königsberg has already been introduced to the reader, but we have scarcely touched upon the radical nature of his philosophy. It is arguable that Kant's contribution to ethics is the most valuable part of his system, but there is no denying that it is his fundamental approach to metaphysics which has had the greater influence. In fact, its influence has extended far beyond the ordinary spheres of philosophy, so that all manner of people from scientists to artists have—often without realizing its source—adopted a Kantian attitude to the material on which they work.

Briefly, this attitude consists in making a special kind of distinction between the world as we know it and the world as it really is: the world as we know it—the world of appearances or the *phenomenal* world, as Kant called it—is related in some mysterious way to the real, or *noumenal*, world, but it is also in part the product of our minds. It is this emphasis on the subjective contribution which we make to our own knowledge that is most characteristic of the Kantian attitude. In one sense, according to this approach, looking at reality is rather like looking through colored glass: *what* we see is conditioned by the *way* we see it. On the other hand, in contrast to the passive empiricism of Locke and Hume, Kant thought knowledge to be an intellectual activity in which we mold the phenomena that appear to our senses, so that they can be made intelligible to our minds. Thus, if we use the comparison of looking through colored glass, we must remember that the glass does not represent a medium through which things appear, but a special way in which we look. This should become clear when we have stated the theory.

Kant, like Descartes before him, had been impressed both by the lucidity and the certainty of mathematics and by the great progress that had been made in physical science. Like Descartes, he was anxious to bring philosophy into line with these sciences and, in so doing, to establish the validity of the reasoning which these sciences employed. We have just seen the challenge which Hume had issued to such reasoning, and undoubtedly it is to this challenge that Kant is primarily replying.

But, nearer home, another German philosopher, Leibnitz (1666–1716), had issued another challenge in different terms. There is a uniqueness about Leibnitz's system which keeps it apart from the main stream of European philosophy; for this reason, we have felt justified in making but a casual reference to him here, despite the undoubted importance and interest of his works. Like most philosophers of what we might call the Newtonian period, he was interested in the problem of the relations between particulars; for it was in terms of such relations that the scientists had expounded their theories. Briefly, Leibnitz held that the world consists entirely of what he called *monads*; this term (derived from the Greek MONOS, meaning "alone") was used to signify isolated non-material units that are incapable of having any actual relations with each other.

Scientific reasoning is possible only because there is a preordained harmony in the universe—a harmony that is founded in the intelligence of the monads. Matter and the relations between material things are merely appearances; but beneath these appearances, the monads are at work realizing their potentialities, like so many Hegelian gods. In this way, Leibnitz tried to penetrate, as it were, the shadowy appearance of the material world and discover the natural forces at work underneath—the forces which the scientists had to assume, but could not analyze. In effect, therefore, this was a challenge to the objective validity of scientific reasoning, which talked in terms of the relations between material things and their interaction upon one another; if Leibnitz were right, physics would have to give way to metaphysics.

Now, the philosophies of both Leibnitz and Hume were a criticism of the old Aristotelian logic with its realist terminology of substance and accidents, essence, causality and so on. The elements of this logic had been accepted more or less without question even by those of a more idealist turn of mind; but now it seemed that a new logic was needed, and to this task Kant applied his great powers of systematic construction. For obvious reasons, we have been able to devote little space in this book to the highly technical subject of pure logic, but, as we approach modern times, it plays an increasingly important part in the development of philosophy as a whole. For the moment, however, we need only concern ourselves with one item in Aristotle's logic—the so-called *categories*.

Aristotle used the term "categories" to signify the basic forms of thought, which he considered to be ten; his list (with examples in brackets) was as follows: *substance* (man), *quantity* (6 ft.), *quality* (white), *relation* (double), *place* (in the Lyceum), *date* (yesterday), *posture* (sits), *possession* (is shod), *action* (acts), *passivity* (is cut). In Aristotle's view, we are unable to form any proposition that cannot be broken up and analyzed under the above headings.

Now, we are not here concerned with the question whether this list is exhaustive or even appropriate; its importance for us lies in the fact that Aristotle thought that every proposition could be analyzed in terms of these ten categories because every particular in the real world was in fact limited to corresponding forms of existence or behavior. To describe any reality, you had to start with the particular itself (i.e., substance); this could be of a certain size, have certain qualities, have certain relations with other particulars and so on; you exhausted the categories when you had completed the basic pattern, as it were, of the real world. It was precisely because the world had this pattern that you were forced to think about it in terms of these categories.

Kant substituted a different list of twelve categories under the four headings of *Quantity, Quality, Relation* and *Modality*; thus, for example, under *Relation* comes *cause and effect*, under *Modality* comes *possibility*. Again, here we are not concerned with the list itself, but for us the important point is that Kant started, as it were, from the opposite end to Aristotle. For Kant, these categories represent not what we find in reality, but what we put into it; they are the modifications which the mind makes to reality in order to make it intelligible. We have used the word "reality," but Kant, as we have said, held that we cannot know the real or noumenal world; we can now see why: clearly, the mind cannot modify what is independent of the mind; it is less paradoxical, however, to suggest that it modifies the appearances which are given to our senses; this leaves the noumenal world untouched.

In coming to this conclusion, Kant had been influenced by his partiality for mathematics. In geometry, for example, he thought that we were able to reach absolute certainty precisely because we were talking in terms of our own logical constructions. As we have seen, a triangle formed of three perfectly straight lines cannot be found in the external world, but we can construct it in our minds, and out of this construction certain logical implications will follow—that the angles, for example, add up to 180°.

This is what Kant calls *a priori* reasoning—that is, to use his own words, "knowledge absolutely independent of all experience."* Kant, of course, did not believe that our reasoning about the external world was *a priori*; as we shall see, he was careful to insist that the content of such reasoning and knowledge came from outside. But he did hold that the categories—the formal structure of such knowledge—were *a priori*, and that it was precisely this *a priori* element which made ordinary reasoning possible. The difference, therefore, between mathematical reasoning and reasoning in a more general sense was a difference of content but not of form: only in mathematics was the content *a priori*.

This can be seen, first of all, in his theory of space; for, space is the content, as it were, of all reasoning in geometry. Space, then, was for Kant a purely subjective concept: "Space," he says, "is nothing but the form of all appearances of outer sense . . . It is, therefore, solely from the human standpoint that we can speak of space, of extended things, etc."† Secondly, it was but a short step from space to time; the one could hardly be subjective and the other objective; and it was tempting to think that time was to arithmetic what space was to geometry. In fact, Kant says: "Time is the formal *a priori* condition of all appearances whatsoever. Space, as the pure form of all *outer* intuition, is so

* *Critique of Pure Reason*, tr. Norman Kemp Smith, abridged, p. 26.
† *Ibid.*, pp. 46 and 47.

far limited; it serves as the a priori condition only of outer appearances."* But time, he continues, is the condition of all "inner appearances" as well; in other words, all our thoughts take place in a subjective temporal framework. In short, the space-time category is the essential mold in which we shape all our knowledge of the phenomenal world.

Having established the principle that it is possible for the content of some of our thought to be a priori, it seemed not so paradoxical to suggest that the form of all of our thought was a priori. We can now see how Kant treats concepts like substance and cause. It is no longer necessary to refer to substance as a vague "I-know-not-what" or paradoxically to dismiss it as beyond our knowledge. We can accept it as an intuition about the working of our minds—and, of course, in philosophy after Descartes, an intuition about our minds has not the scandalous associations of intuitions about the external world. The position was similar with causality: Hume's scepticism could now be met; it did not matter that impressions from the external world could not give us the idea of causality, because it was we who gave the idea to the impressions. The world of science, therefore, like the world of mathematics, was, in the last resort, a construction of the mind; as such, its validity was no longer in doubt.

Logical constructions, however, may be valid without being of very much practical use; it might be thought that science would not get very far by working out relations in the phenomenal world which were simply the products of its own reasoning. But this point did not worry Kant, because, for him, the phenomenal world was the world of experience—the only world with which, for all practical purposes, we have to deal; the noumenal world we can never know. Kant does not use the non-technical language of the British philosophers, but here is a fairly simple summary of his position:

What we have meant to say is that all our intuition is nothing but the representation of appearance; that the things which we intuit are not in themselves what we intuit them as being, nor their relations so constituted in themselves as they appear to us, and that if the subject, or even only the subjective constitution of the senses in general, be removed, the whole constitution and all the relations of objects in space

* *Ibid.*, p. 50.

and time, nay space and time themselves, would vanish. As appearances, they cannot exist in themselves, but only in us. What objects may be in themselves, and apart from all this receptivity of our sensibility, remains completely unknown to us. We know nothing but our mode of perceiving them—a mode which is peculiar to us, and not necessarily shared in by every being, though, certainly, by every human being.*

A little later, he gives a specific example:

We then realize that not only are the drops of rain mere appearances, but that even their round shape, nay even the space in which they fall, are nothing in themselves, but merely modifications or fundamental forms of our sensible intuition, and that the transcendental object [i.e., the object as it really is] remains unknown to us.†

At the same time, he realizes that it would be ridiculous to suggest that reason invents the categories in a purely arbitrary manner:

It is, indeed, difficult to understand how there can be a logical principle by which reason prescribes the unity of rules, unless we also presuppose a transcendental principle [i.e., a principle drawn from the reality of things] whereby such a systematic unity is a priori assumed to be necessarily inherent in the objects. For with what right can reason, in its logical employment, call upon us to treat the multiplicity of powers exhibited in nature as simply a disguised unity, and to derive this unity, so far as may be possible, from a fundamental power—how can reason do this, if it be free to admit as likewise possible that all powers may be heterogeneous, and that such a systematic unity of derivation may not be in conformity with nature? Reason would then run counter to its own vocation, proposing as its aim an idea quite inconsistent with the constitution of nature. Nor can we say that reason, while proceeding in accordance with its own principles, has arrived at knowledge of this unity through observation of the accidental constitution of nature. The law of reason which requires us to seek for this unity, is a necessary law, since without it we should have no reason at all, and without reason no coherent employment of the understanding, and in the absence of this no sufficient criterion of empirical truth. In order, therefore, to secure an empirical criterion we have no option save to presuppose the systematic unity of nature as objectively valid and necessary.‡

* *Ibid.*, p. 54.   † *Ibid.*, p. 57.   ‡ *Ibid.*, pp. 303–4.

In short, we cannot perceive the noumenal world or its structure, but it can be assumed that it does in fact correspond in some way with the phenomenal world that we know. Ultimately, therefore, Kant's metaphysics, like his ethics, rests entirely in the belief that man is essentially rational and that his mental processes, working in a vacuum though they may be, have some sort of correspondence with the reality that they can never reach: the categories and the categorical imperative are both subjective, but, thanks to man's rational nature, they are the same for all men and in harmony with reality as a whole.

There is, however, one great difference between the categories and the categorical imperative: the categories merely provide the form of our knowledge; they do not provide its content. Kant did not believe in a Berkeleyan world of ideas; the phenomenal world was in a real sense the product of the noumenal world, and our knowledge was derived empirically from our contact with this phenomenal world: the material is drawn from without by the senses, and only then is it shaped into an intelligible form by the understanding.

To use Kant's terminology, we derive the original material through our senses by *intuitions*; these intuitions then become the object of *thought* and are worked up into *concepts* by the understanding. With this in mind, we can understand his famous dictum: "Thoughts without content are empty, intuitions without concepts are blind.* Here we have an answer both to Berkeley and to Hume: Berkeley's ideas are without content, and Hume's impressions are blind.

It can now perhaps be seen why Kant worked out his system in this way. He was anxious to safeguard two things: the objectivity of our knowledge and the validity of our reasoning. To do this, he accepted the Cartesian legacy of representative ideas and used it for his own ends: once it was granted that appearances were the objects of our knowledge, the mind had tractable material to work upon, and need not be conceived, in the manner of Locke and Hume, as purely passive in its behavior.

Kant was thus able to give an account of what is surely fundamental

* *Ibid.*, p. 61.

to all mental activity—the movement towards coherence and unification. The active mind—itself a unity of consciousness—was able to assimilate, as it were, to its own unity the data of experience which came to it; just as the appearances of which these data consisted could only be experienced in the subjective medium of space and time, so they could only be understood in the subjective framework provided by the unity of consciousness. Having established this much, Kant had only to fill in the details in order to complete his synthesis. If worked out with care, he thought, the *Critique of Pure Reason* could establish once and for all the canons of certainty and put an end to philosophical doubt.

Obscure though it was, nobody could accuse Kant of any lack of care in preparing his *Critique;* but, for all that, he failed in his main object: the validity of human reasoning was never in fact established. We have already suggested one fundamental weakness in Kant's whole approach: he had to assume a noumenal world of which, by his very hypothesis, he can give no account whatsoever. It is the old difficulty about representative ideas in another form: Locke could not explain how, if our ideas are representative, we can know that they are so or can have any idea of reality at all; Kant could not explain how, if we know only the phenomenal world, we can possibly know that it is phenomenal: the prisoners in Plato's cave, for example, could not know that the shadows were only shadows until they had seen the puppets by which the shadows were cast.

Certainly, Kant seems to have felt this difficulty, but it only made him shift his ground rather uncomfortably when it cropped up. An example of this can be seen in our last long quotation from the *Critique,* where he said that we must hold, as a necessary *a priori* assumption, that there is coherence in nature or, in other words, in the noumenal world. But if there is objective coherence in nature, it would presumably be reflected in the world of appearances; in which case, why invent all this complicated mental machinery in order to impose a unity which is already there?

Perhaps we may be accused of oversimplifying Kant's account, but there is just as much danger that its very obscurity may lead us to put more faith in it than is justified. In fact, we would suggest that this obscurity covers another fundamental weakness: it is doubtful whether the account can be made comprehensible; for it is not at all easy to see how any facts or appearances can be *given* intelligibility. If they are intelligible, then it seems reasonable to say that we can recognize the coherence with which they are arranged; but if they are not intelligible, no amount of arrangement on our part will tell us anything about them —however much it may tell us about our minds.

On the other hand, we can have nothing but praise for Kant's insistence, in opposition to Hume, that coherence and unity are fundamental to knowledge: "If each representation," he says, "were completely foreign to every other, standing apart in isolation, no such thing as knowledge would ever arise."* He showed too that this unity and coherence is bound up with a certain necessary sequence of events: a ship going from one point to another is bound to pass through the intervening points; it cannot suddenly reappear in some quite different place. It was the high aim of Kant's *Critique* to explain how this necessity can play its all-important part in our knowledge.

The main complaint that we have is rather that this aim was too high, and that consequently Kant's method was too radical. If Hume was a sceptic, Kant was something of a rationalist. He thought that it ought to be possible to reduce all our mental activity to a coherent system of rational analysis without any lopholes or gaps. Where he could not extend his system, he was prepared to limit the scope of knowledge itself. Or, to put it the other way round, he made an arbitrary limit to the scope of possible knowledge in order to keep it within the bounds of analysis. Once again, we can detect the influence of the scientific methods of his day. Those methods may have been quite legitimate for science, but they are not the right methods for philosophy. The problem of knowledge, for example, is not simply a logical problem about the rules of. inference—any more than it is simply a psychological problem about the facts of mental behavior. There are numerous ways in which knowledge can be acquired, and, as we have suggested before (pp. 8, 49), the mind is neither entirely intuitive nor entirely discursive in its method of operation.

Moreover, experience seems to show that human knowledge is neither absolute nor fundamentally ambiguous. There are some facts of which we are quite certain, even though we are prepared to find that additional facts or a deeper understanding of the original facts may lead us to modify our original ideas. Thus, for example, we may

* *Ibid.*, p. 82.

have been quite certain that there was a place called New York in America, but afterwards find out that our picture of it was quite wrong; it is not the kind of place that we imagined. Or, again, we may be quite certain that the product of two numbers is larger than either number by itself; we may then find that this is not true of irrational numbers. In the first case, the general fact was true, but the details wrong; in the second case, the proposition was true in so far as we understood the terms, but we discovered later that there are certain numbers which do not behave like rational numbers.

Our knowledge is usually of this progressive kind; it is not always a question of its becoming progressively more certain, but more often of its becoming progressively more explicit. The sceptic's mistake is to deny that such a progress can ever begin; the rationalist's mistake is to refuse to recognize it as progress until it has reached its final conclusion. In fact, human knowledge always seems to be progressing, but never to reach absolute finality.

It was, as we have seen, this indecisive element in knowledge which gave scandal to Descartes and those who followed him. They thought that it was due to the inadequacy of the data which was supplied to our minds, and that we could overcome all ambiguity by assessing these data at what they were worth. It cannot be said, however, that a satisfactory assessment was ever in fact made. So, we must now turn to the alternative view of realism, which explains the facts from the opposite standpoint: our knowledge is indecisive not because the objects of perception are too thin to convey anything but a veneer of truth, but because the objects of perception are nothing but reality itself, and reality is too profound ever to yield its full meaning to our limited intellects.

APPENDIX: The Realist Legacy

In Descartes's method of approach to truth where the *cogito* was the first step, the second step was bound to consist in advancing from the certainty of the *cogito* to the certainty of our knowledge of the external world. We have seen something of the vast amount of philosophical labor to which that second step has given rise. The essential point about any realist account, whether of Aristotle, Aquinas, or certain modern philosophers, is that it makes no attempt to suggest an alternative method of taking that second step, but rather the necessity of taking the first two steps in one. For the realist, the first step is not: "I think," but: "I see a horse," "I smell a rose," "I feel a table," and so on. To this extent, all realist answers to the Cartesian problem are alike. Radically speaking, however many idealist theories of knowledge there may be, realism cannot alter. That is why we have referred to it as a "legacy" and why we shall make no attempt to go into details.

The point may be illustrated by quoting from two modern philosophers who belong to widely divergent schools of thought. Professor Gilson, a Thomist, has written: "Whereas critical idealism is critical in so far as it is idealism, everything can be criticized in a realist philosophy except its actual realism" ("Au lieu que l'idéalisme critique est critique en tant qu'idéalisme, tout peut être critique dans une philosophie réaliste, sauf son réalisme même.").* He suggests, therefore, that the error of idealism is essentially an error of method: "The problem does not arise in this way as a problem until the very moment when actual existence, the object of our search, is lost for ever. Why then is the problem raised? Because of an error of method which realism ought to oppose on the grounds that its method is the true one" (Le problème ne surgit ainsi comme problème qu'au moment où l'existence actuelle qu'il s'agit d'atteindre est perdue pour toujours. Pourquoi donc le problème se pose-t-il? En vertu d'une erreur de méthode a laquelle le réalisme doit s'opposer comme étant lui-même la méthode vraie.").† Professor Ryle, of the analytical school, has written: "When asked whether I do or do not see a tree, I do not dream of postponing my reply until an anatomist or physiologist has probed my insides, any more than he, when asked whether he has seen the zigzag lines on his encephalogram, postpones replying until some other anatomist or physiologist has tested him by a second encephalogram. The question whether I have or have not seen a tree is not itself a question about the occurrence or non-occurrence of experimentally discoverable processes

* *Réalisme Thomiste*, p. 160.   † *Ibid.*, p. 235.

or states some way behind my eyelids, else no one could even make sense of the question whether he had seen a tree until he had been taught complicated lessons about what exists and occurs behind the eyelids."*

Of course, these two philosophers are not saying anything like the same thing: a widely different approach to philosophy itself lies behind these two statements. Gilson's phrase "actual existence," for example, is precisely the kind of phrase that Ryle is trying to eliminate; while Ryle's argument that perception is not the kind of thing to be checked by scientific instruments would settle little for Gilson. But these differences belong to our next chapter. For the moment, we are concerned to suggest in very general terms what they have in common. This may be stated quite simply by saying that they accept as an empirical fact that we have means of perceiving the world around us; when these means fail, just as when our motor-car fails, we immediately look for the reason why; we assume some defect. The very inquiry into causes of error suggests that we know what the normal, correct act of perception is like. Or, to use Professor Ryle's analogy, however many counterfeit coins we may come across in a country, it would be absurd to suppose that all coins in that country were counterfeit; the word "counterfeit" suggests that they must be counterfeit of something.

* *Dilemmas*, pp. 100–1.

PART FOUR

THE NATURE AND LIMITATIONS
OF HUMAN THOUGHT

12. THE MODERN DICHOTOMY

1. Existentialism

Existentialism, in its most recent form, was born out of the Resistance Movement in France; it is indeed a philosophy of experience—the experience of defeat, enemy occupation and torture, of political futility and corruption, an experience which taught nothing but the bitterness of frustration and despair.

As a philosophy, however, its roots go back to the Dane, Søren Kierkegaard (1813–55), a lonely cripple whose profound intellect was the measure of his mental suffering. As a student, Kierkegaard had tried to substitute Hegel for Christ. Soon he found that Hegel had nothing to offer by which he himself could live, nothing by which he could be guided in the decisions of everyday life: "A philosophy of pure thought is for an existing individual a chimera, if the truth that is sought is something to exist in. To exist under the guidance of pure thought is like travelling in Denmark with the help of a small map of Europe, on which Denmark shows no larger than a steel pen-point—aye, it is still more impossible."* Kierkegaard's reaction against Hegel carried him back to Christianity, but to a Christianity which swept aside all systematic thought, whether Hegelian or scholastic.

Martin Luther had preached the absolute transcendence of faith over reason; Kierkegaard saw the intellectual implications of Luther's

* *Concluding Unscientific Postscript*, tr. Swenson and Lowrie, Princeton, 1941, p. 275.

doctrine and accepted them: faith was utter darkness where the light of reason could not penetrate; life lived by faith was, therefore, a life of uncertainty involving a cruel tension between faith and reason. The Old Testament, Kierkegaard thought, contained the prototype of this tension in what he calls "the anguish of Abraham": Abraham was in the dark when he prepared to sacrifice his son Isaac; on purely rational grounds, it seemed a monstrous thing for a father to do; but it was yet demanded by the inscrutable decree of a God who was above and beyond reason. The anguish of Abraham was for Kierkegaard at once the most common and the most profound experience in the life of a Christian.

At the same time, Kierkegaard does not reject thought as such; in fact, his whole approach is based on what he considered to be the rational implications of Christian dogma and the belief in Infinite Being. Reason indeed could and would take us to the brink of faith, but we had to make the decision to plunge or not to plunge; it was a decision of the most terrible responsibility, a decision made in utter darkness and yet one on which everything would depend, a decision which every man had to make for himself. This was the anguish of Abraham in its most acute form.*

Karl Jaspers (born 1883), now Professor of Philosophy at Basle, has shown that this anguish of responsibility is not confined to the Christian. For Professor Jaspers there are three levels of being: firstly, *being-in-itself*, the transcendent totality of truth; secondly, *being-oneself*, the self-conscious existence of the individual, who is aware of the transcendent, but is unable to reach it except through this awareness of his own existence; thirdly, *being-there*, the external world of experience which cannot give us that unity and totality of knowledge for which we yearn. Thus human choice is made objectively in the context of the world of experience, but subjectively in the world of transcendence (since it is *being-oneself* which chooses). So there is nothing in the incoherent

---

* Kierkegaard seems to have modified his views on faith before he died; but I have summarized the thought that is normally associated with his name and which has most influenced his followers.

world of experience to determine our choice; only the coherent reality of the transcendent world could do that.

Again, therefore, human choice is made in darkness, aware of nothing but the immense responsibility which that choice entails. For the awareness of transcendence, with all that it implies, is a given fact of experience which only deliberate self-deception can ignore. Self-deception, or the refusal to accept one's responsibilities as a person, is the cardinal sin for all existentialists.

Another German, Martin Heidegger (born 1889) more in the tradition of Greek and medieval philosophy, is primarily concerned with the problem of Being. This may seem more objective than the approach of Kierkegaard or Professor Jaspers, but, for Herr Heidegger, that aspect of Being with which we are most familiar is our own being; *Dasein* (his word for the mode of human existence) must be the first object of our enquiry. The salient characteristic of *Dasein* is possibility: when we turn in upon ourselves, we find no fixed, immutable nature, but a being moving in time, moving from past actions to future actions, giving a meaning or failing to give a meaning to himself by what he does. Moreover, it is not merely the individual himself whose meaning is involved by his own actions, but all the non-human creation which he employs for his own ends. Herr Heidegger comes from a peasant family in the Black Forest; he knows that barren land takes on a meaning when the farmer cultivates it; the dead wood takes on a meaning when the carpenter fashions it into a table. But what meaning can be found for man out of sheer possibility? What is man's end?

The answer, at first sight, is not very encouraging: the end of man is death. True to the realism of all existentialists, Herr Heidegger insists that we must recognize this at the start and acknowledge the essential worthlessness of all that we do. At the same time, again true to the tradition, he insists that we must not seek to escape responsibility and take refuge in the abstract. The awareness of death is part of the sincerity of action: only sincere action can be meaningful. Dread, or fear without an object, has its place too in Herr Heidegger's scheme of things; and even if he recognizes that human experience is shared by all men alike, he insists, too, that the individual is isolated and lonely, shut up with his own power of choice; for he has to give meaning to himself and his environment, and none can assist him.

Like most forms of existentialism, this is a pessimistic philosophy, but perhaps not so quite so pessimistic as it seems. Complementary to Herr Heidegger's idea of the utter contingency of man is the idea of Necessary Being, for whom man must empty himself. In other words, there is something of the traditional strain of Christian mysticism in Heidegger; but true to his terms of reference as an existentialist philosopher, he concentrates on the man that is given in his own experience. Not many are willing to lose their own souls in order to save them; Herr Heidegger teaches that this "loss of soul," by which man comes to know himself for what he is, is the only logical and sincere course for man to take, whatever may come of the future. But there is also a hint—especially in his later works—that Being will reveal itself and perhaps is revealing itself in the course of time—at least to those who are true to themselves.

To most people today, "Existentialism" means the contemporary movement in France, where the two most prominent names are Jean-Paul Sartre and Gabriel Marcel, whose approaches have something in common, but whose views are diametrically opposed. In fact, M. Marcel prefers not to be called an existentialist. It is significant that both these philosophers prefer to convey their thought in the form of drama rather than in any systematic treatise. Having seen something of totalitarianism and bureaucracy, of men losing their identity in mass movements or office routine, they have a horror of systems of any kind.

Philosophically, again we see the reaction against Hegel—the philosophical parent of state-worship and communism alike. While agreeing with Hegel that reality is in the process of being formed, they argue that for that very reason it cannot be reduced to a conceptual system; for reality is formed by the free choice of the individual. And this brings us again to the now traditional existentialist attitude: the responsibility of choice, the anguish that it involves, and the cardinal sin of refusing to face it—the sin manifested most commonly today in the irresponsibility of mob violence on the one hand and routine apathy on the other, the sin of Belsen and of Vichy.

Jean-Paul Sartre (born 1905), as we have said, prefers to convey his thought in dramatic form, and it is therefore difficult to convey it in any other form without doing him an injustice. He has, however, published a brief and, as he says, inadequate summary of his views in a thin volume which has the English title *Existentialism and Humanism,** and we shall list the main points which he makes in that book. M. Sartre is an atheist, and his philosophy is as significant a logic of atheism as can be found. He starts with the premise that there is no God: from this he argues that existence is prior to essence: "There is no human nature, because there is no God to have a conception of it."* Man, therefore, when born, merely exists. Like the artist, M. Sartre says, he has to choose his own standards: "Man is nothing else but that which he makes of himself."†

The next point, somewhat unexpectedly, is this: our choice involves all humanity, because in choosing for ourselves we are choosing for all men: "I am thus responsible for myself and for all men, and I am creating a certain image of man as I would have him to be. In fashioning myself I fashion man."‡

And now we come to the familiar anguish: this choice without standards causes a terrible sense of responsibility: "When a man commits himself to anything, fully realizing that he is not only choosing what he will be, but is thereby at the same time a legislator deciding for the whole of mankind—in such a moment a man cannot escape from the sense of complete and profound responsibility."§

Again, the moral duty is not to shirk the responsibility of choosing: "Everything happens to every man as though the whole human race had its eyes fixed upon what he is doing and regulated its conduct accordingly. So every man ought to say, 'Am I really a man who has the right to act in such a manner that humanity regulates itself by what I do?' If a man does not say this, he is dissembling his anguish." And then he adds by way of a gloss: "Clearly, the anguish with which we are concerned here is not one that could lead to quietism or inaction. It is anguish pure and simple, of the kind well known to those who have borne responsibilities."‖

The greatest value of M. Sartre's philosophy is, as we have suggested,

* Tr. Philip Mairet, Methuen, 1948.   ‡ P. 30.
* P. 28.   § P. 30.
† P. 28.   ‖ P. 32.

his recognition of the logical implications of atheism. "The existentialist," he says, ". . . finds it extremely embarrassing that God does not exist, for there disappears with Him all possibility of finding values in an intelligible heaven. . . . Dostoievsky once wrote 'If God did not exist, everything would be permitted'; and that, for existentialism, is the starting point."*

Much of Western philosophy, as this book has tried to illustrate, has been devoted to showing the relationship between Absolute Being and human values. In the past, from the time of the Greeks, men recognized these values and looked beyond them for the Being whose presence they seemed to indicate. It is the tragedy of post-war Europe that men are unwilling to recognize values of any kind, whether aesthetic, ethical, or what we might call "ontological"—the value of things in themselves. M. Sartre carries this attitude to its logical conclusion; unflinchingly, he accepts the bleakness and despair which it implies.

Furthermore, M. Sartre shows, as clearly as Socrates, though arguing from a different point of view, that where you have no idea of human nature as a permanent entity, you can have no ethical standards. A common nature suggests a common end and a common means to that end; ethical standards, if they are to have any meaning at all, must represent those means. Thus, God, human nature and ethical standards must be accepted or denied together. M. Sartre, by denying all three, has at least put the problem in its proper terms.

On the other hand, has M. Sartre succeeded in consistently keeping up this denial all through his work? There is no doubt that the sense of moral obligation is at the center of his attitude. Apart from crying out against the cowardice, apathy and brutality of his age, he makes moral demands of his own: "Every man *ought* to say 'Am I really a man who has the *right* to act in such a manner that *humanity* regulates itself by what I do?' " What meaning can he give to these words which we have written in italics—*ought, right, humanity*? What right has he, we may ask, to use them at all? We would say that M. Sartre's profound moral sense is at once the basis and the refutation of his philosophy. Abraham's anguish was certainly the pain of acting in the dark, but the pain is known to all mystics, and the darkness is but the deprivation

* *Ibid.*, p. 33.

of light; when this is recognized, as perhaps Herr Heidegger sees, the light returns:

> For none save those are worthy birth
> Who neither life nor death will shun:
> And we plough deepest in the Earth
> Who ride the nearest to the Sun.*

M. Sartre too perhaps may yet find that it is so.

Passing to the Catholic existentialist, Gabriel Marcel (born 1889), we find not only, of course, a quite different philosophy but also a quite different context of ideas. M. Marcel, like the others, is horrified by the irresponsibility with which modern affairs are conducted and the blunting of sensibility in our ordinary lives. Like the others, he sees modern man as an apathetic creature, bemused by a life of routine punctuated by sensation. The philosophical counterpart of this is an arid scholasticism, which talks too much in terms of general concepts and too little in terms of direct experience. In our account of knowledge, for example, M. Marcel insists that we leave room for the direct interchanges of persons and the intuitive experience which goes with our human relationships; thus a strong personality may profoundly affect our minds and even our mode of life without ever teaching us anything explicit.

Above all, he stresses the importance of faith in the Christian system —faith which is not so much a belief in a certain number of propositions, but a living experience of transcendent reality. Christianity, as we have seen (p. 91), gives the fullest value to human personality, and faith enables man to rise above the impersonal function which he performs in the economy of modern life to a sense of personal vocation on the supernatural plane. To develop M. Marcel's thought would take us further into the realm of theology. As any reader of M. Marcel can testify, this would be a stimulating experience, but unfortunately it is beyond the scope of this book.

It is never easy to estimate a contemporary movement, and the exis-

* Roy Campbell, "To the Survivors."

tentialist approach makes it almost impossible to summarize. We have said enough, however, to show the main characteristics that these philosophers have in common and at the same time to illustrate what widely different forms the appeal to experience can take. It is the natural tendency of philosophy—and of theology, for that matter—to inbreed, as it were, and continue generalizing from its own generalization, so that it loses touch with the reality with which it began. In this way, nineteenth century philosophy worked itself out in Hegel and Kant. Historical conditions have given a cruel poignancy to the reaction; there is a danger in all reactions, especially when they are violent. For all that, the return to experience is a healthy sign; we can only hope that it will survive in its more constructive form.

2. Logical Positivism

Logical positivism too may be said to make its appeal to experience, but experience of a very different kind. The existentialist appeal (if we omit M. Sartre) was to moral experience and the awareness of transcendent being; the positivist appeal, taking its cue from Hume, is to the phenomena that constitute the world around us, or, in other words, to the empirical data of which science can give some account. The philosopher's task, then, is to analyze our use of language in terms of this data, and in doing so to adhere rigidly to the method which has been found so valuable in science.

Now, before we explain this philosophy, we must be quite clear about what is meant by "scientific method." It is the function of the scientist to observe phenomena; and by "phenomena" we mean quite literally "appearances." These appearances, in physics for example, most frequently take the form of registrations on a scale. The physicist takes various readings in various different circumstances and by collating the readings he forms a theory, say, about the behavior of light. He may find it convenient to express this theory by saying that light travels in waves. This is what is known as a "model"; in other words, it is a convenient way of picturing the situation.

The physicist is not necessarily saying that light *really* follows a wavy path; he merely suggests that such a picture fits in with the observed facts—the observed facts largely consisting of numerical values registered on a device constructed for the purpose. These facts, then, are essentially indications; they are not ultimate facts. Thus, to give another example, the physicist can give us a formula for the structure of the atom, but he would not claim to tell us—except again by hypothetical models—what the atom is really like. For the purposes of experiment, therefore, it is important that the realm of what we call ultimate facts should not be confused with the realm of pointer indications. The integrity of the scientist demands that they should be kept separate.

Applying this principle to philosophy, the positivist contends not only that it is not the business of philosophy to try to penetrate beneath phenomena, but that man is by nature incapable of doing so. Nothing is meaningful, he says, unless it is, at least in theory, capable of being sensed. Thus it is meaningful to say that New York exists because you can go there and see for yourself; but it is meaningless to say that beauty exists, for you are unable, even in theory, to set eyes upon her. By such standards, most of past philosophy and certainly all metaphysics have no meaning. What then is the function of philosophy? It is simply to analyze and elucidate—to analyze the statements of common sense and remove any ambiguities that they may involve, or to analyze traditional philosophy and reveal the futility of its aims and methods. In other words, philosophy is reduced to logic; and, significantly enough, it is in the narrow sphere of pure logic that the greatest advances in modern philosophy have been made.

Logical Positivism originated with a group of philosophers in Vienna, of whom Carnap, Schlick and Neurath were the most prominent, and found its home in England, with a very special corner in Oxford. At the present time, its leading English exponent is Professor A. J. Ayer, who left Oxford to be Grote Professor in London. Professor Ayer himself has modified his views since he published the first edition of his famous book, *Language, Truth and Logic* in 1936, but his essential attitude of mind remains the same. In this book he stated the fundamental principle of logical positivism: "The criterion which we use to test the genuineness of apparent statements of fact, is the criterion of verifiability";* his more recent modifications do not deny the principle, but allow broader interpretations of the word "verifiability." Thus, he may allow barriers of time and space to be theoretically broken—meaningful statements can be made about the past or the moon—but the essential point remains that a statement has no meaning unless it refers to something that can be *sensed* at some time or place. To put it another way, it must be the kind of thing which a scientific instrument could, at least in theory, detect. Any statements to which this criterion cannot be applied are either emotive, tautological or just nonsensical.

Let us now consider some of these exceptions. Ethical statements belong to the first, emotive class: thus, "This is good" simply means "I approve of this" or "This gives me a satisfactory feeling." Professor Ayer insists, however, that he is not taking a subjectivist view of ethics —like Kant, for example. In fact, his main point is that it is a logical fallacy to explain ethical terms in any terms which are non-ethical. This is what he says:

We begin by admitting that the fundamental ethical concepts are unanalysable, inasmuch as there is no criterion by which one can test the validity of the judgements in which they occur. So far we are in agreements with the absolutists. But, unlike the absolutists, we are able to give an explanation of this fact about ethical concepts. We say that the reason why they are unanalysable is that they are mere pseudo-concepts. The presence of an ethical symbol in a proposition adds nothing to its factual content. Thus if I say to someone, "You acted wrongly in stealing that money," I am not stating anything more than if I had simply said, "You stole that money." In adding that this action is wrong I am not making any further statement about it. I am simply evincing my moral disapproval of it. It is as if I had said, "You stole that money," in a peculiar tone of horror, or written it with the addition of some special exclamation marks. The tone, or the exclamation marks, add nothing to the literal meaning of the sentence. It merely serves to show that the expression of it is attended by certain feelings in the speaker.

If now I generalise my previous statement and say, "Stealing money is wrong," I produce a sentence which has no factual meaning—that is, expresses no proposition which can be either true or false. It is as if I had written "Stealing money!!"—where the shape and thickness of the

* Revised ed., p. 35.

exclamation marks show, by a suitable convention, that a special sort of moral disapproval is the feeling which is being expressed.*

Just as words of ethical meaning or tone do not add any facts to a proposition, so we add nothing by saying that a proposition is true:

> Reverting to the analysis of truth, we find that in all sentences of the form "p is true," the phrase "is true" is logically superfluous. When, for example, one says that the proposition "Queen Anne is dead" is true, all that one is saying is that Queen Anne is dead. And similarly, when one says that the proposition "Oxford is the capital of England" is false, all that one is saying is that Oxford is not the capital of England. Thus, to say that a proposition is true is just to assert it, and to say that it is false is just to assert its contradictory. And this indicates that the terms "true" and "false" connote nothing, but function in the sentence simply as marks of assertion and denial. And in that case there can be no sense in asking us to analyse the concept of "truth."†

Philosophy itself, according to Professor Ayer, belongs to the second class—the class of tautologies, since it is but analysis and tells us nothing new. It may help to illustrate this if we give a typical analysis of world objects which was popular a few years ago.

On the empirical principle that we can only know what we sense—a legacy, of course, from Hume—and on the allegedly scientific principle that we sense not things but "sense-data" (i.e., brown patches, noises, etc.)—a more ancient legacy from the theory of representative ideas—we must not say that we have any knowledge of cows, trees and tables, but only of the sense-data to which we attach these names. Thus, our first "knowledge" of a table amounts to a brown patch of a certain size, shape, etc., and our subsequent knowledge of the "same table" amounts to similar appearances, differing in size, shape and perhaps even in shades of color, as we look at it from different points of view, but providing some kind of consistent pattern; so what I call "the table" amounts to a "class of appearances," to use the once popular jargon which, I think, Lord Bertrand Russell invented.

This, then, is a typical example of positivist analysis; it would claim that it tells us no new facts about the table or about reality as a whole, but that it simply "unpacks," to use Professor Ryle's phrase, the com-

---

* *Op. cit.*, p. 107.   † *Ibid.*, pp. 88–9.

monsense statement into its fundamental component parts. It follows that the proposition "a table is a class of table-like appearances" is meaningful only in the sense that it is tautological. This analysis has, of course, the advantage of avoiding words like "substance" which denote what positivists would regard as occult, metaphysical entities without any real significance; for substance cannot be sensed.

All other propositions are either nonsense or at best only probable. "No proposition, other than a tautology, can possibly be anything more than a probable hypothesis."* At the same time, any purely metaphysical statements cannot be said to be even probable; they are just meaningless. Thus, "God exists," or, to repeat, "Beauty exists," mean nothing because neither God (in the metaphysical sense of pure spirit) nor beauty can conceivably be the objects of sense-perception.

The most significant fact, of course, about Professor Ayer's book is that it is a book, not on logic, but on metaphysics. No less than all other metaphysicians from the time of Thales to the present day, he is regarding the world as a particular kind of place and human knowledge as a particular kind of operation, or, if this is too definite, he is at the very least regarding the world as a particular kind of place as far as human knowledge is concerned.

He is also making very definite and far-reaching statements not only about the nature and limitations of human knowledge, but also about the meaning of ethical and aesthetic propositions. Certainly the principle of verifiability cannot itself be verified, unless we are to say that it is self-evident or revealed in the way language is actually used; but, if this be the argument, how are we to account for the fact that philosophers and others over so many years have used so much of the kind of language to which Professor Ayer, on this principle, objects?

Moreover, any philosophy which holds that nothing meaningful can be said except in terms of empirical fact or logical analysis, can give no account of values of any kind. This is the one piece of common ground which logical positivists share with their existentialist contemporaries on the continent; their philosophy is perhaps a similar, if less obvious, manifestation of modern disillusionment and despair. Of course, psychologically, there is a vast difference between the two approaches:

* *Ibid.*, p. 38.

M. Sartre's whole philosophy is based on the fact that he has a natural craving for the things which these values represent, but cannot find them; the positivists seem to suggest that we can get along quite nicely without them, provided we adhere to the rigid discipline of logic.

They are, in fact, supported by modern theories of ethics and aesthetics which explain away such "values" in terms of purely subjective attitudes of mind. Some, for example, say that it is all a matter of psychological adjustment: a good poem or picture is that which produces in us some kind of equilibrium which we find pleasant; or, on the question of ethics, some say that doing one's duty is equivalent to getting rid of some kind of guilt complex. Apart from the distinct psychological flavor of these theories, basically, as the reader may have noticed, we are back in the mental climate that pervaded Greece, and especially Athens, towards the end of the fifth century B.C.

13. WITTGENSTEIN AND LOGICAL ANALYSIS

If Ludwig Wittgenstein is a product of the same climate, his is a more open, constructive approach than Professor Ayer's. He adopts a less downright position in his attitude to traditional metaphysics and concentrates on the technique of analysis; thus, with the growth of his influence, logical positivism, if such labels are to be used, passes into logical analysis. Professor Ayer himself acknowledges his debt to Wittgenstein, who was closely connected with the Vienna School which so much influenced Ayer; but we have given an account of Ayer's philosophy first partly because its very decisiveness makes it easier to understand and partly because, as we have said, the tendency at the present moment is to return to Wittgenstein rather than to develop Ayer.

In 1912, Wittgenstein came from Vienna to Cambridge, where he studied under Bertrand Russell. After the First World War, when he served with the Austrian Army, his life alternated between academic prominence at Cambridge and complete retirement from public life: at one time he was a schoolmaster in an Austrian mountain village and even in 1943, during the six years that he held the Chair of Philosophy at Cambridge, he went to work first as a porter, then as a research assistant at a London hospital. He died in 1951 at the age of sixty-two.

He was an ascetic for whom philosophy was something much more than an academic pastime; he was a man whose philosophical ideas, passed on by word of mouth and his students' notes, fired his disciples long before the one written work that he had published became widely known. Since his works are still in the process of being edited by Miss Elizabeth Anscombe, it is impossible to give any final account of his philosophy. Here, we shall confine ourselves to this one early work, *Tractatus Logico-Philosophicus*, which first appeared in English in 1922. In his preface Wittgenstein says:

The book deals with the problems of philosophy and shows, as I believe, that the method of formulating these problems rests on the misunderstanding of the logic of our language. Its whole meaning could be summed up somewhat as follows: what can be said at all can be said clearly; and whereof one cannot speak thereof one must be silent. The book will, therefore, draw a limit to thinking, or rather— not to thinking, but to the expression of thoughts; for, in order to draw a limit to thinking we should have to be able to think both sides of this limit (we should therefore have to be able to think what cannot be thought).

The limit can, therefore, only be drawn in language and what lies on the other side of the limit will be simply nonsense.*

Wittgenstein sets out his thesis in a series of propositions, each numbered according to its logical position in relation to the rest. Thus the book begins:

1.   The world is everything that is the case.
1.1   The world is the totality of facts, not of things.
1.11   The world is determined by the facts, and by these being *all* the facts.
1.12   For the totality of facts determine both what is the case, and also all that is not the case.
1.13   The facts in logical space are the world.
1.2   The world divides into facts.
1.21   Any one can either be the case or not be the case, and everything else remains the same.
2.   What is the case, in fact, is the existence of atomic facts.
2.01   An atomic fact is a combination of objects (entities, things).
2.011 It is essential to a thing that it can be a constituent part of an atomic fact.

* *Op cit.,* p. 27.

2.012   In logic nothing is accidental: if a thing can occur in an atomic fact the possibility of that atomic fact must always be prejudged in the thing.

We shall just add three later propositions:

2.04   The totality of existent atomic facts is the world ...
2.061   Atomic facts are independent of one another.
2.062   From the existence or non-existence of an atomic fact we cannot infer the existence or non-existence of another.

Philosophy, then, deals with facts, not things; these facts, like the atom, are recognized by their structure: thus, in the formula H_2O, oxygen, hydrogen and water are the terms in which the fact is expressed; they stand to the fact as electrons or protons stand to the atom; we know nothing about them in themselves, any more than we know anything about electrons in themselves. The atomic fact is complete and self-contained; to elaborate further on the formula would be merely to elucidate what is already contained in it; no amount of elaboration will enable us to pass by inference from one fact to another. It is the function of philosophy, therefore, to unpick these atomic facts and elucidate them by giving us the relevant logical formula in which their structure can be most accurately expressed. Wittgenstein, therefore, devoted his life to working out a logical system by which this task could be most easily accomplished.

Now, we have not attempted in this book to discuss logic as such; it would have been idle to do so in such a brief compass. It must be remembered, however, that a revolution took place in modern logic—and consequently in modern philosophy—with the publication in 1910 of *Principia Mathematica*, the joint work of Bertrand Russell and Alfred North Whitehead. This was an attempt to replace Aristotelian logic by a more scientific system, worked out in terms of mathematical symbols. This was the new tradition which Wittgenstein was following.

Wittgenstein based his work on two main principles. The first was the principle of the medieval philosopher, William of Ockham, the principle known as "Ockham's Razor." Briefly, this was an attempt to get rid of a multiplication of metaphysical entities, by laying it down that the fewest possible terms should be used in any philosophical analysis. The second was the more revolutionary principle that language cannot adequately describe reality unless the structure of the language is equivalent to the structure of the fact which it sets out to describe. Combining these two principles, Wittgenstein attempted to discover the simplest form of language structure which would strip commonsense statements of the disguise of colloquial expression and present the naked forms of thought, where they could be examined without linguistic or emotional confusion.

It is important, however, to realize that Wittgenstein did not claim that his was *the* logical system or indeed that any logical system could make such a claim. Logic, he thought, is merely a system of measurement; it is therefore arbitrary, except in the sense that some systems are more informative and easier to use than others. The effectiveness, then, of Wittgenstein's own system has no necessary bearing on the essential tenets of his philosophy; so we may be permitted to pass over the complicated detail of the logic and examine his views of the function of philosophy itself:

> 4.112 The object of philosophy is the logical clarification of thoughts.
> Philosophy is not a theory but an activity.
> A philosophical work consists essentially of elucidations.
> The result of philosophy is not a number of "philosophical propositions"; but to make propositions clear.
> Philosophy should make clear and delimit sharply the thoughts which otherwise are, as it were, opaque and blurred.

He goes on to say: "*The limits of my language* mean the limits of my world."* And again: "What we cannot think, that we cannot think; we cannot therefore say that we cannot think."† In other words, thoughts are equivalent to their verbal expression; speaking is simply thinking aloud. What then, we might ask, is it like to have thoughts that are opaque and blurred? Presumably the answer would be that it is exactly equivalent to expressing oneself illogically; the two phrases

---

* *Ibid.*, 5.6. † *Ibid.*, 5.61.

would be held to say the same thing. Significantly enough, this may be said to be true in mathematics: at least, I can say that I understand an equation if I can go through the stages of working it out; I do not say, "I know the answer but cannot find the right words for it" (unless I have cheated and looked it up in the back of the book). But this is precisely what we do say in other contexts—for example (to take an obvious and extreme case) in trying to convey the meaning of a work of art. In fact, the very process of elucidation suggests that we can see beyond our language; we can see that it is inadequate for the thoughts that we are trying to express. In some cases even, we feel that it is quite impossible to convey our meaning with definite precision; but we still think it worth while to try to convey it obscurely. Words may be signs, but they are not necessarily like the precise signs of mathematics; they can signify truths which lie beneath the surface at a level where precise analysis is no longer possible. Wittgenstein seems both to assert and deny this in his paradoxical conclusion to the *Tractatus*:

6.521　The solution of the problem of life is seen in the vanishing of this problem ...

6.522　There is indeed the inexpressible. This *shows* itself; it is the mystical.

6.53　The right method of philosophy would be this. To say nothing except what can be said, i.e. the propositions of natural science, i.e. something that has nothing to do with philosophy: and then always, when someone else wished to say something metaphysical, to demonstrate to him that he had given no meaning to certain signs in his propositions. This method would be unsatisfying to the other—he would not have the feeling that we were teaching him philosophy—but it would be the only strictly correct method.

6.54　My propositions are elucidatory in this way: he who understands me finally recognizes them as senseless, when he has climbed out through them, on them, over them. (He must so to speak throw away the ladder after he has climbed up on it.) He must surmount these propositions; then he sees the world rightly.

7　Whereof one cannot speak, thereof one must be silent.

The parallel with Professor Ayer will at once be apparent. Both philosophers devote themselves to writing what, on their own showing, is senseless. Neither of them, of course, believes that what he has written is senseless, nor do they intend the reader to believe it; but their techniques of convincing the reader are different: Professor Ayer drives his point home as forcibly as possible without adverting to the fact that he is cutting the ground from under his feet; Wittgenstein makes a disingenuous avowal in the hope that it will pass for a profound statement. Of course, in so far as Wittgenstein's statement is meaningful—and he would not have made it, had he not intended it to be so—it may well be profound; but profundities have no place in his system; they remain incorrigibly opaque and obscure. But perhaps it is not meaningful; perhaps we ought to accept the more downright comment of Professor Barnes of Durham: "The notion of elucidatory nonsense is one that only a very subtle mind in a very stupid moment could have conceived."*

It is worth noting that Bertrand Russell is himself unhappy about this aspect of Wittgenstein's work. This is what he says in his own introduction to the *Tractatus*: "What causes hesitation is the fact that, after all, Mr. Wittgenstein manages to say a good deal about what cannot be said, thus suggesting to the sceptical reader that possibly there may be some loophole through a hierarchy of languages, or by some other exit. The whole subject of ethics, for example, is placed by Mr. Wittgenstein in the mystical, inexpressible region. Nevertheless he is capable of expressing his ethical opinions. His defence would be that what he calls the mystical can be shown, although it cannot be said. It may be that this defence is adequate, but for my part, I confess that it leaves me with a certain sense of intellectual discomfort."†

For all that, we must remember that the *Tractatus* was an early work. It seems that Wittgenstein's ultimate answer would be on the lines of what Russell calls a "hierarchy of languages." Thus confining his original logic to the sphere of physical science, he would wish other logics to be evolved for the various other fields of intellectual investigation. If this is so, Wittgenstein's work, so far from confusing science with metaphysics, will have the entirely beneficial effect of demonstrating

* *The Philosophical Predicament*, Black, p. 104.
† *Op. cit.*, p. 22.

more exactly where the line of demarcation should be drawn. The truth will no doubt emerge when Miss Anscombe has completed her great task of editing Wittgenstein's hitherto unpublished writings.

A Test Case: The Concept of Causality

Whatever may turn out to be the ultimate influence of Wittgenstein's philosophy, it would be disingenuous to deny that his method itself contains a challenge to much that is cherished by traditional metaphysics—a challenge which the traditionalist cannot ignore. We have quoted Wittgenstein's views on the function of philosophy: "The right method of philosophy would be this. To say nothing except what can be said, i.e. the propositions of natural science, i.e., something that has nothing to do with philosophy: and then always, when someone else wished to say something metaphysical, to demonstrate to him that he had given no meaning to certain signs in his propositions."*

Now, without admitting the rightness of this procedure as an ultimate ideal for philosophy, we must grant that something is wrong with traditional metaphysics if it cannot stand up to logical criticism. We propose, therefore, to examine such criticism in an important context and see what value it has. The reader will perhaps have noticed that much of traditional metaphysics—and in particular the proof of transcendent being—depends on the concept of causality. This was the concept which caused most scandal to Hume and so it remains the reddest of rags to most of his followers today. It will be appropriate, therefore, to say a special word about it.

Berkeley, it will be remembered, was the first to suggest that the concept of cause corresponded to nothing more than an association of ideas: the heat of the fire is not the cause of my feeling pain, but the mark or sign which forewarns me of it (*vid.* pp. 145–6). Hume developed this: "Having thus discovered or supposed the two relations of *contiguity* and *succession* to be essential to causes and effects, I find I am stopped short, and can proceed no further in considering any single

* 6.53.

instance of cause and effect" (*vid.* pp. 152–4). For Kant, of course, the concept was simply one of the subjective categories (*vid.* pp. 162–4). Professor Ayer interprets Hume as follows:

> He [Hume] has been accused of denying causation, whereas in fact he was concerned only with defining it. So far is he from asserting that no causal propositions are true that he is himself at pains to give rules for judging of the existence of causes and effects.* He realized well enough that the question whether a given causal proposition was true or false was not one that could be settled a priori, and accordingly confined himself to discussing the analytic question, What is it that we are asserting when we assert that one event is causally connected with another? And in answering this question he showed, I think conclusively, first that the relation of cause and effect was not logical in character, since any proposition asserting a causal connection could be denied without self-contradiction, secondly that causal laws were not derived from experience, since they were not deducible from any finite number of experiential propositions, and thirdly, that it was a mistake to analyse propositions asserting causal connections in terms of a relation of necessitation which held between particular events, since it was impossible to conceive of any observations which would have the slightest tendency to establish the existence of such a relation. He thus laid the way open for the view, which we adopt, that every assertion of a particular causal connection involves the assertion of a causal law, and that every general proposition of the form "C causes E" is equivalent to the proposition of the form, "Whenever C, then E," where the symbol "whenever" must be taken to refer, not to a finite number of actual instances of C, but to the infinite number of possible instances.†

Professor Ayer goes on to say that he does not accept Hume's precise definition of "cause," but makes it clear that he disagrees only on the exact terms of the formula to be used, not on the principle of what kind of definition is required. For our purposes, the important points are the three which we have just quoted. Firstly, there is no *logical* relation between cause and effect—e.g., there is no *logical* contradiction involved in my denying that the sound which I hear is caused by the needle scratching on the revolving gramophone disc; all I can say is that when I remove the needle, the sound ceases. Secondly, causal laws

---

* *A Treatise of Human Nature*, bk. 1, pt. iii, s. 15.
† *Language, Truth and Logic*, revised ed., pp. 54–5.

are not analytically derived from experience—i.e., I can say analytically that color is always extended, because when I say "I see a blue color," I always mean "I see a blue patch of some shape and size" (thus, my empirical idea of "color" necessarily involves the empirical idea of "extension"); but I can quite easily think of an event without thinking of its cause. Thirdly, there is no necessity in the supposed relation; however many times day follows night, I can never give any necessary reason why the sun should rise tomorrow.

Finally, we remember that Wittgenstein's whole position in the *Tractatus* centers on the denial that we can pass by inference from one atomic fact to another; we can only elucidate a fact by analyzing it in terms which are always, in the last resort, tautological. One brief quotation will suffice:

5.133   All inference takes place *a priori*.
5.134   From an elementary proposition no other can be inferred.
5.135   In no way can an inference be made from the existence of one state of affairs to the existence of another entirely different from it.
5.136   There is no causal nexus which justifies such an inference.
5.1361 The events of the future *cannot* be inferred from those of the present.
        Superstition is the belief in the causal nexus.
5.1362 The freedom of the will consists in the fact that future actions cannot be known now. We could only know them if causality were an *inner* necessity, like that of logical deduction.

This last point touches on another side to this question—the relation between the ideas of cause and free will; it need not detain us long. Mr. G. J. Warnock, who is sympathetic towards the analytical method, has shown that these ideas can exist quite happily side by side:

In order to maintain that the occupant of the next room *decided* to turn on the lights it is not necessary, nor indeed is it possible, to deny that their lighting up was an ordinary instance of the laws of electricity. And to say that the golf-ball finished short of the green because the player wanted to keep out of the bunkers does not make it either incorrect or impossible to explain its flight in terms of the elasticity of the ball and club-face, the velocity of impact, and the state of atmosphere and ground.*

In fact, it would be true to say that the idea of free will would have no meaning in a universe in which there were no causal laws: I cannot aim to drive short of the bunker unless I am convinced that my hitting the ball in a particular way will have the desired effect. We are back with Aristotle: there are different kinds of causes, but they all combine to make intelligent behavior possible (*vid.* pp. 58–9).

There is another red herring which we must remove from the path before we proceed with our discussion. It is frequently supposed that the final blow to the traditional conception of cause and effect has been dealt by the physicist's claim to have discovered that the behavior of phenomena cannot in principle be predicted with accuracy.

The argument is roughly on these lines: physical phenomena and our means of detecting them are such that we can never measure the phenomena without at the same time interfering with the very process which we are attempting to measure. To suggest a rather crude parallel, suppose that we could not measure the speed of water running through a pipe without inserting an instrument into the water and thus reducing the very speed which we intended to measure; it might then be impossible to measure the original speed accurately. Similarly, according to this theory, the measurements of the physicist must in certain fundamental cases contain a margin of error.

Clearly, this is a physicist's theory about physics. It may be true that physical phenomena and the resources available to man are such that the physicist must despair of measuring those phenomena accurately; but it is not for a philosopher to pronounce on such a theory. At the same time, the philosopher's conception of causality is not in the least invalidated by the physicist's failure accurately to detect a causal nexus; in fact, the philosopher's views are confirmed by the physicist's attempt to explain *why* there must be a margin of error in his measurements; a certain consistent, intelligible state of affairs is assumed.

Now, to return to Professor Ayer's three points. Let us begin with the second. Do we have any direct, empirical knowledge of causality?

* "Every Event Has a Cause"—in *Logic and Language*, ed. A. G. N. Flew, Blackwell, 2nd series, p. 96.

The answer surely is that we do: we are conscious of our own causal acts. If I throw a ball, I am aware of myself imparting energy to that ball; it would be a most misleading sophistication to say that I am at one moment aware of a movement in my arm and at another of a movement in the ball. Or again, if I scratch myself, I have an equally clear knowledge of the cause and a rather more intimate knowledge of the effect. Once more, Hume's universe of momentary sensations is simply not the universe of experience. It is perfectly possible, therefore, for me to understand the behavior of, say, a piston in a steam-engine by analogy from my own experience: I can say that there is an analogy between the way the steam pushes the piston and the way I throw the ball.

This, however, is only part of the answer; it relates to a special kind of cause—the cause of movement or what Aristotle calls the efficient cause. But the real point is that if thinking about the world is to be considered a proper activity, events must have explanations, and these explanations must imply a necessary relation between cause and effect. If I say that my friend died of arsenic poisoning, I must imply that there is something about arsenic which necessarily endangers the health if it is taken in sufficient quantity; and the science of medicine depends on the fact that there is a necessary relation between cause and effect in such cases. In this sense, "event" implies "cause" as much as "color" implies "extension."

Moreover, the etymology of the word "event" suggests "a coming-out-of" (Latin: *evenio*); an "isolated event"—if the phrase be strictly applied—is a contradiction in terms. Or, if this seems too academic an argument, we can equally well appeal to experience: what is an isolated event? When you pluck the string of a violin, is the movement of the finger one event, the movement of the string another, the vibrations in the air a third, my hearing them a fourth? Or, are we, for a start, to break up the movement of my finger into a series of isolated nervous and muscular events? In the first case, I cannot talk intelligibly about "hearing the violin"; in the second, the phrase "moving the finger" begs a number of insoluble questions. Either case would seem to take us out of the world of experience—the world of ordinary speech and common sense—into a logician's madhouse.

Professor Ayer's other two points are bound up with his whole conception of the nature of logic and the relation of our minds to the universe; they depend on the theory that all truth is either verifiable or tautological: for him, "necessity" must either be logical or empirically witnessed if it is to have a meaning. But to say this is to beg the question and empty it of meaning from the start.

Let us begin with the second alternative, that "necessity" would have to be empirically witnessed. In the professor's own words, Hume discovered that "it was impossible to conceive of any observations which would have the slightest tendency to establish the existence of such a relation." We can answer quite simply that it would indeed be highly paradoxical if we were able to make such observations, for the very good reason that the intelligibility of our observations depends on the implicit assumption of some causal nexus: the chemist, for example, talks about the properties of oxygen because he assumes that there is some real connection between the circumstances in which he places the chemical (the burner, for example, beneath the test tube) and the subsequent behavior of that chemical, and also between that behavior and the impression (of color, size, etc.) which it makes on his own sense organs. Even a simple observation like "that is a cow" suggests some necessary connection between what we observe to be the head and the tail and implies, as before, that our eyes are reacting to the object in question with a very definite kind of coherence which cannot do without the idea of causality. If, therefore, the intelligibility of our observations depends upon the implicit idea of cause and effect, it would be a very obvious kind of logical fallacy to treat this dependence as reversible and say that the intelligibility of the idea of cause and effect depends upon our observations. Hume, therefore, not only invented the quite unreal "isolated sensation," but also failed to see what is implicit in all sensation, if it is to be understood as an intelligible activity.

To return to Professor Ayer's first point: it is equally misleading to say that the relation of cause and effect is not logical in character because "any proposition asserting a causal connection could be denied without self-contradiction." Let us say that I find a dead frog in my bed. I accuse Peter or Harry or John of having put it there. Each can deny his guilt without contradiction; it is not contradictory to say: "John did not put it there." It is not even contradictory to say: "Nobody put it there; it might have jumped in and died." But it is contradictory to say: "Perhaps there is no explanation at all"; because the whole enquiry starts with a *thing-to-be-explained*, and if we cannot make such a start, we cannot use our minds at all, let alone talk philosophy. It may, then, be true to say that any *particular* cause can be denied of any event without self-contradiction, but that is quite different from saying that the possibility of any cause can be denied of any event. It is an elementary principle of logic that a term used collectively has a different meaning from the same term used distributively; we would say that Hume has committed the fallacy of disregarding this principle.

Basically, as Aristotle saw, the words "cause," "effect" and "necessity" belong to the philosopher's vocabulary rather than the physicist's. Perhaps some of the confusion over these words arises out of a naive conception among earlier scientists who regarded physical energy as some kind of material stuff whose function it was to translate cause into effect; as though the thrower really did impart some separate thing to the ball when he threw it. When "energy" was found to be a mere scientific model, philosophers thought that the whole vocabulary of cause and effect ought, from the philosophical point of view, to be placed in the same category.

This temptation will be avoided, however, if we use the Aristotelian vocabulary; for Aristotle's four "causes" ought really, as we have said, to be translated as "explanations"—the point being that a thing is fully explained when, and only when, these four types of explanation have been given. Thus, "cause," in the scientific sense—Aristotle's "efficient cause"—is the answer to only one of four questions which we are entitled to ask about any given thing; at the same time, when we ask a philosophic question about the efficient cause of, say, the ball's movement, we are looking for an explanation in terms of some thing or person distinct from the ball itself; we are not asking for a scientific account of the manner in which the agent acted upon the ball.

There remains one final point: granted that the mind naturally looks for explanations and is entitled to speculate about things and events in the universe only if it assumes some coherent pattern of cause and effect, is it entitled to ask for similar explanations about the universe itself? I am part of the universe and to that extent can react intelligently to what happens within it, but how can I possibly project myself outside the universe in order to say something about the universe as a whole? The prisoners in Plato's cave could work out relations between the shadows on the wall, but how could they know that the shadows were caused by the puppets that moved along behind? The question is obviously of the greatest importance for any philosopher who attempts to prove the existence of infinite being from the existence and nature of the universe.

Before we attempt a positive answer, it must be stated that at least there is no contradiction in the theist's position. It is part of the theist's philosophy that man himself is in part spirit—that man belongs in part to a realm of existence which is not confined by the limits of the material universe. For him, therefore, there is at least no contradiction or even paradox in saying that he is capable of grasping the universe from the outside, as it were.

On the more positive side, I think that the theist might himself take the offensive somewhat on these lines: "Ever since Kant, philosophers have tried to decide the limits of human reasoning; but this is a highly paradoxical thing to do; if there were such limits, we could not possibly be aware of the fact, let alone say where those limits lie. I admit that my thought is limited, but not in your sense of the word. You say that there are only certain kinds of things which the mind can know: I say that all reality must be meaningful to the mind, but that there are some things too profound for it to grasp fully; I know this because my very knowledge of such things includes the awareness that my knowledge is incomplete. I find that whenever I ponder upon reality, the clarity of my vision decreases in proportion to its depth; the horizon of the mind is like the horizon of sight: I can say that there is a horizon, but I cannot define its position. At the same time I find that knowledge of things always takes me beyond those things; in the same way, the knowledge of the universe takes me beyond the universe. I cannot prove that this is so, except by appealing to most of philosophy and all of the arts; but during our discussion, I expect to find a point where you yourself are using your mind in this way; it is not easy to avoid doing so for long."

In our final chapter, by summarizing this book and the history which it contains, we hope to achieve a balanced view of the workings of the human mind. In the last two chapters we have discussed the two extreme points of view which characteristically modern philosophers adopt—the existentialist concentration on the intuitive, and the positivist concentration on the discursive approach. These schools of thought have both reacted—though in opposite directions—from the idealist metaphysics of men like Kant and Hegel, which had lost touch with experience. The positivists say that we must be content with what is given on the surface of experience and not try to look for an inner meaning; the existentialists say that to remain on the surface is a form of escapism which does violence to our nature and that we shall lose the meaning below the surface if we try to place it in tidy parcels on top. On this showing, there is a complete *impasse*: the existentialists cannot give any logical form to their meaning; the positivists can give no meaning to their logic.

On the other hand, the general situation is perhaps not so unhealthy as it may seem; both schools enjoy something of the freshness of reaction. We have praised the existentialists for their appeal to experience; we must also acknowledge—even if we have no space to illustrate the fact—that the logical analysts are clearing away some of the dead wood which has obscured philosophical thought for a considerable time. Unquestionably, much of traditional philosophy will have to be re-stated in more exact terms if it is to survive. Challenge, indeed, and discussion are essential to philosophical progress. Philosophy has a natural tendency to choke itself with its own abstractions. From time to time the tares have had to be removed at the cost of some wheat. There are times, however—and there is a danger that our age may prove to one of them—when the cost is too heavy; the wheat has been lost in the reaping; only the machine remains.

14. THE LESSON OF THE PAST

In the first chapter of this book, we saw that European philosophy began with the efforts of Thales to find some explanation for the world as a whole; we saw the difference between the scientist, who observes the phenomena of nature, and the philosopher, who attempts to explain what these phenomena imply; we saw, in the case of the Pythagoreans, that experience of a special kind—whether we choose to call it religious or mystical—can deeply affect the conclusions at which a philosopher may arrive. In all this early philosophy, we saw Homer's descendants employing all their great imaginative powers in the attempt to explain the ultimate secrets of the universe. Very soon the reaction set in; it was easy to pick holes in their systems; and it was soon seen that scepticism was the safest refuge from the critics. This early age was the prototype of all that was to come—periods of systematic construction followed by periods of criticism and analysis. By such means—in fact, by a kind of Hegelian dialectic—the great treasure of European philosophy has been accumulated.

The theme of Part 1, *The One and the Many*, was also, in a sense, the underlying theme of the book as a whole. It signified something about the world and something about our way of looking at the world. The world is complex, but not utterly confused. It is complex in the senses that a machine is complex: some parts may be missing, but those that we have can be arranged in some coherent order. The great question is whether it is also complex in the sense in which a work of art

203

is complex: does its pattern signify something beyond itself, or is it simply to be taken on its face value alone? Anaxagoras's theory that Mind might be behind the universe opened up possibilities that were pursued for a very long time.

Socrates and Plato made much of the fact that most of our language consists of words that have a general application: every noun, except the proper noun, describes a number of things which are thought to conform to type; every verb describes a type of activity or state which we can recognize. And, provided that we use these words in a general way and do not tie them down to any particular thing, we can safely make statements which can be expected to remain valid for all time. On the strength of this Plato worked out his Theory of Forms.

If this theory seemed too naive, we found that we could take refuge in Aristotle's compromise whereby the universal had no separate existence, but depended upon the particular. This compromise had the advantage of giving a realist interpretation of the world around us; it gave full value to what is the object of at least our most unambiguous experience. At the same time, it was, as it were, a realism in depth. It stated that a great many other things must be true about another, invisible world, if this visible world is to be intelligible. Since this world is not self-explanatory, we must carry our explanations back until we find an explanation that is; moreover, unless we do this, all our other labors are in vain; for no single explanation is of any value unless it is itself part of a whole system of explanations issuing from a self-explanatory principle.

There is, however, a danger in this construction of systems; we called it the "systematic fallacy." It is a temptation, once the imagination has seized upon a systematic plan, to force the pattern of reality to conform to our preconceived ideas of it. Moreover, our intellectual operations are such that the more we reason discursively, the more we tend to lose our grasp of the reality about which we are reasoning. Thus we saw that Aristotle's system was too rigidly scientific to be a philosophy by which men could live. Plato had the distinction of being the one pagan philosopher who found room for love.

Love was the keynote of Christianity, and at first it seemed to eliminate all else; but religion could not do without theology—an account of the supernatural in rational terms—and theology could not do without philosophy, whose function it was to supply these terms; and it was natural that Christian philosophers should first turn to Platonism, with its theme of the progress of the soul in the path of love and its ultimate ideal of contemplating the Good in another, more perfect world.

But although Christianity was other-worldly, in a theology which taught that God had taken on human flesh there could be no dualistic philosophy of matter and spirit; if Plato had a more Christian view of man's activity and final end, Aristotle had a more Christian view of man himself. Thus the pendulum swung back, and St. Thomas's great system of Christian thought was evolved, based firmly on Aristotle, but infused with something of the Platonic spirit: this world was no illusion, but a reality to which the Creator had given life; man himself was no imprisoned spirit, but essentially composed of matter and form; at the same time, the pattern of the world emanated from the mind of God, and God guaranteed, as it were, its stability and coherence.

In the Middle Ages, if there were disputes about the philosophy of the Church, the basic theology was taken for granted and occupied a central position in all the thought of the time. The Renaissance brought back the quite different orientation of the pre-Christian world: the ultimate appeal was not to the authority of dogma, but to the light of human reason. At the same time, the prevailing influence was not the classical humanism of Greece—the humanism of artists like Sophocles and Phidias—but the scientific humanism of Newton, Kepler and Galileo: Descartes was inspired by the clarity of mathematics, Locke, Hume and even Berkeley by the immediate certainty of empirical science. Hume, by pressing the scientific method as far as it would go, left no meaning for philosophy, so that it could no longer even account for the methods which science itself was using so successfully.

It was this *impasse* which Kant sought to break through. His was the final attempt to base a system on the fact that nothing could be taken for granted except our own thoughts; it was the apotheosis of the subjective approach. In this sense, Wittgenstein follows in the Kantian tradition. Of modern philosophers, therefore, the existentialists are the most radical in that their appeal (if we omit M. Sartre) is not to our own isolated experience, but to our experience of things and other people whose reality we can directly grasp. In other words, this is a radical attack on the habit, in vogue since Descartes, of treating scientific and philosophical knowledge as though they were the same kind of thing.

Such, then, is a very rough sketch of the main lines on which European metaphysics has developed. Before we try to draw any conclusions from it, we must be clear as to what kind of conclusions we should expect.

We have already warned the reader against looking for the wrong kind of certainty in philosophy. All forms of knowledge do, of course, imply that facts can be known with certainty; but it is not often realized how ambiguous that word "certainty" is. In one sense, Plato was quite right in saying that the most compelling kind of certainty belongs to abstract propositions, but both he and many other philosophers have failed to realize that we attain to this special kind of certainty only because it is knowledge of a secondary kind. In fact, the abstract proposition is a means to knowledge, rather than knowledge itself. Knowledge of abstractions can be clear and precise simply because we have isolated certain aspects of a particular in such a way as to make them more intelligible to our minds. By this means, we can know the present more fully by applying generalizations from the past. Our simplest observations, in fact, are accompanied by this process: if, for example, I see a cat that I have not seen before, my past experience of cats helps me to know it. Now, these generalizations from my past experience of cats will be rough if I am not a lover of cats, more accurate if I have made a special study of them; but, however accurate it may be, there will always be details which I have omitted for the sake of tabulating the experience in my mind. To tabulate is inevitably to over-simplify.

Now philosophy is a form of tabulation. So, inevitably, the history of philosophy is the history of over-simplification. This, of course, is true of all the sciences; but it causes a special problem in the case of philosophy. For the other sciences have definite boundaries, the limitations of which are taken for granted; thus a biologist's account of a horse is not thought defective because it does not take into account the beauty of its proportions. But philosophy sets out to explain life itself;

its subject-matter has no natural limit. Thus, as we have seen, philosophers disagree as to what we should regard as relevant data; their conclusions are often determined by their answer to this very obscure question.

It would be wrong, therefore, to expect philosophers to be able to produce a clear formula of the kind that is expected of the physicist or chemist. The philosopher must be ever testing his theories by the facts of experience, until some coherent view of life begins to take shape in his mind. There may come a point when he is prepared to say that he is certain that his view is correct, at least in outline. He will hope to clarify the details, and he will expect to be forced to modify his conclusions in response to new arguments and fresh experience.

If we are right in saying that our intellectual operations are partly discursive and partly intuitive, then we should expect that the philosopher, who is bound to use his whole mind on the whole of reality, will not reject any truth that forces itself upon his experience, however difficult to analyze it may be. In this way his knowledge will grow not merely in certainty, but also in depth; and, as Plato saw, the deeper our knowledge, the more difficult it is to analyze. Analysis, of course, is still necessary; we must check the accuracy of our thought and attempt to make clear what is obscure. But, by a paradox at the roots of human thought, analysis, if it be properly conducted, will at once clarify what we have dimly grasped and take us into further depths that are yet more obscure. Thus Socrates, unlike the Greeks who condemned him, had a profound awareness of his own ignorance, but was prepared to die for the knowledge that he had.

In this light, let us add a few further comments on two allied problems which, as we have seen, have cause so much trouble to philosophers: the status of universals and the nature of identity. These problems are allied in two ways: firstly, the particular and the universal are complementary to each other and together they embrace the whole of the reality that we directly know; secondly, they raise the question of metaphysical entities in an acute form: do we really explain anything by talking about the objectivity of universals or the unity that proceeds from an underlying substance; or are we just using words to conceal puzzles that we cannot solve?

To begin with, we must surely admit that it would be very odd indeed if the history of these problems over the last 2500 years were merely the history of a wild-goose chase. These problems indeed seem to arise out of the very nature of thought and reality; they are difficult because they are fundamental. The word "one," for example, is ambiguous, because we use it in a different sense of different levels of reality: a stone, a plant, an animal and a man have a different kind of unity. Indeed, we might say—as, incidentally, many modern philosophers are saying—that the whole of our language and thought is permeated with this kind of ambiguity; if this is so, analogy must be at the roots of knowledge. If we apply this to the universal, we can easily see that it is wrong to think of the universal as an object in the sense in which a particular tree is an object; that was Plato's error, and Aristotle pointed it out.

It is equally wrong to treat universals as if they had no foundation in reality; even Locke granted this much. Thus we might select a collection of apples according to their size, shape, color, age, origin and so on; the sizes of any given lot selected according to size would be similar in reality; the shapes of a lot selected according to shape would be similar in reality, and so on, whatever particular method of selection we might choose; we can in fact select only according to such characteristics as there are to be selected. So far, then, the method of selection is at least objective.

On the other hand, the decision to select according to any particular characteristic is ours. The question, therefore, remains: to what extent are the divisions which we make in nature natural divisions? Is the distinction, for example, between "bush" and "tree" arbitrary? Or do these words stand for independent types? To give another example, does not the half-way position of the tomato prove that there is no clear distinction between fruit and vegetable? Here the nominalist seems to have a very strong case. According to Aristotle's conception of the universal, we should be able, at least in theory, to count the number of universals that exist, but who is to say whether "tree" and "bush" should be counted as one or two? Aristotle, it seems, has not allowed sufficiently for the subjective element.

But if we allow this much to the nominalist, have we not surrendered all right to talk about metaphysical entities? Now, we have already seen that Aristotle himself regarded the universal as having a special kind of existence; universals, he held, do not exist in the sense in which particulars exist. We have also suggested that particulars themselves have varying degrees of unity; this is only another way of saying that they too exist in different senses of that word; the existence of some is fuller, we might say, than the existence of others. If this is so, it would be reasonable to suppose a similar ambiguity in the existence of universals: types in nature might be held to be more or less distinct according to a similar, analogous pattern. If we return to our example of the apples, we see that this is borne out by experience: it would generally be considered to be less arbitrary, for example, to pick out those of a like size than those which had red patches—unless the red patches signified something more fundamental about the apples (e.g., that they belonged to a common stock or species).

If this be granted, the fundamental position of the realist remains unshaken: the distinctions are still objective. On the other hand, he must modify his views on the nature of so-called metaphysical entities. The universal can still be said to exist objectively, but the meaning of the word "exist" has to be qualified more fully than even Aristotle was prepared to allow. Similarly, if we accept the view that "unity" is an ambiguous concept, we must modify our definition of substance. In such a case, the realist would have learned from the nominalist; he would have learned that his original position was naive and oversimplified; at the same time, he would not have surrendered the fundamental principles on which that position rests.

This is not the place to develop this or any other new theory; we merely offer it as an example of the way in which we may learn from the past. We can, if we wish, accept the fundamental principles of the Platonic or Aristotelian system, but at the same time grant that the criticisms of Locke and others have revealed much that was crude and in need of re-statement. Again, Kant may have helped us to see the point that we have just been making—that there is a definitely subjective element in our abstractions. But we are not thereby bound to accept the extreme conclusion which Kant urges: the return to experience—the return that we should always be making—helps us to see his criticism in a rather different perspective.

We do not think that Aquinas was right in saying that the particular could not be known, but he was certainly right in suggesting that it is obscure. The intuitive mind, when it meets a particular, is quick to send the discursive mind off on its path of exploration, and messages usually flash in with encouraging speed. But we have pointed out that the intuitive mind should also do a little work on its own; it has often hit upon the greatest truths by staying behind to watch. The habit of contemplation has been a characteristic of most great thinkers—whether in philosophy or in science—from Socrates to the present day. It is also the habit of poets, painters and other artists; and poetic truth—that direct, if confused grasp of reality—is often of the most compelling kind.

This has an important bearing on what we have just said about the part which analogy plays in our thought. Analogy can more often be seen than actually worked out. It is perhaps pre-eminently in the idea of analogy that the approaches of the poet and the philosopher meet. Professor Day Lewis has written: "The poet's task, too, is to recognize pattern whenever he sees it, and to build his perceptions into a poetic form which by its urgency and coherence will persuade us of their truth";* knowledge by analogy is the philosophical counterpart of this poetic recognition of pattern.

Thus, in the end, we find that the philosophic analysis of particulars and universals leads us to a conclusion which is consistent with the approach that the poet has always adopted. It is at the same time a conclusion about the nature of thought, and it is fitting that such a conclusion should allow for the two forms of approach; otherwise, we would seem to be splitting up the mind artificially into unrelated parts.

If this is true of metaphysics, it is even more true of ethics, where it is even harder to reduce the data of experience to any scientific form. Here, if anywhere, we see the combination of depth and obscurity. The moral sense is notoriously difficult to analyze and, at the same time, notoriously powerful in the history of human behavior. Attempts to reduce ethics to a neat science have inevitably failed. This seems to be confirmed when we examine a naturalistic system like Mill's. We noted the tendency of such a system to empty itself out. We can analyze what men generally think to be right and wrong, but we cannot analyze the idea of obligation itself. And yet, as we saw with Professor

* *The Poetic Image*, pp. 36–7.

Ayer's theory, if we refuse to admit the idea of obligation as anything more than a particular kind of emotion, we are forced to deny what is deepest in our experience; to adopt such an attitude is simply to treat analysis as an end in itself by arbitrarily discarding what will not easily submit to its methods.

Kant, on the other hand, was almost obsessed by the absolute demands made by the moral law. Since he also saw that the value of moral action depended on its being free, he had no alternative, in his desire for a water-tight system, but to place that moral law in the hands of the individual himself. By this method of reasoning, Kant emphasized certain aspects of moral experience which we are in great danger of forgetting today: he realized that moral imperatives are categorical and that the demands of morality are unique in type; they are not, therefore, to be considered as variants of the attraction of desire. Nothing has caused so much trouble in ethics as this confusion between obligation and desire—the misleading model which suggests that we act rightly because the "pull" of obligation is stronger than the "pull" of desire.

Kant's theory, however, had difficulties of its own: we can give no coherent account of a legislative will breaking its own laws; at every point, our moral experience and our language about it suggests that people and things are good and actions are right independently of our thinking them so; freedom does not consist in the ability to decide for oneself what is right or wrong—such freedom is no more than the paralyzing dilemma of M. Sartre—but in recognizing what is good and doing it for its own sake.

At this point, it seems we are forced to recognize that "good" and "right" are not terms that we can apply independently and in isolation. If we are to account for the absoluteness of the categorical imperative, which Kant saw so clearly, then every instance of good and right must be linked to a common system of values. Socrates saw this in his appeal to absolute standards of morality in opposition to the relativism of the sophists; Kant saw it—despite its awkwardness for his system—in his appeal to a kingdom of ends. It is also the essential thought behind Aquinas's fourth argument for the existence of God—the argument from degrees of perfection. It lies, in fact, at the center of any theistic philosophy, as M. Sartre pointed out when he said: "The existentialist

. . . finds it extremely embarrassing that God does not exist, for there disappears with Him all possibility of finding values in an intelligible heaven."

The logical demand of ethics, therefore, brings us back to the logical demand of metaphysics. In both cases, the Many are intelligible only in the light of the One, and, if human life is to be intelligible as a whole, the One must be the same for both.

There seems to be only one alternative to this conclusion, and that is to deny that human life is intelligible at all. Professor Ayer in an essay written a few years ago adopted this position:

> For those to whom it is intolerable that facts should be contingent, that things should just happen to be as they are, it is also likely to be intolerable that the choice of values should rest ultimately with themselves. They may not need religious sanctions in order to observe the ordinary social rules of morality, but unless they do feel that life has some meaning in itself they are inclined to feel that everything they do is trivial and that all conduct, including moral conduct, is arbitrary. What they obtain from religion is not the answer to their question concerning the meaning of life, but only, here again, the fallacious assurance that there is an answer. If they were satisfied with their own values, if they found life meaningful as they actually lived it, they would not need this assurance.*

We have touched upon this attitude at various points of the book. Here, we can only repeat that it cuts the ground from under the feet of any kind of philosophy or any thought which attempts to make anything intelligible. Professor Ayer's final sentence is meaningless: how can we find life meaningful as we actually live it except by looking for some principles by which to live? It would be a very nightmarish world where men acted at random and then sought a reason for their random actions.

Moreover, the idea of men's "being satisfied with their own values" suggests complacency in a very unattractive form. Can we honestly say that such an aim enters into the moral life at all? Does not the phrase really imply an accepted independent standard which we make our own? The answer to these questions is to be found by introspec-

---

* *Partisan Review*, March 1950.

tion rather than by discursive analysis. One test would be to ask ourselves whether we would have other people accept the same values as ourselves: if we would make such a demand, then we could not justify it upon Professor Ayer's principles; if we would not, then the whole science of ethics is an absurdity.

Professor Ayer's attitude of mind is, as we have explained, borrowed from the scientist's attitude as he stands waiting without prejudice for any observations that may occur. The scientist's self-discipline is admirable for the purposes of his own technique; but the philosopher, however he may try to avoid the issue, must commit himself to some principle or another; the logical positivist, with his criterion of verifiability, is no less committed than the theist. Wittgenstein's *Tractatus* points a useful moral. Here was a philosopher determined at all costs to eliminate everything but the technique of analysis; but, as Bertrand Russell pointed out, he could not conceal his ethical opinions, and, as we saw, he had to resort to a meaningless paradox in order to justify his book.

There remains one further question: granted that we accept that the structure of the world and our own experience demand an explanation in terms of an Ultimate Being who transcends the universe and ourselves who are in it, are we to say that we have done nothing more than prove the utter contingency of our own existence and, in consequence, the utter inadequacy of our own reason? Are we to stand, like Kierkegaard, on the outer limit of reason and prepare to plunge with the "anguish of Abraham" into the darkness of faith?

The answer once again depends on our view of human knowledge. In the account that we have given, there is no place for any outer limit of reason in Kierkegaard's sense any more than there is in Kant's sense. The vision of the mind has its vanishing point, but that point is sufficiently beyond contingent being for the mind to realize that it is contingent. Moreover, if we reach necessary being as an explanation of what is contingent, we must say that while necessary being is in itself independent of contingent being, contingent being is dependent upon it. Necessary being, therefore, must be immanent as well as transcendent. It must also shine through its own creation in order to be recognized.

So, if knowledge by faith is a special knowledge of the same reality, it must enlighten reason, not darken it. According to Christian doctrine, faith is a gift of God, but it still requires an act of acceptance. This act is not a reckless plunge into darkness, but a moral response to a rational demand—a demand that carries with it the light by which it may be understood. In this response, there is a tightening of the will by which it grasps what is offered to it; and the will, as we have said, is not some separate faculty, but rather one aspect of the intellectual act which is proper to man.

The reader may note that this is the second time in this book where we have resorted to theology to explain a philosophical difficulty; the first was in answer to Aristotle's argument that the Absolute could have no interest in contingent man, and that there could be no love between them. The Christian answer, as we saw, was the doctrine of the Mystical Body, by which it is believed that God has enabled man to share in the life of the Blessed Trinity. The two points are not unconnected. Metaphysics, if it is not to end in a hopeless desire for the unattainable, demands a means whereby we can reach the Absolute and rejoice in Its contemplation; ethics, if it is not to be reduced to a dry science of computation, demands that moral progress be the fruits of a personal love; reason as a whole demands that this moral progress be the way to contemplation, and that the final act of man be love as well as knowledge. Whether we accept it or not, there is surely nothing irrational in the idea that the theologian must step in to guide the philosopher along the last stage of his journey. It might even be said to be the only consistent view that can reconcile the limitations of human reason and the aspirations of human nature.

APPENDIX

TWO DIFFICULTIES: FREE WILL AND
THE PROBLEM OF EVIL

I have implied in this book that reason demands belief in an Absolute Being. It would be a little cavalier, therefore, to ignore two problems which trouble a number of thinkers who might otherwise accept this position. At the same time, a discussion of this kind, out of any immediate historical context, seemed hardly to fit in with the plan of the book as a whole. For this reason I have added this section as an appendix.

We saw in our chapter on Socrates (Part 1, Chapter 2)—which incidentally should be borne in mind in connection with this whole question of free will—that the sense of moral obligation is meaningless in a creature whose actions are automatically determined. Moreover, from the Christian point of view, any system of reward and punishment for creatures who are not free would be not only meaningless, but also cruelly unjust. The first difficulty under this heading, however, of which we do not perhaps hear so much nowadays, comes from a paradox within this Christian conception itself: to know something new is to change; therefore, as Aquinas himself argues, God, who does not change, must be omniscient, so to speak, from the start; how then can we be free, when God knows what we are going to do?

The paradox really arises from a difficulty of language—the difficulty, on which Aquinas lays so much stress, of finding words with which to talk about God without confusion (though, of course, this linguistic difficulty merely reflects the fundamental incomprehensibility of God

Himself). In this case, the problem, as stated, talks about God as though He existed in time. Now, time is inconceivable without change; therefore Necessary Being must exist outside time. So words like "before" and "after" have a meaning in the context of human life, but have no meaning in the context of divine life. The sequence of human life truly exists as a sequence, but God, since he is outside the sequence, must see it as a whole and not piecemeal.

To give a very rough analogy, in looking at a comic cartoon on the cinema screen, we see each section as a whole, although we know that it takes a number of drawings to produce the effect of each such action: for us, Popeye eats spinach and then hurls the giant to destruction, but for the artists responsible, the time sequence is very much more involved. The analogy is, of course, misleading in the sense that our actions produce no illusion in God's mind; but it does suggest how it is impossible for a sequence to be seen as a whole without prejudice to its actual existence as a sequence and, further, that when we see it as a whole we may still know that the effect has been produced by a series of consecutive events. We can say, then, that the sequence "yesterday-today" exists for us and, in a sense, for God too, but our way of knowing it is different from God's: our knowledge is consecutive in time, while God's is simple and outside time.

Similarly, the sequence of our moral lives exists for us and for God; but God can see the sequence as a whole without prejudice to the fact that it does really exist as a sequence for us and that God knows it as existing for us in this way. When we make a choice, therefore, the whole sequence of events exists for us as we experience it, and so for us the uncertainty of our decision is not illusory. It is, of course, not false to say that God is certain of the issue of our choice, but it is impossible for us to say this without suggesting a temporal relation by which God's knowledge comes before our choice, although the word "before" has no real meaning in this context. In short, it makes no sense to say that God foresees what we are going to do; for such language commits the logical solecism of talking about God as though He existed in time.

Admittedly, we have not in any proper sense of the word explained the relation between our action in time and God's knowledge out of it; we have merely tried to show that the two are not incompatible. In order to do more, we should have to understand both terms of the relation: but, as we saw in the last chapter, such a claim to understand the nature of God would itself be a logical contradiction.

It may now seem that having freed ourselves from one difficulty, we have sunk much more deeply into another; in emphasizing the timelessness of our dependence upon God, we seem only to have shown the radical limitations of our freedom; in trying to explain it, in fact, we have explained it away. So we are now forced to consider in what exactly this freedom consists. It is a most important question; for "freedom" has perhaps suffered more than any other word from the political jargon of our time. It does not mean, for example, simply "absence of constraint." Nobody really means to say that a free country is a country without laws. The idea of freedom, in fact, is complementary to the idea of law and order. The State has a certain function to perform in the complex plan of human society; roughly speaking, that function consists in enabling all its citizens to lead the fullest life possible both individually and as a community, so that each citizen enjoys his rights without encroaching on those of his neighbor. The State is most free when this function is most satisfactorily fulfilled.

Now, as we have seen, man has a position in the order of creation analogous to his position in the structure of the State. He has a proper end, a function which it is his nature to fulfil. Where the function of a state is ensured by civil law, the function of the universe is ensured by natural law, and, in the case of man, as we said, natural law is enforced by the sanctions of divine justice. In the State, the citizen who defies laws that are for his political good is denying himself (as well as others) the benefits of harmonious living in a community; the anarchist does violence to his own citizenship.

When it comes to violation of the natural law, man inflicts upon himself a much more fundamental injury; for the natural law is not a series of wise injunctions, but it is simply another word for the basic conditions of human well-being. It follows that moral freedom does not mean freedom to do what we like (which would be the negation of freedom in its very lawlessness), but freedom to realize that end which it is our nature to fulfil. Now, this whole system of natural ends and means is rooted in the order that proceeds from Necessary Being; so that the existence of God, so far from compromising our freedom, is an essential condition of it. It is because we have a conscience, because we have a sense of values and some knowledge of what we ought to do, that we are able, by trusting these values and the system of which they are a part, to live with a sense of purpose. When that sense of purpose is lost, as we saw in the case of M. Sartre's Existentialism (vid., pp. 179–180) the sense of freedom, so far from opening the way to happiness, crushes a man within the confines of his own person and drives him into the anguish of despair.

We may say, then, that freedom consists firstly in the ability to realize one's natural end. But there is more to it than that. When we talk of freedom of will, we mean something more positive than absence of restraint in the attainment of the good. If we left it at this, it would seem that the animals are freer than man, since they cannot help functioning according to their nature. In fact, however, freedom is precisely that characteristic which most strikingly differentiates human actions from the instinctive behavior of the animals.

Moreover, at this point the hierarchy of nature seems to take a much longer leap than any that can be found in its lower reaches; the analogy of being widens; an entirely new form of unity appears, and it is a unity which is beyond the world of the natural scientist; for, try how he may, no scientist will ever be able to chart the depths of human personality. As we saw, the natural hierarchy ascends in increasing degrees of spontaneous activity: the cabbage has a life of its own denied to the rock; the dog can run about and play in a way unknown to the cabbage. With man, however, it is not merely that he has a new form of consciousness and sensitivity, not merely that he can form concepts and think, but that in a real sense he carries with him his own character and destiny to shape as he will:

> The fault, dear Brutus, is not in our stars
> But in ourselves . . .

—the words are an echo not merely of one play, but of almost all the greatest literature of the world.

We have now to see how these two freedoms in fact operate. How are we to reconcile the demands made by the moral law, which are implicit in the first freedom, with that spontaneity and freedom of choice which is the characteristic of the second? We have already suggested that the first freedom is in fact a condition of the second: choice is inconceivable without a given standard by which to choose. If we had to choose the standard itself, that choice too would be dependent on other standards—and so on *ad infinitum*; in fact, we could never even begin.

As it is, as Aquinas says, we always choose what appears to be good. Even the most heinous crime is committed because the criminal—assuming that he is sane—expects to get some good from it—even if it is only the pleasure of revenge (which is not, of course, good in itself, but appears good to him at the time). This, however, brings us face to face with a logical difficulty: choice implies a standard by which to choose; given the standard, how can we help complying with it? If revenge is the strongest motive, how can we act according to any other? Alternatively, if we do act according to any other motive, it only proves that revenge was not in fact the strongest. In either case, our choice is determined by the standard which, as we have said, was not ours to choose.

This point has already been touched upon in connection with Kant's categorical imperative (*vid.*, p. 104). Ambiguities of language, we suggested, tend to create in our minds a quite unreal situation; we do not in fact choose to get up in the morning in the same sense in which we choose the brown suit. Everybody knows that what is really required is what we call "moral effort"; it is a simple act of the will, a concentration on doing right. It is not really a choice at all; it is a question of acting or not acting. Of course, many moral decisions are much more complicated than this example may suggest; we may, for example, begin simply with an uneasy feeling that we are not acting as we should in some particular circumstances, but are genuinely uncertain of the right course.

The moral act then is divided into two stages: in the first, the moral demand is that we should apply our minds to the situation with as much integrity as we can muster; secondly, having reached a decision in the light of such principles as are clear to us, the demand is that we put the decision into practice. Essentially the principle is the same in both cases. Even in cases that are far more complicated—and the reader may feel that we are still making rather convenient simplifications—I believe that the same essential principle will still be found to apply;

but to analyze further would take us too deep into psychological questions which can hardly be discussed in the space at our disposal.

How, then, does this moral effort fit in with the conception of human nature which we have given? We said that the special unity which gives such dignity to the human person lies in the spontaneity of the will; the good man, we added, will be more integrated, more of a whole than the bad man (vid. p. 75). The unity of the personality, therefore, is in part only potential; it has to be reached by a tightening of the will in a series of moral actions. The case of the man lying in bed is a trivial enough example of that process in operation. The whole situation presupposes a standard; we can only feel a moral obligation to do what presents itself as part of a whole rational system of belief: we feel that we ought to get up and go to work because implicit in this are other duties—providing for our family, carrying out our contract with our employer and so on. This system of belief is not necessarily explicit at any time, but no rational person, however little he may realize the fact, can live without it.

Moral principles, however, although they are the condition of moral action, do not automatically determine the decision of the agent: between the principles and the decision there lies that moral effort which is at the very roots of free will. There is always a certain tension in man that tugs his conscience towards the good. In every moral act, this tension is either tightened or relaxed. Every time, he becomes more or less of a self. The good man is one who has so tightened the tension, has become so much of a single-minded self, that any pull in a contrary direction has to be very strong to make any impression upon him.

Now, as we have seen, while there must be a motive for any particular moral action, there can be no second motive for that tightening of tension which leads us to act upon the first motive, apart from the sense of obligation, which is essentially part of any moral situation that arises and is not something separate and outside it.

Psychologists, however, quite rightly remind us that there may be a highly complex collection of amoral influences at work at the same time, some strengthening the sense of obligation and others weakening it. The man in bed may pride himself on his early rising or be afraid of his wife; at the same time, it may be a cold morning or he may have a hangover; again, he may have been brought up to get up late, he may have inherited the characteristics of a late-rising father, or he may even have fallen out of bed as a baby and developed a complex about getting up at all. All these influences no doubt play an extremely important part in any moral decision, but the sense of obligation remains the essential element; this sense is quite distinct in its own nature from these various influences, although in practice, of course, it is frequently difficult to distinguish between the disinterested moral motive and all the other factors.

It should hardly be necessary to point out that all this is meant to apply to men who are normal. Moral insanity is recognized as a disease by law and the general agreement of human society. This only serves to emphasize that moral sense is presumed to be a normal human characteristic. Those who are not normal may either have no moral sense at all (which is probably very rare), an irrational or fanatical moral sense, or one that is so weak that the person is incapable of acting upon it. Such a disease may be only temporary. In fact, in the actions of those who are normally sane, it may sometimes be difficult to distinguish between responsible acts of free will and other acts where amoral influences rendered the will powerless. It is no doubt true that injustice has often been done in the past through ignorance of psychological disease, where the abnormal have been punished as though they were normal. Clearly, it is highly desirable that psychological research should try to prevent this happening in the future. It is most important, however, that the distinction between the normal and the abnormal should be fully understood and remembered. Quite apart from anything else, psychiatry itself is bound to fail if it works on the false assumption that man is *nothing but* a series of complexes which it is the psychiatrist's function to adjust and keep in tune. As we learn from Plato, the skillful physician must be acquainted with good health as well as disease.

We are now in a position to sum up what we mean by free will and see its relation to Necessary Being. Free will appears at that point in the natural scale where the scale rises from the animal's spontaneity in the quantitative sphere of movement to man's spontaneity in the qualitative sphere of rational choice. A dog's action changes its environment; a man's action changes himself.

Man cannot work out a new nature for himself or nullify the con-

ditions of his birth and surroundings, but he can become or not become the kind of man that God, so to speak, wants him to be. Within
the limits of his own species and according to its laws, he can, as it were,
participate in the divine act of creation by responding or failing to respond to those demands upon his conscience which challenge him to
reach that unity of self which is implicit in him at birth, and thus to
fulfil the potentialities of his nature. When he fails, he does not do
anything positive or new which limits the necessity of the divine plan,
but simply makes it impossible for himself, within the workings of that
plan, to achieve the happiness which is the natural fulfilment of a
spiritual being. Since, however, man is imperfect but can recognize
imperfection for what it is and thus be dissatisfied with it, his happiness
must lie in the contemplation of what is perfect; as Aristotle saw, contingent being must always be orientated towards Necessary Being as
its ultimate end. Thus by the inevitable logic of creation, the freedom of
creatures consists in their willingness to accept the position that they
have been given in the scheme of things and to act according to the
laws of their being—their willingness, in other words, to accept that
dependence which is logically bound up with the creative act.

The Problem of Evil

This thorny problem is as old as philosophy itself. Every thinker has
been struck by the presence of two conflicting forces in the world, the
one that we admire and in our better moments strive to make our own,
the other that we abhor but frequently accept—to our subsequent
shame and regret. These forces are perhaps felt most deeply of all
within ourselves—in that moral conflict of which we have been speaking.

Some philosophers, therefore, have adopted what is called a dualist
view of the universe; they have believed, that is, that two equally
powerful beings exist, and that the world is a manifestation of their
eternal conflict. This solution gives rise to many more problems than it
solves; perhaps the most fundamental objection is that if the power of
each of these beings is limited by that of the other, neither is infinite
or necessary; neither, therefore, carries with it its own explanation, and

so the problem of the world's existence has merely been put a stage further back: we still have to explain the existence of these conflicting powers.

Once again, we must warn the reader that when inquiring into the nature and purposes of God, it would be illogical to expect a complete explanation of all that puzzles us. On the other hand, the arguments for the existence of God, like any other arguments, must collapse if there is any contradiction inherent in their logic or in their application to experience. We should expect a mystery, but it should be the kind of mystery that does not cover up a logical contradiction which is otherwise insoluble, but that lies very definitely on the side of reason.

A mystery is acceptable to reason only if it is the kind of mystery that we should in the circumstances expect; when, for example, we inquired into the relationship between Necessary Being and free contingent being, we were content to allow our inquiry to end in a certain mystery, once we had seen that there was no contradiction involved and that the mystery appeared, so to speak, at the right place. If we are walking in the Alps and can just see that a cloud covers a large mass where Mont Blanc ought to be, we are quite happy; but if our map tells us that there ought to be an open valley in that direction, there is a strong presumption that we are lost. Can we, then, with regard to this problem of evil, orientate our map so that the land disappears into the cloud where we would expect it to do so?

Now the whole question contains two separate, if allied, difficulties: firstly, why does God allow sin, when He might perhaps have created us in such a way that we could not have sinned? Secondly, why, if He is infinitely good, does He allow suffering?

Let us consider the first question. Sin is the defiance of the Creator's will—a defiance which, as we have said, brings punishment upon itself in accordance with the justice that is inherent in the whole creative plan. Now, let us make it quite clear in the beginning that it makes no sense to say that God might have given us a perfection almost as complete as His own. In the last chapter, we saw clearly enough that by God we mean Being in a unique sense; some creatures may be more or less perfect, but their perfection is still infinitely removed from God's. The real point, then, is to see what is implied by the nature of a creature as such.

We have just seen that a creature with free will is nobler than one without: a creature with free will contributes to the attainment of his own end and thus, we might say, reflects God, Who is His own end. Man can accept that end as good in itself and rejoice in what he has chosen. Since, however, the creature is by definition imperfect, that choice must, it seems, entail the possibility of sin. Since it is inconceivable that he should be able to upset the Creator's plan in itself, the only scope that he can have is to refuse to accept the position that is offered to him. By that refusal, he merely blights his own growth; he fails, in other words, to realize the potentialities that he has been given. His action, therefore, is essentially negative. Since all potentialities are part of God's creation and are therefore good in themselves, the failure to realize them is a loss; but the loss is not suffered by God, who has no need of man, but only by the man whose potentialities they are.

Now, since the creature's free choice logically consists in the passing or failing to pass from potency to act, there must come a point where the choice is final: like the growth of a flower, it cannot be reversed. At the same time, again like the flower, the process is always implied in the result. This explains St. Augustine's paradox: "It is a great liberty to be able not to sin; but a greater liberty not to be able to sin."

For the Christian, that is to say, man comes to the full realization of his freedom when he enjoys the vision of God and, being absorbed in God, can no longer sin; but that joy is possible only because he is endowed with "rational desire," as Aristotle calls it, and, thus endowed, can have the happiness of knowing that this is the choice that he has made. This may suggest the reason why God did not create us already in the act of enjoying His presence; it would, it seems, have denied us that voluntary transition from potency to act which is necessary to free creatures—to creatures, that is to say, who would be capable of that happiness which He desired for them.

The possibility of sin, therefore, is implied in the gift of free will. At the same time, sin is essentially negative; it does not compromise the divine omnipotence.

It might be worth making a further point from our actual use of the words "good" and "evil." They imply, as we have said, that we admire the one and abhor the other; as St. Thomas says, we naturally choose the good; evil is always a thing to be avoided, even though we may do what is in fact evil because of some attraction, some semblance of good, which it has for us. Now, it seems inconceivable that an evil being could have had any part in the creation of a nature which is radically disposed to abhor evil as such.

We have, of course, to make a very clear distinction between what seems to be the proper functioning of human nature and how it functions in practice: we cannot refute the moralists who say that human nature is "prone to evil"; but the implication always is that it ought not to be prone to evil—that something has gone wrong. We might, for example, say that motor-cars always break down when we want to go on an important journey; but this is only to imply that the very point of motor-cars is that they should carry us to any destination whenever we want. Similarly, the whole moral vocabulary suggests that man is made for the Good, but that, more often than not, he makes a very poor attempt at getting there. Before Christianity appeared with its doctrine of original sin, the Greeks, among others, had stories which suggested that at some point in time there had been a fundamental breakdown in human nature from which we had never recovered. There is considerable agreement, in fact, among pagans and Christians alike that man was at first rooted in the Good and then, for some reason or other, became severed from these roots. The very moral consciousness of man demands some such explanation as this.

This brings us to the second main difficulty which the problem of evil contains: the question of suffering. This question in turn has two quite separate parts: human suffering on the one hand, and animal pain on the other. We shall discuss them in that order.

It is sometimes argued that, moral questions apart, pain is necessary to our physical welfare: if, for example, we did not feel the pangs of hunger, we should die for lack of food; or again, if it did not hurt us to put our hands in the fire, we might often suffer physical injury before we realized what was happening.

It seems true enough that pain does indeed play a useful part in our own physical lives and in the lives of the animals. It is *in fact* true that we could hardly live without the warnings that pain gives us; but there seems to be no necessary reason why this should be so. On the physical plane of which we are talking, it is not clear that our instincts and those of the animals could not have been made to react appropriately to what was for and against our physical interest without the intervention of pain. Even as things are, in the ordinary physical functions of the healthy, sometimes the role of pain seems only auxiliary, and sometimes it does not seem to have any useful role at all: the pangs of hunger, for example, seem to play only an auxiliary role in that the instinct of self-preservation would probably be enough to make us eat; the pangs of childbirth are an example of the second type, where they do not seem in any way to assist the natural process which they accompany. In short, the explanation of pain as a functional necessity is, at best, inconclusive and, in some cases, quite irrelevant.

Furthermore, it is important to realize that this attempted explanation implies that pain is not evil in itself; for, if it were essentially evil, it could not conceivably play a necessary part in the divine plan. Now, this seems contrary to the inmost convictions of man. For example, if it were true, the antithesis between pleasure and pain could not be said in any way to correspond with the antithesis between good and evil; and yet such a correspondence seems to be assumed in our whole conception of punishment and reward, and, indeed, in our fundamental attitude of repugnance to evil and pain on the one hand and acceptance of good and pleasure on the other. In brief, we do seem to imply that pain is a physical evil which has a very real connection with moral evil.

This would appear to be a very much more satisfactory approach to the problem of human suffering at least. When a plant will not grow straight, a certain force has to be exerted in order to put it right. When a man does not go straight in the moral sphere, it seems appropriate—and perhaps even inevitable—that the process of returning to his proper path should be painful. This process, it will be noted, is the result of sin and not of the divine plan in itself. If we accept the doctrine of original sin, it seems reasonable to suppose that, once man had sinned, pain would play an essential part in the world in which he found himself.

We might go further than this and say that in the moral sphere, the *possibility* of suffering does seem to perform a necessary function. It is doubtful if one could conceive of a world where there was a possibility of sin but no possibility of suffering; at least it is fairly certain that in such a world there would be more sin—more moral evil, that is to say—than in the painful enough world that we know. This, of course, is not to suggest that suffering is good in itself and essentially necessary to the right working of God's creation, but rather that it is dependent upon sin which, as we have seen, was inevitable as a possibility, but not as a fact. We might add that, as things have turned out, suffering does help to bring home to us the nature of sin: quite apart from personal considerations, we can most easily grasp the enormity of evil when we see it in terms of human suffering.

It seems, therefore, that suffering is related to sin in three ways: it brings home to us the nature of sin; it encourages us, out of self-interest, to avoid it; most fundamentally of all, just as happiness necessarily follows upon the right working of our nature, so suffering is the inevitable result when that nature becomes distorted.

Bound up with the last point is the idea of atonement: it is not merely, to put it in its essential Christian form, that the man who defies God must suffer the pain of being absent from Him, but that he must also suffer if he wishes to repair the injury that he has done. It does seem in fact that this is the only conceivable way in which a creature can make reparation. One might be tempted to ask: why does God demand reparation at all? Why does He not just forgive? This is one of the questions to which we can expect no complete answer, because it touches not merely upon the purpose of God, but also upon what we can only call His personal attitude to us as persons.

On the other hand, some light shines through even this cloud: even in ordinary human affairs, the idea of reparation is normally included in the idea of justice; this idea seems fundamental; it is very difficult to see how it could have been invented; and so it may well be that to deny that reparation is necessary in the nature of things and to look for nothing but unconditional forgiveness from God is to yield to sentiment rather than reason.

If we turn from the religious aspect of philosophy to the historical aspect of Christianity, we see that the end of the Incarnation was the Cross. The redemption of man by the suffering of Christ is the central dogma of Christianity. God, so to speak, found the violation of His justice to be so fatal to man that he sent His own Son into the world to die for our sins. This may be outside the philosopher's field; but if we have any leanings at all towards Christianity, this is the one fact that we cannot escape about it.

Moreover, if we accept the evidence, with which our own experience and human history abounds, that human nature has at some time been corrupted at its roots, then, some compensating historical act seems almost inevitable; otherwise, creation must be written off as a failure. This has a very real bearing on our problem, because if we accept the Christian doctrine that in man the old growth of original sin has to die before the new growth of the Redemption can take root, it follows that there must be a tension between good and evil deep down in his being and that this tension is bound to be painful.

Closely allied with this is another Christian doctrine, especially prominent in St. Paul: we are told that Christ not only called all men to share in the fruits of the Redemption but also to share in that act of Redemption itself; every man, it is said, has his own cross to bear. Now, if the doctrine of the Redemption is accepted as true, it can hardly be denied to be the greatest event in history.

It follows that the greatest thing that any individual can do is to accept his share in that redemptive act. Admittedly, this doctrine cannot be proved to be true by pure reason; but it does throw light on two related anomalies in human experience that have always proved so baffling and this in itself is a rational point in its favor: these anomalies are firstly, the ennobling effect of suffering, despite its being felt to be an evil, and secondly the deep satisfaction that can be given us by works of literature and art whose theme is suffering in its most intense form—a satisfaction in no way callous, but combined with a profound sense of pity for the victim and horror at the suffering itself.

To illustrate this, we can go back to the pre-Christian era: the Greeks of the fifth century, for example, had a deep conviction that it is the lot of man to learn by suffering (PATHON MATHEIN), and at their dramatic festivals the audience enjoyed, as we can still enjoy, plays like the Oedipus Tyrannus with its apparently sordid theme of patricide and incest. Not only did they enjoy them, but they thought that they were better men for doing so. We feel the same; in fact, these very tragedies, particularly the Oedipus, play an important part in the education of some of our more intelligent children today. Obviously, this has no explicit connection with any Christian doctrine; it does, however, point to something deep in human life which is not inconsistent with the belief in the existence of God, and which is more than consistent with the belief in the God of Christianity.

To sum up this problem, human suffering cannot logically be said to be caused by God. It is not illogical, however, to see it as an inevitable consequence of sin, where sin is the work of contingent being endowed with free will. Moreover, it fits in with the facts of human experience to say that, while suffering is not good in itself, yet, granted the existence of sin, it is one of the surest means by which man can reach his ultimate end and happiness.

Such a view may be a consolation to us, but it does not seem of very much help to the animals. It is sometimes suggested that they were in some way involved in the fall of man and they had to take the consequences too. Apart from the fact that this view does not explain the apparent injustice, there seem to be strong scientific reasons for supposing that animals inhabited this world long before man, and, if anything, caused more distress to each other than they do now.

Others have argued that animals have reflexes which suggest expressions of pain to us, but that in fact they do not suffer. This again is difficult to accept. It is no doubt true that a dead frog will writhe in apparent agony if pricked in the appropriate place; but this does not seem conclusively to prove that the agony of a live frog in similar circumstances is not genuine. Such reflexes can be artificially produced equally well in human beings, but we do not therefore dismiss all such manifestations in man as purely automatic.

What is, of course, true, is that, although animals almost certainly have unpleasant sensations, we can have no idea what these sensations are really like. It seems clear that animals have no power of forming abstract ideas; they cannot, therefore, reflect on the present, past or future. This rules out in their case an essential element in human suffering: we cannot conceive what it would be like to suffer pain without reflectively knowing that one was suffering at the time. It is almost equally difficult to see what it means to suffer pain without any conscious reference to past or future; in fact, it does sometimes happen with men that they receive some sudden injury and immediately show signs of pain, but do not suffer any pain until they realize what has happened.

Now, as I have said, I do not believe that all this amounts to proving that animals do not suffer at all, but it does make it very difficult to get the problem into perspective. One curious thing about it is that it does not seem to have worried people until comparatively recently. Whether we have become less brutal than our ancestors, whether Darwinian theories have given us a fellow-feeling for the animals, or whether we are just sentimental seems very difficult to decide. Personally, I do feel it to be a problem, and I know of no satisfactory answer. On the other hand, it does not seem so deeply to scandalize the reason as to justify us in rejecting a system of thought which otherwise fits in with the facts of experience; this seems particularly true when we consider that the very terms of the problem are so obscure.

BIBLIOGRAPHY

I have composed the following list with the beginner particularly in mind, but it must be appreciated that most philosophical works are not easy. Plato, however, can be recommended as the most readable and rewarding of philosophers to begin with.

Early Greek Philosophy

John Burnet: Greek Philosophy Part 1 (Thales to Plato)—Macmillan, 1914.

A. H. Armstrong: An Introduction to Ancient Philosophy—Methuen, 1947; Newman, 1949.

F. Copleston: A History of Philosophy (Vol. 1: Greece and Rome), Burns, Oates, 1944; Newman, 1946.

Plato: Republic (tr. A. D. Lindsay)—Everyman, No. 64.

Plato: Symposium, Meno, Phaedo, etc. (various translators)—Everyman, No. 456.

G. C. Field: The Philosophy of Plato—O.U.P. (Home University Library) 1949.

Aristotle: Nichomachaean Ethics (tr. D. P. Chase)—Everyman, No. 547.

Aristotle: Politics (tr. William Ellis)—Everyman, No. 605.

W. D. Ross: Aristotle—Methuen, 1937 (revised edition).

Medieval Philosophy

E. Gilson: The Spirit of Medieval Philosophy—Scribner's, 1940. Sheed and Ward, 1950.

F. Copleston: *Medieval Philosophy*—Methuen (Home Study Books) 1952; Philosophical Library, 1952.

E. Gilson: *Introduction à l'Étude de S. Augustin*—Paris, 1943 (2nd ed.).

E. Gilson: *The Philosophy of St. Thomas Aquinas*—Cambridge, W. Heffer and Sons, 1929.

F. Copleston: *Aquinas*—Penguin Books, 1955.

Descartes

Descartes: *Discourse on Method and Meditations*—Everyman, No. 570.

British Empirical Philosophers

The important writings of Locke, Berkeley, Hume, and excerpts from Reid and Mill are conveniently selected in one volume: *British Empirical Philosophers* (ed. Ayer and Winch)—Routledge and Kegan Paul, 1952.

Mill: *Utilitarianism, Liberty and Representative Government*—Everyman, No. 482.

Karl Britton: *J. S. Mill*—Penguin Books, 1956.

D. J. O'Connor: *John Locke*—Penguin Books, 1952.

Kant

S. Körner: *Kant*—Penguin Books, 1955.

All Kant's own works are difficult; the following are the most suitable standard editions:

Kant: *The Critique of Pure Reason* (tr. N. Kemp Smith)—Macmillan, 1934.

Kant: *Prolegomena* (tr. P. E. Lucas)—Manchester, 1953.

Kant: *The Critique of Pure Reason* (tr. N. Kemp Smith)—Macmil- 1909 (6th edition).

(Hegel is too difficult a philosopher for a beginner).

Marx

Marx: *Capital*—Everyman, 848 and 849.

Sheed: *Communism and Man*—Sheed and Ward, 1938.

Existentialist Philosophers

F. Copleston: *Contemporary Philosophy*—Burns, Oates, 1956; Newman, 1956.

H. J. Blackham: *Six Existentialist Thinkers* (Kierkegaard, Nietzsche, Jaspers, Marcel, Heidegger, Sartre)—Routledge, Kegan Paul, 1951.

Most of their original works are too difficult for beginners, but these two are short and fairly easy:

Jean-Paul Sartre: *Existentialism and Humanism*—Methuen, 1948.

Gabriel Marcel: *The Philosophy of Existence*—Harvill Press, 1948; Philosophical Library, 1949.

Logical Positivism and Analysis

F. Copleston: *Contemporary Philosophy*—Burns, Oates, 1956; Newman, 1956.

W. H. F. Barnes: *The Philosophical Predicament*—Black, 1950.

Ayer: *Language, Truth and Logic* (revised edition) Gollancz, 1951.

Ayer: *Problem of Knowledge*—Penguin Books, 1956.

Ryle: *Concept of Mind*—Hutchinson, 1949 (a rather difficult book).

Ryle: *Dilemmas*—Cambridge University Press, 1954.

INDEX

Page numbers in italics indicate the principal treatments of a subject.

235